PERSIA
THE
IMMORTAL
KINGDOM

Roman Ghirshman
Vladimir Minorsky
Ramesh Sanghvi

PERSIA
THE IMMORTAL KINGDOM

PHOTOGRAPHY BY
William MacQuitty

The publishers wish to express their profound appreciation of the help that has been so graciously provided by His Excellency The Minister of Court, Mr A. Alam, and of the advice and guidance given by Their Excellencies Mr A. Aram, Mr S. Shafa and Mr M. Pahlbod. They are grateful also to Mr H. Bahadori; Mrs Atabay, Curator of the Imperial Library; Miss Tehrani; and to the staffs of the Ministry of Information and the Ministry of Arts and Culture; also to the Imperial Iranian Embassy in London, and in particular to Mr A. Shapurian and Mr I. Amini.

Special thanks are due to Professor J. A. Boyle, of the Department of Persian Studies, Manchester University, for his expert and unstinted assistance in preparing for press the late Professor Minorsky's text on the Medieval Era in Persia.

Acknowledgments are made to Penguin Books Ltd, the publishers of Professor Roman Ghirshman's *Iran* (1954). Philip K. Hitti's *History of the Arabs* has been a useful source of information with regard to the Islamic period.

The publishers are grateful also to Mr Basil Robinson, Keeper of Metal Works, the Victoria and Albert Museum, for his contribution as Art Advisor; to Miss Shahnaz Ala'i, who undertook the major editorial responsibilities for bringing out this book, Mr William Taylor, Dr Surya Goswami and Mr S. Athar Ali for arranging the material for publication; and to Mr R. H. Pinder-Wilson and Mr Terence Mitchell, of the British Museum, for their kind assistance.

All photographs have been specially taken by William MacQuitty, FRGS, with the exception of the following, which have been supplied by Orient Commerce Establishment: pages 162, 165, 168, 170, 172–3, 178–9, 182–3, 184–5, 186–7, 191, 192, 200 (top), 204, 212.

The drawing by Eric Schroeder on page 132 is from Arthur Upham Pope's *Persian Architecture* and is reproduced by permission of George Braziller Inc, New York. The brick and tile patterns on that page are from the same author's *Survey of Persian Art*, and are reproduced by permission of Jay Gluck, Ashiya, Japan. The drawings on pages 102, 104, 106–7 and 137 are from Sir John Chardin's *Voyage en Perse* (1811). Those on pages 36, 60, 65, 72, 87, 88, 92 and 140 are by Quad; and on pages 37, 40, 42, 64, 68, 74, 79, 80, 93, 94, 97, 107, 121 and 124 by Lawrence Broderick. The decorative caligraphy throughout is by Madeleine Dinkel. The reconstruction of Persepolis on pages 54–5 is by David Watson and Vana Haggerty, and the plan on page 48 and the map on page 50 are by Diagram.

The maps on pages 33, 34, 39, 40, 65, 68, 75 and 100 are the work of Vernon Mills Associates.

The example of Cuneiform script on page 44 is by Gordon Cramp, from a text supplied by Dr George Morrison, of the Oriental Institute, Oxford University.

Finally, the publishers would like to thank Mitchell Beazley Ltd, who designed and produced the book, and especially Peter Kindersley, Wendy Bann, Nicholas Maddren, Michael Powell, Clare Hoare, Elsie Day, Daphne Wood and Malcolm Smythe.

Filmset by Filmtype Services Limited Scarborough England
Printed by De Lange/Van Leer NV Deventer Netherlands
Bound by Proost en Brandt NV Amsterdam Netherlands

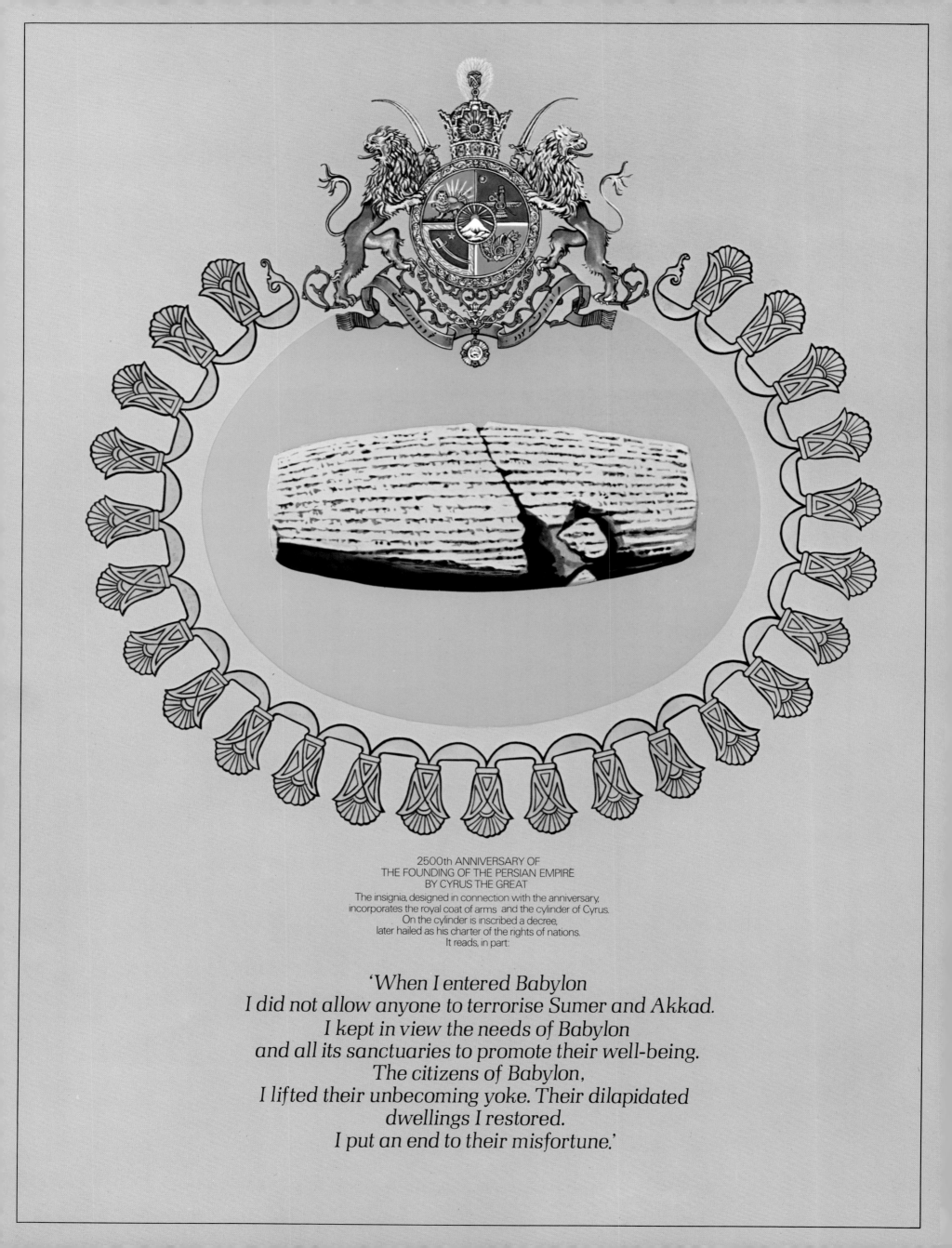

2500th ANNIVERSARY OF
THE FOUNDING OF THE PERSIAN EMPIRE
BY CYRUS THE GREAT
The insignia, designed in connection with the anniversary,
incorporates the royal coat of arms and the cylinder of Cyrus.
On the cylinder is inscribed a decree,
later hailed as his charter of the rights of nations.
It reads, in part:

'When I entered Babylon
I did not allow anyone to terrorise Sumer and Akkad.
I kept in view the needs of Babylon
and all its sanctuaries to promote their well-being.
The citizens of Babylon,
I lifted their unbecoming yoke. Their dilapidated
dwellings I restored.
I put an end to their misfortune.'

Some 2,500 years ago, Darius, Shahanshah of Iran, described
his realm, the greatest empire known to the world at that time,
and the duties of its ruler in this way: 'This is my
kingdom . . . the land of brave men and handsome horses. May Ahuramazda keep
it under His protection for evermore. O Thou, who rulest
after me as king over this land, if thou wishest to keep it lasting
and prosperous, avoid falsehood and mete out punishment
to the liar. Be benevolent, forbearing and just.'

In all the centuries since, God has protected this land
from untold perils. It still remains today a proud, flourishing and independent
country — a bastion of peace in this troubled
region of the globe.

Today the ordinary citizens of the Western world may not be aware
of Iran's importance to the peace-loving nations of the globe.
It shows clearly, however, with a single glance at a map.
My country is the geographical key to the entire Middle East, to Pakistan,
to India and to Africa. Seldom in the long course
cf history has one nation been burdened with so great a responsibility.
We are conscious of its magnitude, and we know
that it is as glorious as it is heavy.

Consciousness of our historic and humanitarian mission has been essential
in enabling the Iranian people to preserve
their independence and integrity throughout our eventful
and sometimes calamitous history. Perhaps no other nation on earth
has been subjected so often to occupations, devastations,
and periods of decadence, yet so quickly
able to recuperate and renew itself.

Good fortune and adversity, strength and weakness followed each other
through twenty-five centuries of Iranian history.
There is a legend, still existing in our folklore, of the Salamandar (phoenix),
an immortal bird which in old age burned itself
on its own funeral pyre and rose from the ashes
with renewed youth and vigour to live through another cycle.
Nothing could be more symbolic of Iran
than the phoenix; it epitomizes this nation.

HIS IMPERIAL MAJESTY MOHAMMED REZA SHAH PAHLAVI, SHAHANSHAH OF IRAN

'O Man,
Whoever Thou Art,
and Wheresoever Thou Cometh,
For I Know Thou Wilt Come:
I Am Cyrus,
Who Founded the Empire of the Persians.
Grudge Me Not, Therefore,
This little Earth That Covers My Body.'

INSCRIBED OVER THE TOMB OF CYRUS,
CYRUS THE GREAT, KING OF KINGS, 529 BC.

INTRODUCTION

Twenty-five centuries have passed since Cyrus addressed himself with humility to the Ages – twenty-five centuries of a civilization that has brought inestimable contributions to mankind. In this year of 1971 the nations of the world will recognise this great inheritance by placing in the New York headquarters of the United Nations a memorial to Cyrus the Great and the humane and civilized precepts he introduced in the sixth century before Christ, often described as the first charter of Human Rights.

To the archaeologist and the historian Persia has presented some tantalising mysteries. Others still remain. We know, however, that in the beginning people of Aryan stock came down out of Central Asia and settled in land below the Caspian Sea and in the course of four centuries reached the foothills of the Bakhtiari mountains, close to the Persian Gulf, where the first kingdom of Persia was founded. The plateau to which they came must have offered a severe challenge to their hardihood, their determination, and their ingenuity. Two immense salt deserts combine to drive a wedge into an arid plateau, dividing it in two. Three forbidding mountain ranges, Zagros, Alburz and Makran, rise up like fractured walls on three sides, the Persian Gulf separating them from what now is Arabia. This plateau lies along historic migratory routes, and is the natural land bridge between Asia and Europe. To the east lie India and China; to the south were Sumer and Babylon; and to the west stood Egypt and Phoenicia, with the European civilisations of Greece and Rome beyond. It is scarcely to be wondered at that Iran, placed as it was at the geographical heart of the ancient world, became early in its history one of the principal centres of civilisation and culture. The eclectic nature of Persian culture has often been emphasised, often to the detriment of the distinctive Persian genius. This is partly because for many centuries the basic staples of Western education were the Greek and Latin classics, which created perhaps in the minds of early scholars a natural if unwitting bias in their favour and an indifference to the classical cultures of peoples less familiar. Iran's history, in contrast to that of many insular nations, shows that at no time was she unresponsive in cultural exchanges with the outside world, that she was as ready to yield something of her own heritage as to absorb influences and ideas beneficial to herself.

Moreover, dispassionate research has established the consistency and coherence, the singular creative force and vivid genius of the Iranian mind and culture. One has only to consider the magical and airy luminosity of Persian domes and cupolas, arching overhead as lightly as the Iranian sky, yet standing as majestically erect as any of the massive mountains, to realise with what infinite sensitivity the Iranian spirit has pervaded and tamed the landscape.

The Achaemenian past is no myth of national chauvanism. In examining more closely this ample past, astonishment is transformed quickly into respectful understanding. Only such illustrious names of the classical world as Alexander and Pericles justly compare with those of Cyrus the Great and Darius I. Under these giants of the Achaemenian dynasty, Persia became the hub of the greatest empire the world had ever known. Within their powerful, well-organised and ably administered universal state they built with titanic energy networks of roads, coastal ports and beautiful cities, the ruins of which are marvels to behold. The

Continued on page 12

Below: A model showing the preparations at Persepolis for accommodating the many distinguished guests at the ceremonies in connection with the 2500th anniversary of the Persian monarchy. The ruins of Persepolis itself are seen at the top of the picture. Below, set in an extensive plantation of trees and forming an immense star, are the tents for the guests. In the foreground is the ceremonial area.

Right: Detail of a bas-relief in the apadana at Persepolis, showing the head of a Mede paying tribute to his king.

Above: A general view of the remains of Persepolis. At the top, on the left, is the Palace of Darius, and on the right, the apadana with its tall, decorative columns. Below, in the centre, is the huge Hall of a Hundred Columns.

sense of aesthetic form and civil conduct which they adopted for themselves was liberally shared with all races and nations who came within their orbit. Readers of the histories of such nominal rivals as Herodotus and Xenophon know with what respectful language they describe the courage and decorum of even common Persian soldiers. Moreover, according to Plutarch, when the epigraph at the tomb of Cyrus was interpreted for the conquering Alexander, he was deeply moved and ordered the damaged tomb to be repaired. Far from being merely a natural reverence for the past, modern Iran's tender regard for her ancestral foundations rests on the fact that the Achaemenian period truly was the dawn of conscience, character and conduct in the Persian life-style.

The heritage of the Achaemenian age also included a conflict of political ideas between Persia and Greece. With the establishment of the Achaemenian universal state the historical quest for an egalitarian millenium took hold of thoughtful men well ahead of the accepted Biblical date, and was already in the ascendancy when democracy for a minority first became a clear political idea in the city-state of Athens. Plato produced his *Republic*, and Aristotle his *Politics*. Aristotle differentiated between tyrants, who rule without the consent of their subjects, and inherent monarchs, such as the Macedonian king he himself served. The former, he said, rule for their own good, while the latter rule for the good of the State. (Which of these teachings the master's protégé, Alexander, was attempting to follow is open to doubt.) The 'democratic' sentiments of Plato and Aristotle did not extend to certain strata of Greek society based primarily on slavery. For the slave was to be nothing more than an instrument in his master's hand, creator of prosperity. To use

Aristotle's own analogy, 'The slave is a tool with life in it, and the tool a lifeless slave'.

In contrast, the Iranian people instituted their monarchical form of government. The rationale behind the institution of monarchy was that the powers they invested in each monarch came from a profound conviction that the sovereignty of individuals is best maintained by an individual sovereign, as opposed to the rule of partisan fervour and factionalism. Although the Iranians themselves were deeply religious, the religio-stratocracies of their neighbours, notably the Babylonians, made little appeal to Iranians, for whom the connection between monarch and people was vital and organic. In the eyes of the people, the Iranian monarch was personally responsible to them alone: his fidelity would mean their collective well-being, and their trust was his mandate. His constant purpose was to use, in Ruskin's elegant phrase, 'every power entrusted to him for the good his people; and to be, not in name only, but in heart and hand their king'. That historical forces and immoderate or enfeebled monarchs did not always treat this great trust kindly cannot in the long view detract from the obvious successes of a system so constituted.

After the triumphs of the Achaemenian age, successive waves of predatory foes assailed the Persian state, bringing with them ruin and subjection to the Persian people. Yet enough remains for the modern world to be astonished at the resilience with which Iran reacted time and time again, reasserting her national frontiers and recreating the cultural traditions established by her Achaemenian forebears.

In the course of their long history, the Iranian people have followed pre-eminently the precepts of two of the world's great religions, the first of which found its earliest expression in the Achaemenian period. The precise date of the prophet Zarathustra's appearance in Iran is a matter of scholarly debate. (Zoroaster is a Greek linguistic corruption of his Persian name.) Some place him as early as the ninth or tenth centry BC, but generally he is believed to have been contemporary with Siddhartha (later the sacred Buddha) in India and with Confucius in China. The influence of his teaching on Achaemenian development is thought to have been considerable, though there is evidence of corrupt embroideries by contending priests, the Magi. But the original Zoroastrian concepts have been of profound consequence to the enlightenment of man, as has been the significance of those concepts in the history of ideas. They have provided basic data for varieties of Greek philosophy, notably for the ideas of Pythagoras and Heraclitus, and appear extensively in the sacred books of Judaism, Christianity and Islam. Believers in 'progressive revelation' and students of comparative religion alike confirm the wide diffusion of these ideas. In Western philosophy Nietzsche gave the prophet's name to the protagonist of his great book, *Thus Spake Zarathustra*, in order, he said, to honour this ancient Persian seer, who was the first to propound the cyclical theory of history. And in *The Phenomenology of Spirit* Hegel began his study of religion with the Religion of Light, of which he acknowledged Zoroastrianism to have been 'the historic expression'.

But Zarathustra's contribution to philosophy and religion is only a part of Iran's intellectual legacy to Islam and to the Western world. The contributions made to Islamic culture in particular by Persian scholars, scientists, poets and artists are incalculable. When, after centuries of

Continued on page 16

accumulated wisdom, experience, and sensibility the carefully acquired skills and inborn grace of the Iranian people flowered in the Persian Renaissance, that era proved to be one of lasting and transcendent beauty, abundant in its vitality, copious in the resources of its imagination and learning. In the history of medicine, of science and of philosophy, Ar-Razi (Rhazes) and Ibn Sina (Avicenna) are among the immortals. Avicenna's monumental work, *Al-Qanun fi'l Tibb (The Canon of Medicine)* was translated into Latin in the twelfth century and until the sixteenth remained a standard work in European universities. Rudaki is generally recognised as the first of the classical Persian poets; and, Daqiqi had, when he died, completed a thousand couplets of an epic of the Iranian monarchy. This work, known as the *Shahnameh (Book of Kings)*, was completed by the famous poet Firdausi, who collected the old Iranian legends and retold them in some 60,000 couplets, exceeding by seven times the length of Homer's *Iliad*. This vast work is regarded by Persians as their national poem; almost every Iranian knows some couplets by heart and many can recite hundreds of lines. The *Mathnawi* by Rumi has been hailed by Westerners as the *Divine Comedy* of Islam. Rumi's English translator, the Cambridge scholar R. A. Nicholson, called him 'the greatest mystical poet of any age'; and of Rumi's contemporary, Sadi, like himself a poet and a Sufi, Emerson declared that 'He speaks to all nations, and like Homer, Shakespeare, Cervantes, and Montaigne is perpetually modern'. To Emerson Sadi's *Gulistan (Rose Garden)* was 'one of the bibles of the world', and in it he found 'the universality of moral law'. The work of the renowned Hafiz had perhaps an even greater impact. Another American, John Payne, regarded the 'sweet singer of Shiraz' as 'one of the three greatest lyrical poets of the world', the equal of Dante and Shakespeare. A German translation of his *Divan* begot Goethe's *West-ostlicher Diwan* in imitation and, as Cyprian Rice says, 'Ruchert, Herder and others set themselves with great zeal and application to study Persian mystical verse and to make it the leaven of the new poetical and philosophical movement in their country'.

The immense and world-wide influence that radiates from the Persian genius – how that genius blossomed, bore fruit, and spread in philosophy and science, architecture and literature, miniature painting and carpet weaving, as well as in other arts – remains a source of wonder and of gratitude throughout the rest of the world. This commorative volume, which marks an event of majestic importance in the age-old story of Iran, records the achievement of this immortal people in a historic and national context. Indeed, it seeks to present not only the past, but also the modern Persian Renaissance which, in more senses than one, is a resurrection of the genius of the people of this immortal kingdom.

1971

16

*The Achaemenian empire unified the whole
of western Asia, which enjoyed administration
under central control, good means of transport
and communication, and a perfectly
balanced system of tax collection...
These... institutions of the Achaemenian civilization
were to have a lasting impact
on other countries.*

Roman Ghirshman

THE CLASSICAL AGE

Right: Some thirty-five miles north of Teheran is the Karaj dam, 550 feet high, which is the main source of the city's water supply. The strange and dramatic terrain above the dam gives an indication of the cataclysmic upheaval by which the Iranian plateau was formed millions of years ago.

Following pages: Below the steep and jagged slopes of the Elburz mountains runs the placid Karaj river. In the spring its waters, swollen by the melted snows of winter, become a torrent.

The geographical situation of the Iranian plateau has determined to a large extent the course of its civilisation. Iran is a triangle bounded by mountains rising round a central depression, a desert region, set between two depressions, the Caspian Sea and the Persian Gulf. She serves as a bridge between Central and Western Asia, and also as a promontory linking the inner Asian steppes to the plateau of Asia Minor and beyond to Europe. The Zagros mountain chain, 620 miles in length and running north-west to south-east to a depth of 120 miles, lies in numerous folds overlooking hot and arid plains. A spur from the central Zagros runs into the Mesopotamian plain, causing a bend in the river Tigris. This hatchet-shaped spur dominates the plain below. This is the land of ancient Luristan, the base from which the Kassites invaded Babylonia in the second millenium BC and made their power felt for full five centuries. The Elburz chain, of which Mount Demavend is the highest peak, begins at the southern shores of the Caspian Sea and reaches the historic Iranian province of Azerbaijan in the west. The Medes and the Persians, the Kurds, the Mongols and the Turks had their first homes in the valleys of the Elburz, and the Median dynasty rose here. The eastern Elburz are the mountains of Khorasan, the granary of Iran. The low mountains offer, here too, natural gateways for penetration. Khorasan has been for thousands of years a crossroads of peoples, and till the end of the nineteenth century it was repeatedly raided by the Turcomans. The valley of the Atrek and the plains of Gurgan, between the mountains and the Caspian, are natural ways of migrations, as is the region between the Caspian Sea and Lake Rezaiye (Urmiya). These north-east and north-west areas were the birthplaces of several dynasties: the Arsacids, Safavids and Kajars. The mountains bordering the triangle are completed by the southern chain, the Makran in the east, a range pierced by two passes, leading to Bandar Abbas and Baluchistan. In the central part of the plateau, which itself is crossed by two inner mountain chains, lie two deserts: Dasht-i-Kavir in the north and Dasht-i-Lur in the south.

Life on the plateau could develop and prosper only in valleys, oases and on the wide plains of inner and outer Iran under these geographical conditions and their climatic consequences. Ancient Susiana spread over the plain of Khuzistan. The plain bordering the Caspian Sea is a lush tropical area, and hence has always been densely populated. The outer plains also played a role in the growth of Iranian civilisation, which from the earliest times grew in the scattered oases in the mountain ranges which encircle the plateau and catch rain clouds. All the capitals of Iran have been built along the two principal routes that skirt the edges of the two great mountain ranges of the Zagros and Elburz. The land there is alluvial and, despite the intense cold in winter and the heat in summer, yields abundantly wherever man can bring water. Thus the question of water has always been vital. No less important is artificial irrigation. Since the time of the Achaemenians, civilisation has depended as much on the subterranean canals, (the *ghanat* and *khariz*) for its sustenance and growth as on the wisdom of kings or the valour of soldiers. This water and the rainfall in the Zagros and Elburz mountains made it possible for the people to chart the two principal trade routes with cultivation and oasis settlements. On the route along the Elburz stand Ecbatana (Hamadan), the capital of the first Median kingdom, and also Kazvin, Tehran, Rayy, Damghan and Herat. Isphahan, Pasargadae, Istakhr, Persepolis and Shiraz lie on the other trade route to the south. Stone-Age man, almost as soon as he came down from the mountains to the plains, settled along the same lines, which constitute an arc round the Dasht-i-Kavir. The religious centres of the country, Meshed and Qumm, also lie along these lines.

Iran is primarily an agricultural and stock-breeding country. She also possesses a rich abundance of varied mineral resources. Her annals provide evidence of these riches. Her quarries provided marble and alabaster for the Summerians, who, as early as the fourth millennium BC, also depended upon her forests for timber. The Assyrians came to her territory for iron, copper, tin, lead and horses. The gypsous, oil-bearing rock on both slopes of the Zagros were known to Herodotus. Thus, her land is rich, and richer still in reserves, despite the unkindness of her climate and the scarcity of water.

Before the coming of the Iranians, Iran was a land consisting of plains and plateau, a natural prolongation of Lower Mesopotamia on the one hand and the western marches of Central Asia on the other. It was the cradle of a great civilisation, that of the Elamites – a nation which was neither of Indo-European origin, like the Iranians, nor of Semitic origin. From the fourth millennium BC until the seventh century BC, a period of some three thousand years, there flourished in this land, later to be known as Iran, the advanced culture of the Elamites, the originality of which impressed its western neighbours, the Sumero-Babylonians. The Elamites were brilliantly creative, the equals of the Sumero-Babylonians, who appear to have drawn fresh inspirations from them. The flowering of their culture was marked particularly by achievements in architecture and town planning. Their metalwork and jewellery, as well as their artistic creations, were much sought after in international trading in this part of Hither Asia, and the fabrics of Elam gained her designers and weavers a high reputation for quality. From early times Elam set up trading links and exported her raw materials, such as stone, metal and wood, or objects made from these materials, while developing an entrepôt trade in lapis-lazuli, the semi-precious stone mined in Badakhshan, close to the Pamirs, which was in great demand in Mesopotamia, Syria and Asia Minor. With trade came the most influential concept ever devised by man – the art of handwriting. Thus the oldest known script was developed in this land, the future Iran; it is known as the 'proto-Elamite' script and was in use in the fourth millennium BC.

The development of Elamite culture can be traced from the period at which the first husbandmen and farmers began to inhabit the plain up to the epoch of a fully-developed urban civilisation peopled by a society under orderly government. And this civilisation was to pass on to the new-comers, forerunners of the Persians, the wisdom of the older civilisations. Elam, fertilised by thousands of years of advanced culture, became the educator of the youthful inheritors who took over and faithfully preserved this priceless heritage, and in their turn enriched it with their own peculiar gifts.

What do we know about the Persians who came and settled on Elamite territory in Susiana and to the East in the foothills of the Zagros mountains?

In 843 BC Shalmaneser III, King of Assyria, captured the country of Parsua to the south of Lake Urmiya (Rezaiye), the land of the Persians, twenty-seven of whose 'kings', who were only tribal chieftains, brought 'gifts' to him. One hundred and fifty years later, about 690 BC, Persian cavalry fought with the Elamite army at Susiana against Sennacherib of Assyria. Then about 640 BC, according to the annals of Assurbanipal, who conquered and sacked Elam after capturing the religious centre of Dur-Untach (Tchoga Zanbil) and crossing the river Idide (now known as Ab-e Diz), the Assyrian army pushed on into the district of Hidalu (the present day city of Shushtar), a short distance from Masjid-i Sulaiman. There, Kurush, or Cyrus I, King of the Persians, the grandfather of Cyrus the Great, presented himself before the Assyrian general, to whom he gave his elder son Arukku as a hostage in token of his recognition of the suzerainty of the King of Assyria.

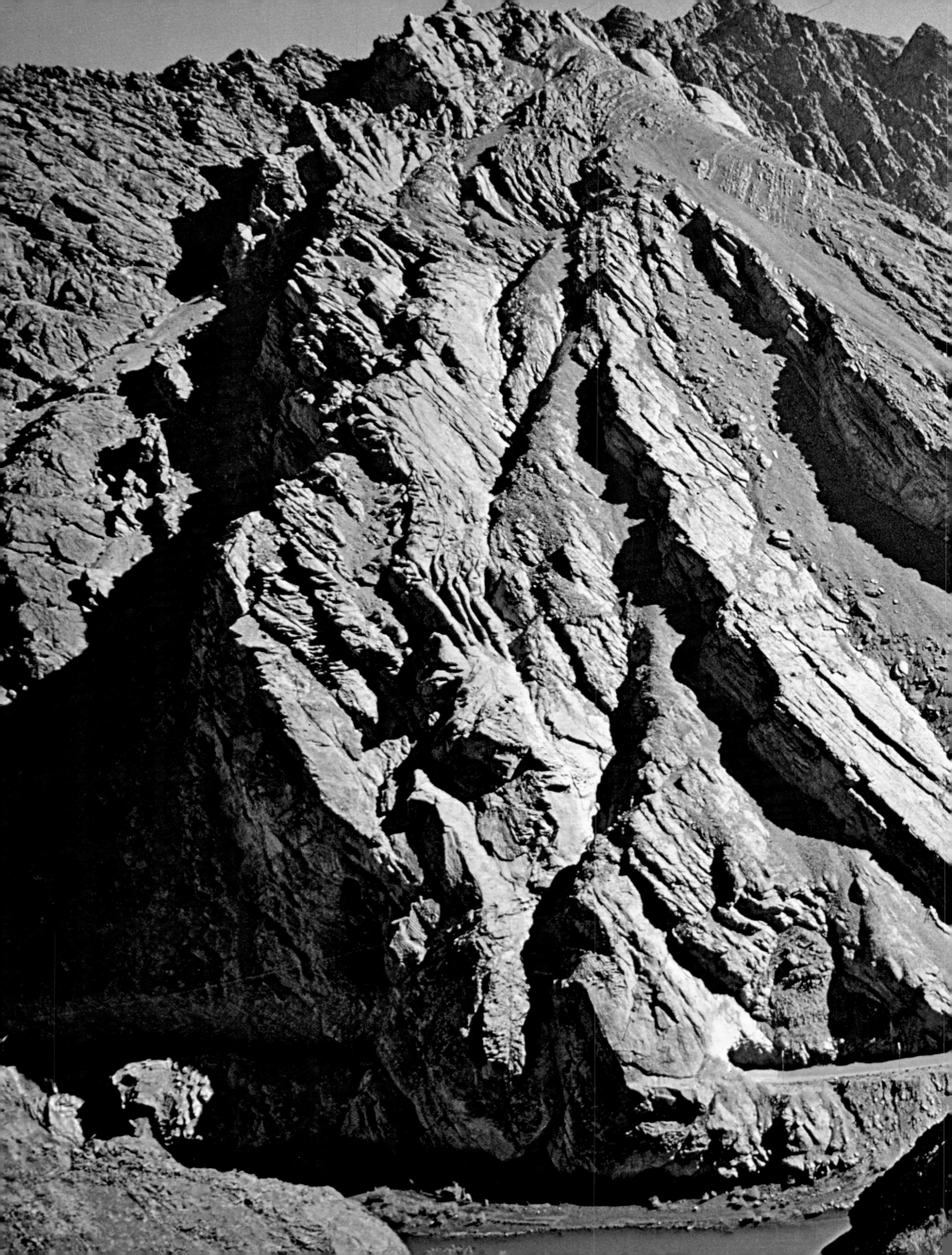

These three stages in the early history of the Persian nation are known to us from written sources. The exact date at which the Persians and the Medes arrived on the plateau is not known, but the onomastics of the area to the north of Lake Urmiya seem to lend weighty support to the supposition that it took place at the end of the second millennium BC, besides giving credibility to the theory that these two nations passed through the Caucasus as, according to Herodotus, did their near relations, the Cimmerians and the Scythians some centuries later. It is thought that the Persians left the north-west of Iran as early as the seventh century BC, and that after 'infiltrating' the folds of the Zagros mountains they settled down close to Ashan in the country of Parsumash, which takes its name from theirs and corresponds to the spurs of the Zagros mountains to the east of Susa, on territory belonging to Elam, a kingdom which allowed these tribes to enter and assigned to them a sparsely inhabited region. On the outskirts of Susa a Persi-Achaemenid village dating back to the same period has been identified.

How did these tribes manage to settle themselves in this new country, which less than two centuries later fostered the beginnings of the Persian kingdom, a kingdom that was destined to become the leading empire of the world?

Recent researches in this area have thrown a completely new light on this obscure period of the beginnings of the Persian tribes. Explorations in the foothills of the Zagros and the Bakhtiari mountains have revealed their settlement, in valleys separated by mountain chains, belonging to tribes which were independent of one another. Each site has a consecrated terrace reached by staircases, on which a fire temple was erected. Objects found there confirm that they were built in the Achaemenian era. This temple was only a podium on which a fire altar was placed for religious ceremonies. All these details correspond to the description given by Herodotus of the religion of the Persians; he says that they had no temples, but sacrificed to Zeus (Ahuramazda) in the open on the high places. Close to the terraces there are ruins of strongholds where the tribal chieftains lived, and not far away are the remains of townships.

So it was that the Persians settled as dependents of the Elamites in the land of their choice, which was to become their true homeland, wherein each great family and tribe remained virtually independent. The great achievement of Achaemenes, who founded the dynasty, and of his immediate successors, was to give cohesion to these tribes, whose final union was promoted by their common language, traditions and aspirations. Political surmises, the progressive weakening of the Elamite state, and its ultimate destruction by the Assyrians, created an environment in which the ambitions of the Persians were promoted both vis-à-vis the Elamites and, later on, the Medes, a closely related people who became their vassals.

It follows that the hypothesis which has enjoyed wide acceptance hitherto, and according to which the Iranians made their appearance on the Plateau as conquistadores, conquering by virtue of their armour and their cavalry, has to be relinquished. The traces of their earliest settlements provide credible evidence that the settlement both of the Persians and of their cousins, the Medes, in the north-west corner of the plateau was a process of unhurried, peaceful penetration. And this process was conducive to cross fertilisation between them and the great civilisations of the ancient East.

The Persians, after their settlement at the foothills of the Bakhtiari mountains, formed the small kingdom of Parsumash. The founder of this unity was Achaemenes. His son, Teispes (675–640 BC), called himself the 'king of the city of Anshan'. At the time of his death, the Persian kingdom consisted of the province of Parsumash, in which were incorporated the cities of Anshan and Pars. Teispes divided his kingdom between his two sons: Ariaramnes (c. 640–590 BC), who became 'great king, king of kings, king of the Land of Parsa', and Cyrus I (c. 640–600 BC), who was 'great king' of Parsumash. It is from Ariaramnes that we have the first authentic inscription of the Achaemenian period of Iranian history. Engraved in cuneiform signs and in the Old Persian language, this gold tablet, a chance find

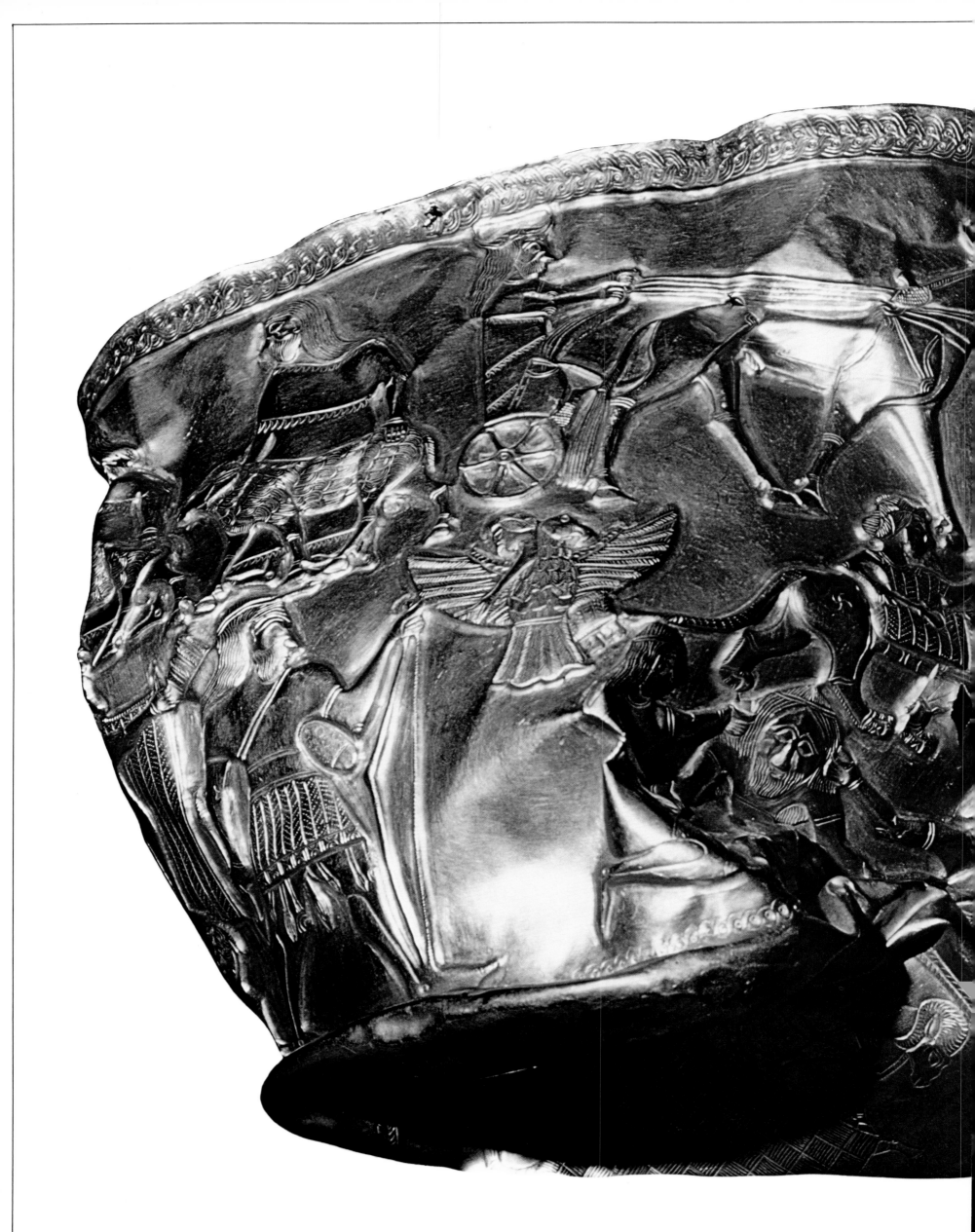

Left: Golden bowl decorated with a repoussé design of religious significance (9th century BC).

Right: Bronze figure of an Elamite god (3rd–2nd century BC).

Following pages: The ziggurat of Dur-Untash at Tchoga Zanbil in Khuzistan. Only two of the original five storeys of this huge religious ediface still survive. It was built about 1250 BC, being made of brick, and measures 346 feet square and 174 feet in height. The site was excavated by Professor Roman Ghirshman between 1951 and 1962.

from Hamadan, describes the title of Ariaramnes: 'This land of the Persians which I possess, provided with fine horses and good men, it is the great god Ahura-mazda who has given it to me. I am the king of this land'. The tablet is symbolic evidence of the great progress made by Persian tribes who had just passed from the semi-nomadic state into that of a semi-sedentary people at the beginning of the seventh century BC. Their alphabet, expressed in cuneiform signs, is a very real advance on the ideo-graphic and syllabic writing of Assyria or Elam. This is an achievement of the Persians at the very dawn of their history. From the beginning of their civilisation, the Persians showed the originality of their creative spirit, which could adopt a foreign idea and reshape it on the lines of their own genius.

This is not the only example of the Persian genius, which had just begun to flower. We learn from the Assyrian annals more about the extent of the territory of Parsumash, which included the district in which is found the modern town of Masjid-i Sulaiman, now a centre of oil production. In this very place are the remains of an imposing artificial terrace, built up against the mountainside. Excava-tions have disclosed several staircases, one over twenty-five metres wide, which lead up to the terrace. This whole structure is an innovation on the plateau – in fact, in the entire area. Neither the Elamites, nor the Babylonians, or the Assyrians, or the original inhabitants were ever associated with construction of this type. The only people in the area who employed this method of wall construction were those of the kingdom of Urartu. The Persians were neighbours of the Urartu before the eighth century, when they left for the Bakhtiari mountains, and it is for this reason that we attribute the terrace of Masjid-i Sulaiman to the Persians. Another similar structure has been found fifteen miles to the north-west, at Bard-i Nishundah. It is possible that the first royal cities of the Persians stood on these two sites, built perhaps by Achaemenes or Teispes. We are inclined to see in the terrace of Pasargadae a similar construction. Thus the terraces of Masjid-i Sulaiman and Bard-i Nishundah, as well as that of Pasargadae, would be 'ancestors' of the terrace of Persepolis.

Ariaramnes was succeeded by his son, Arsames, whose golden tablet, apparently also found at Hamadan, describes him as: 'great king, king of kings, king of Parsa'. Cyrus I, the other son of Teispes, who was granted the province of Parsumash, was succeeded by Cambyses I. Cambyses dethroned Arsames as 'king' and made him a vassal. Cambyses I was married to the daughter of Astyages, King of Media, whose overlordship he had to accept. From this union was born Cyrus the Great, who, on succeeding to the throne, decided on open conflict with the Medes. He could not count on the aid of his Babylonian ally; he was dependent on his own forces alone. These had already been consolidated as the result of a movement for union between tribes of both Iranian and non-Aryan origin.

The victory over Media was not the kind of bloody and destructive triumph which Assyrians or Babylonians inflicted on a vanquished people. Not only was Ecbatana spared, but it remained the capital. Astyages was treated with great generosity, and the Median officials, in association with a number of Persians, were kept on at their posts. In fact, the change in the seat of power took place so discreetly that for western people the Persian was still the Median king. With the victory of Cyrus over Astyages, a new era opened for the Persians, whom fate had united with the Medes.

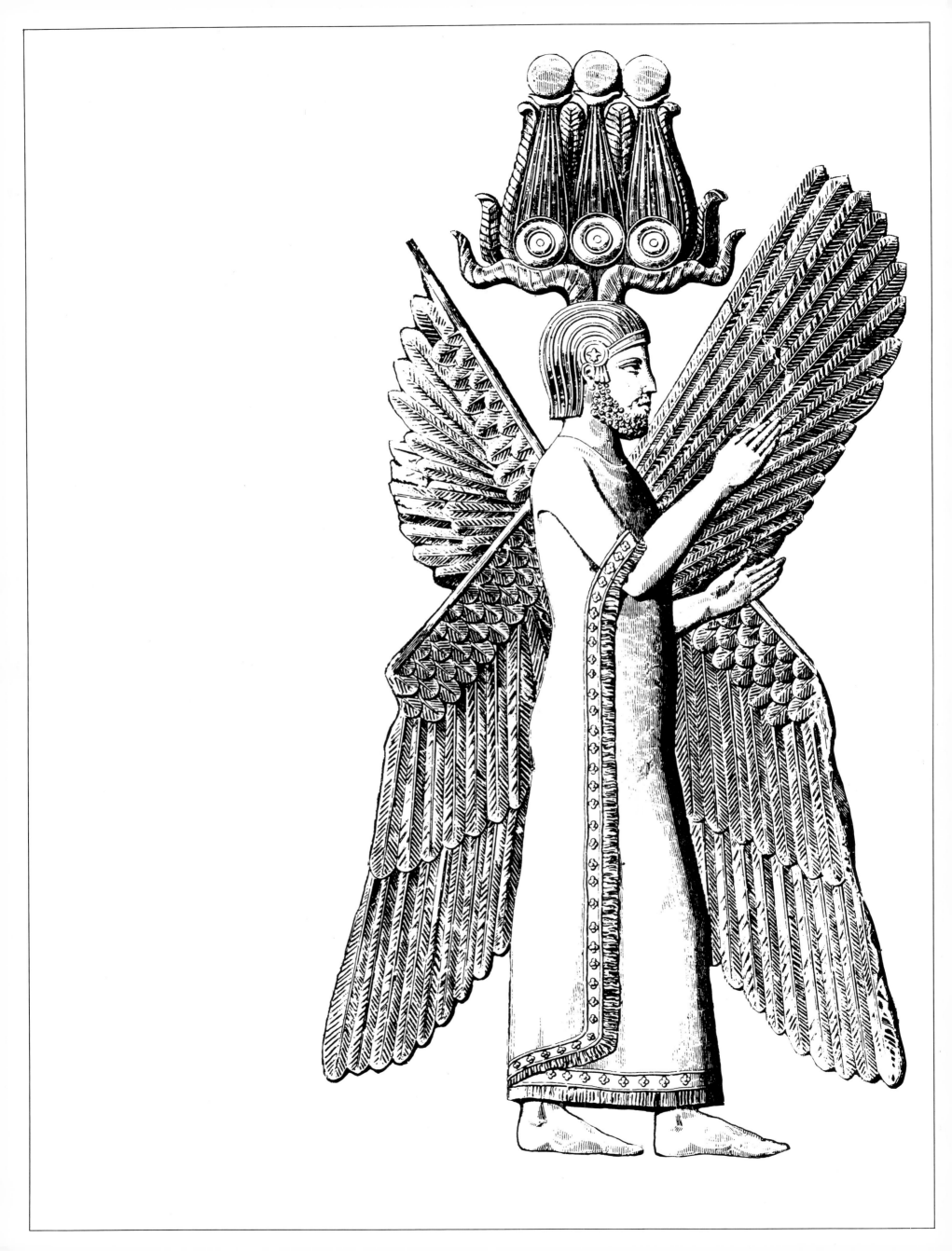

Cyrus...was 'father' to the Persians; the Hellenes, whom he conquered, regarded him as 'master' and 'law-giver', and the Jews as 'the anointed of the Lord'.

Cyrus (559–530 BC) has been known to the historian as Cyrus the Great, though often he is referred to as Cyrus II. He was an outstanding leader and able strategist. Once the Medes and the Persians were united under his sway, he found himself at the head of an empire whose geographical situation and natural wealth enabled him to play the part of intermediary between the civilisation of the west and that of the east. Cyrus was faced with two political objectives: in the west he aimed at the possession of the Mediterranean coast with its seaports, which were the terminals of the great trade routes crossing Iran, and to secure Asia Minor where, in addition to the wealthy state of Lydia, the Greeks had built their maritime bases; in the east he aimed at security. The new state over which he now presided had absorbed part of the older cultures, and stretched to the confines of the Oxus and Jaxartes. Nomadic tribes were still a potential danger to the safety of Iran and her possessions. To secure the defence of his eastern frontier, Cyrus had to subjugate them. Throughout his life he pursued these two aims, and sacrificed himself in the end to the second.

Once he was the ruler of the Median kingdom, and master of Assyria, Urartu and eastern Asia Minor, Cyrus faced the challenge of the powerful kingdom of Lydia, ruled by Croesus since 561 BC. Cyrus invited Cilicia to accept peacefully his overlordship, and when the latter accepted he had successfully cut the route along which Lydia could expect help from her Egyptian and Babylonian allies. Cyrus then made an attractive offer to Croesus. If he would agree to accept Persian sovereignty, Cyrus would leave the throne and kingdom of Lydia to Croesus. When this offer was refused, Cyrus assembled his troops in Assyria, crossed the Tigris, and marched towards Cappadocia. On the way he seized Harran, then an important commercial centre. Lydia, in its battle against Cyrus, was aided by Egypt, Babylonia and Sparta. However, Cyrus moved so quickly that the allies of Lydia had little time to render military assistance. Croesus was compelled to measure his own strength with that of Cyrus. Two battles were fought between the Persians and the Lydians. In the second the Lydians were defeated and Croesus sought refuge in his capital, Sardis, which was believed to be impregnable. However, Cyrus beseiged Sardis and captured it. Lydia became a satrapy under a Persian governor, and Croesus was reprieved. Cyrus then proceeded to the wealthy Greek cities on the coast, which had been subjects of the

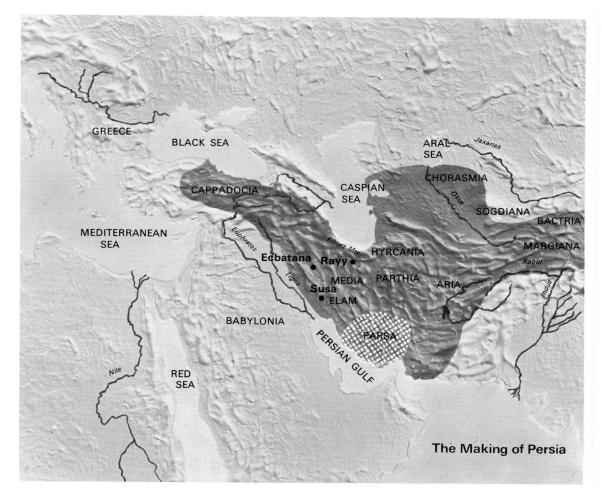

The Making of Persia

Lydian king, and invited them to accept Persian overlordship. The Greek cities, except for the city of Miletus, refused, and proclaimed a rebellion. Cyrus conquered them all, one by one. He divided the littoral into two satrapies – the Ionian, joined to Sardis, and the Black Sea satrapy, named 'those of the sea'. This encounter with the Greeks was the beginning of a policy which was to be pursued by the Achaemenian successors of Cyrus, and which ultimately led to the crusade of Alexander the Great to the east.

The conquest of Asia Minor completed, Cyrus led his armies to the eastern frontiers. Hyrcania and Parthia were already part of the Median kingdom. Further east, Cyrus conquered Drangiana, Arachosia, Margiana and Bactria. After crossing the Oxus, he reached the Jaxartes, where he built fortified towns with the object of defending the farthest frontier of his kingdom against the nomadic tribes of Central Asia. The victories in the east led him again to the west and sounded the hour for the attack on Babylon and Egypt.

The fall of Babylon was not marked by any major clash of arms. It fell without resistance, the royal citadel alone holding out for a few days. The coming of Cyrus to Babylon was foreseen by the Jewish exiles,

who had hailed him as a liberator. Nabonidus, the defeated king, was taken prisoner, but Cyrus – as was his custom – treated him with great clemency, and when the dethroned king died in the following year, 538 BC, Cyrus himself took part in the national mourning which was proclaimed by him. The victory over Babylonia expressed all the facets of the policy of conciliation which Cyrus had followed until then. He presented himself to the Babylonian people not as a conqueror, but as a liberator and the legitimate successor to the crown. He took the title of the 'king of Babylon – king of the land'. He restored to the temples all the statues of the gods which Nabonidus had brought into the capital. At the great New Year festival he took the hand of the god Bel, following the custom of the Babylonian kings, and by this gesture legalised a new line of Babylonian kings. The control of Babylonia meant the overlordship of its dependencies, particularly Syria. Cyrus pursued a benevolent policy towards the Syrians. The Phoenician kings submitted to him and offered their ships for military use against the Greeks. However, the most outstanding feature of his policy concerned the Jews, who had been kept captive and prohibited from returning to Jerusalem. Cyrus, in the

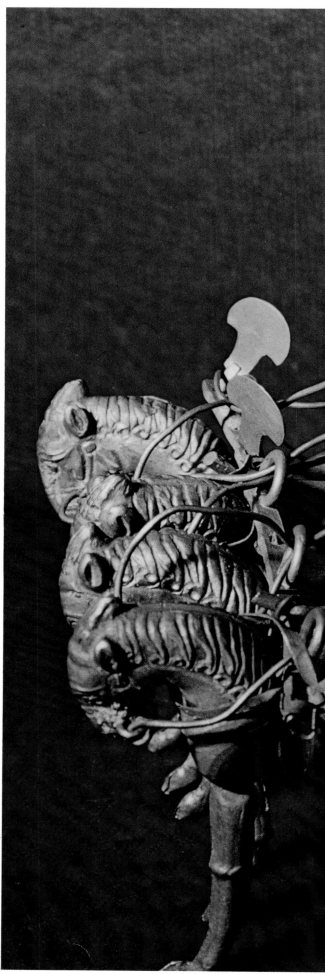

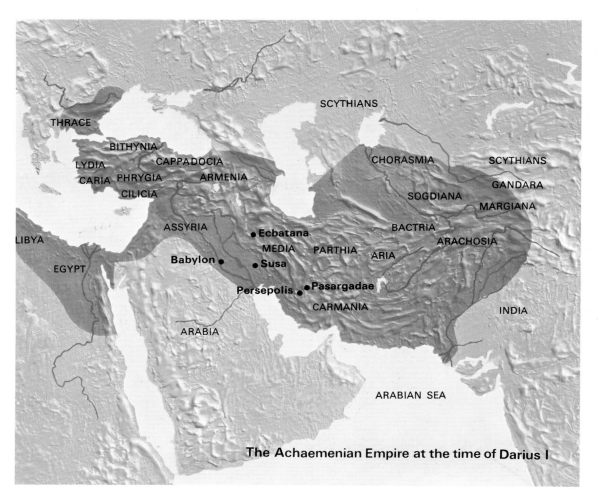

THRACE
BITHYNIA
LYDIA
CAPPADOCIA
CARIA PHRYGIA ARMENIA
CILICIA
SCYTHIANS
CHORASMIA SCYTHIANS
GANDARA
SOGDIANA MARGIANA
ASSYRIA BACTRIA
LIBYA • Ecbatana ARACHOSIA
MEDIA PARTHIA
Babylon • ARIA
• Susa
EGYPT
Persepolis • • Pasargadae
CARMANIA INDIA
ARABIA
ARABIAN SEA

The Achaemenian Empire at the time of Darius I

very first year of his rule over Babylonia, decreed that the Jews could return to Judea, thus ending their captivity. He ordered that their temple at Jerusalem should be rebuilt, and all the gold and silver vessels which belonged to them should be returned. In 537 BC more than 40,000 Jews left Babylonia and returned to the Promised Land. This step was a part of the policy which Cyrus sought to put into practice throughout his life with a view to bringing peace to mankind. At the time of the conquest of Babylon, Cyrus issued a decree on his aims and policy, later hailed as his charter of the rights of nations. Inscribed on a clay cylinder in cuneiform, it was discovered in 1879 and is in the British Museum, London. It reads in part: 'When I entered Babylon . . . I did not allow anyone to terrorise Sumer and Akkad. I kept in view the needs of Babylon and all its sanctuaries to promote their well-being. The citizens of Babylon . . . I lifted their unbecoming yoke. Their dilapidated dwellings I restored. I put an end to their misfortune'. This was a true reflection of his aim of bringing peace to mankind.

From Babylon, Cyrus planned to conquer Egypt. It was at this time that he was forced to resume military operations against the nomads on the eastern marches of his

empire. Leaving his son, Cambyses II, in charge of the preparations for the Egyptian campaign, Cyrus left for the east. Shortly afterwards he fell in battle. His body was brought to Pasargadae and placed in a tomb, the appearance of which is reminiscent of the graves of the first Iranians to enter the plateau, and recalls their original Nordic home. Thus died Cyrus the Great, who conceived of Iran as a state, and turned that concept into reality. Its survival no less than its independence, was his legacy to posterity. This architect of the universal state was a simple man. On his tomb he instructed this inscription to be placed. 'O man, whoever Thou art, And Wheresoever Thou Cometh; For I know Thou Wilt Come, I Am Cyrus Who Founded the Empire of the Persians. Grudge Me Not, Therefore, This Little Earth That Covers My Body'.

Few kings have left so noble a reputation as Cyrus. A great captain and leader of men, he was generous and benevolent. He had no thought of forcing conquered countries into a single mould, and had the wisdom to leave unchanged the institutions of each kingdom he attached to the Persian Crown. Wherever he went he acknowledged and honoured the gods of the different religions, and invariably represented himself as the

Below: A votive four-horse chariot made of gold, from the Oxus treasury (5th—4th centuries BC). The dress of the occupants shows them to be Iranians. It is believed that miniature chariots of this type, which differed from those used in war, played a part in temple ceremonies.

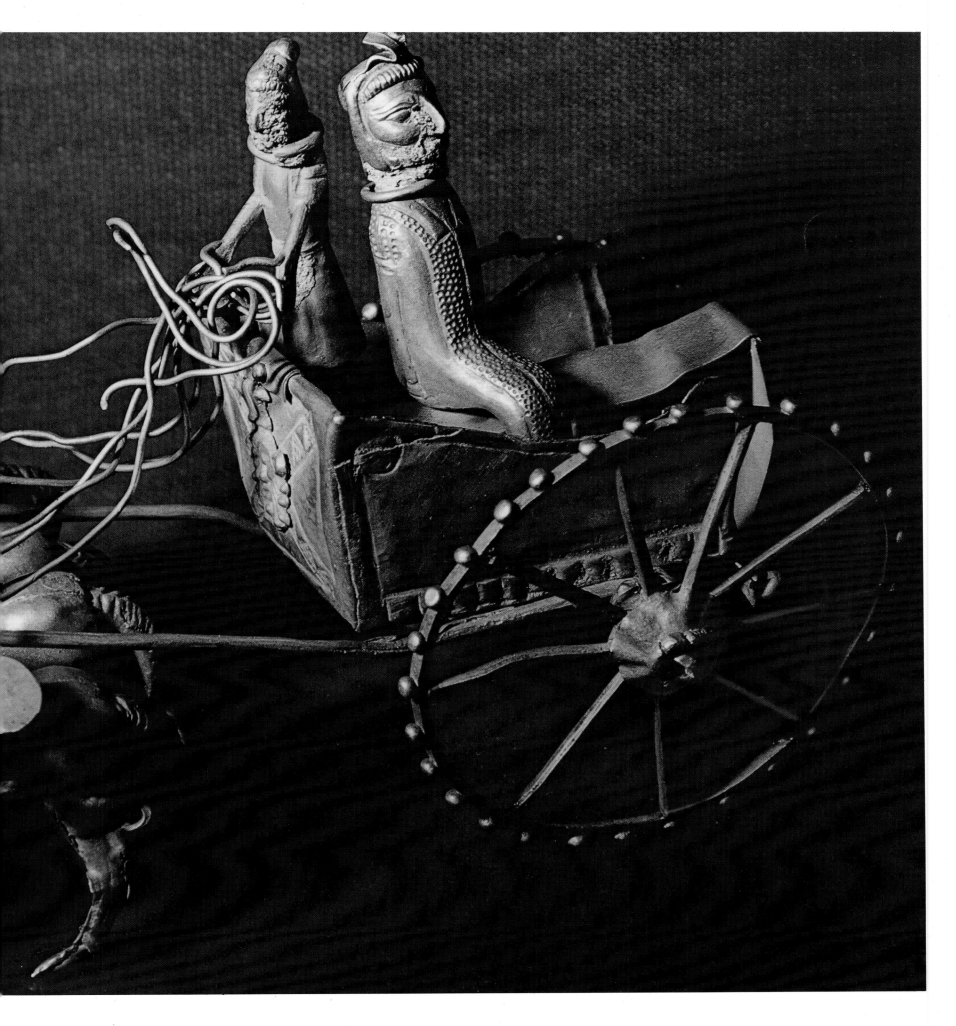

successor of the native rulers. Alexander was not the first to adopt this policy; he had only to imitate the example of Cyrus to be acclaimed by his new subjects. A new wind blew across the world, carrying away the cries of murdered victims, extinguishing the fires of sacked cities and liberating nations from slavery. This was the result of the policies pursued by Cyrus. He was upright, and we never see him, like the Romans, ally himself to a rival people, treat them as an equal, and then turn upon them in a moment of weakness and subject and oppress them. He was 'father' to the Persians; the Hellenes, whom he conquered, regarded him as 'master' and 'law-giver', and the Jews as 'the annointed of the Lord'. A great conqueror, he was always magnanimous towards a defeated enemy,

whom he sought to convert into a friend. In a historical context, writing in Babylon, he himself says: 'Marduk had visited all the land in search of an upright prince, a king after his own heart, whom he took by the hand. He named his name ''Cyrus of Anshan'', and to the kingdom of the whole world he called me by name'.

In less than three decades Cyrus had created a universal state. He had spent most of this time in the campaigns in the east and the west, and had little time for other activities, such as urban development. His subsquent capitals, Ecbatana and Babylon, were used by him at different times. He built Pasargadae, according to tradition, on the site of his decisive victory over Astyages. The name means 'the camp of the Persians', and if this amendment is

correct, it gives a faithful picture of the town. It was, indeed, a vast camp, surrounded by retaining walls, within which, amid parks and gardens, arose palaces and temples. The entrance to the park was flanked by two winged genii. The great audience chamber is decorated with orthostats showing priests bringing animals for sacrifice and genii with eagles' claws. The columns are surmounted by protomes, horses, bulls and lions. Elsewhere the columns were of wood, brightly coloured in blue, green, red and yellow. On the doorposts the king is depicted carrying a sceptre, with part of his clothing inlaid with gold. A fire temple in the form of a square tower is identical with that which stands in front of the tomb of Darius at Naqsh-i Rustam. Some distance away are two stepped fire altars around which religious ceremonies took place in the open air.

Pasargadae is an impressive manifestation of Persian art. In a sense it is a composite, with its Assyrian and Urartian winged bulls, Hittite orthostats, Babylonian polychromy, and Egyptian symbols. Yet fundamentally it reflects a national culture of a high order, in which all foreign influences have been recast and transposed in a coherent and balanced manner, making it a new art in which architectonic features are predominant. The artists have introduced the use of alternating white and black stone in appreciation of the play of colours in sunlight and shadow. We see a notable advance in the treatment of folds of draperies and in the representation of the human form. Each detail, whether original or of foreign provenance, is infused with Iranian spirit, and for many scholars the art of Pasargadae is an even greater achievement than that of Persepolis. Recent research seems to confirm that some of the architects or builders of the palaces were Greek.

'Ahuramazda and other gods help me,' said Darius. The new king invoked the aid of the great god and presented himself as the legitimate successor of Cambyses II, who had died without issue.

Darius the Great ascended the Achaemenian throne twelve years after the death of Cyrus. Cambyses, the eldest son of Cyrus, had ruled in the intervening period. He had come to power after a dispute with his younger brother, Bardiya, who was killed by him. Cambyses was unlike his father in temperament and attitude. His sole achievement was the conquest of Egypt, planned by Cyrus. Cambyses had planned several other conquests: against the Carthaginian power in the western Mediterranean; against the oasis of Ammon, which controlled the route to Cyrenaica, and against Ethiopia. The first was never undertaken, the second partially failed, and the third was not undertaken either. However, in the course of the Ammon expedition, he succeeded in securing the submission of the Greeks of Libya, Cyrene and Barka. A part of the Greek world thus came under Persian domination during his rule. While the king was on his expedition to conquer Ethiopia, a revolt broke out in Persia itself, led by the pretender Gaumata, the Magian, also known as the false Bardiya or Smerdes. The pretender closely resembled, in physical appearance, Bardiya, the king's brother, who had been killed. His success was startling, since all the provinces of the empire accepted him as the new ruler. It is

not known if Cambyses, learning of this revolt, accidentally wounded himself in the course of an epileptic fit, or committed suicide.

Darius was the son of Hystaspes, who in turn was the son of Arsames, who was the grandson of Teispes. According to legend, there were seven young nobles who decided to end the rule of Gaumata, and Darius was their leader. They overthrew Gaumata, who was taken prisoner and executed. Darius was elected to replace him as the lawful heir to the Achaemenian throne, claiming that he was a legitimate descendant of Achaemenes himself.

When the young king came to power, revolts had broken out in all quarters of the empire which Cyrus had built. For the first two years of his reign he struggled to re-establish law and order in the Achaemenian state. During these twenty-four months, he fought nineteen battles and defeated nine kings. To record his victory, he had a gigantic bas-relief cut on a high cliff on the road between Kermanshah and Hamadan. This represents him under the benevolent protection of the great god, Ahuramazda, whose head and shoulders arise out of a winged sun-disc. The king, followed by two arms bearers, tramples under foot the prostrate body of the false

Bardiya, while behind him, attached by a long rope, stand eight 'false kings'. Round this scene is sculptured, in several columns, the story of the revolts and the king's victory over them. The inscription, written in Old Persian, Babylonian and Elamite, states that Darius was the ninth Achaemenian king. In this number are included both branches of the dynasty – that of Achaemenes, Teispes, Cyrus I, Cambyses I, Cyrus II and Cambyses II on the one hand, and Ariaramnes and Arsames on the other – which agrees with other known records. 'Ahuramazda and other gods help me', said Darius. The new king invoked the aid of the great god and presented himself as the legitimate successor of Cambyses II, who had died without issue.

The military achievements of Darius were extraordinary. He re-established the unity of the Achaemenian empire from Egypt to the Jaxartes with the aid of a small army which had remained faithful to him. Though young, Darius had had considerable experience in military affairs. He had carried his lance in the expedition which cost Cyrus his life. He had been a commander of the Ten Thousand Immortals – the Royal bodyguard – under Cambyses, when the latter was on his Egyptian campaign. The Ten Thousand Immortals stood by Darius in his campaign to reunite the empire. He showed his gratitude to them in a spectacular manner; in each new palace he built, whether it was at Susa or Persepolis, he had representations of these Immortals sculptured in stone, or depicted in colour on enamelled brickwork, so that their memory should be perpetuated. Though a great military genius himself, it was his fate to be known to posterity as a great administrator, law-giver and builder of the magnificent urban civilisations which prospered under his Achaemenian empire.

Darius evolved new administrative methods after making an analysis of the set-back suffered by the policy laid down by Cyrus. He decided to replace this 'over-liberal' policy and establish the state on more solid foundations. The revolt in the empire convinced him that he could rely only on the trust of the Persian people who were loyal to their king. They, therefore, must govern as masters, and direct the affairs of all the countries included in the empire. Yet there was no question of a policy of force. In any event, this would have been impossible, since the ruling people were in an obvious minority. A statesmanlike policy was essential: each people was to keep its own language, its individuality, its institutions and its religion and to enjoy the benefits of the

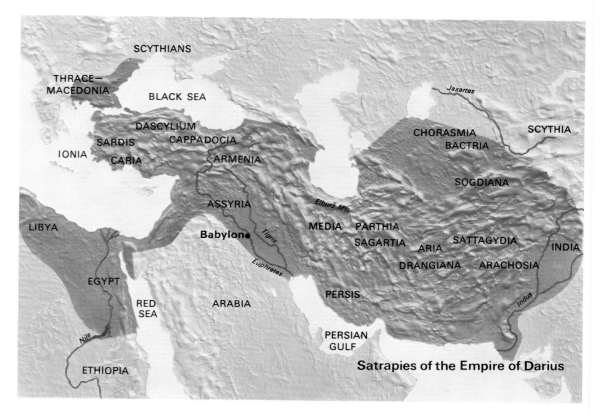

SCYTHIANS
THRACE—MACEDONIA
BLACK SEA
DASCYLIUM
SARDIS CAPPADOCIA
IONIA CARIA
ARMENIA
ASSYRIA
LIBYA
Babylon
MEDIA PARTHIA
SAGARTIA ARIA
EGYPT
RED SEA
ARABIA
PERSIS
PERSIAN GULF
ETHIOPIA
Jaxartes
CHORASMIA SCYTHIA
BACTRIA
SOGDIANA
Elburz Mts
Tigris
Euphrates
Nile
SATTAGYDIA INDIA
DRANGIANA ARACHOSIA
Indus

Satrapies of the Empire of Darius

state of which it formed part; but the state could be administered only by a Persian delegated by the Great King. The whole empire was, therefore, divided into twenty provinces, each under a satrap or 'protector of the kingdom', who was directly responsible to the king. The principle of satrapy was undoubtedly evolved by Cyrus, and followed by Cambyses. Darius applied it to the empire, and organised it on a new basis. Next to each satrap he placed a commander in chief of the armed forces stationed in the satrapy, who, equally, was responsible directly to the king. He created a third post – that of a high official – whose duty it was to collect taxes. By royal edict, each province had to contribute a fixed sum annually to the royal treasury in accordance with its resources. The satrapies paid their dues in precious metals and in kind, such as horses, cattle and food. The administrative machinery was completed by the appointment of a secretary to supervise all the actions of the satrap and provide the liaison between him and the central authority. The king was willing to take no chances. He further evolved an organisation of inspectors. They were completely independent and were provided with their own armed forces in case of necessity. They were called 'the ears of the king', and travelled all over the empire, making surprise visits to the administrators and examined their conduct of affairs. This unique institution was copied in later years by many, including Charlemagne, whose

missi dominici or 'royal envoys', performed the same duties as the 'ears of the king' appointed by Darius. Darius aimed at the creation of a centralised and powerful national state out of a mass of countries, provinces and lands which had been joined together. He, therefore, had to replace the form of government set up by Cyrus. His administrative and fiscal organisation respected national rights and imposed a semblance of unity.

The imperial structure of the universal state required more than a political framework. Large kingdoms had been built in the world before the Achaemenians set up their universal state. However, they could neither be converted into empires nor last for more than a generation. Darius was the first monarch to understand that an imperial state can only exist if it can evolve a technological policy to keep the empire closely knit. He, therefore, concentrated on the creation of a network of transport and communications. He built roads across the length and breadth of his empire which spread from Thrace to the western parts of India. These new roads were intended primarily for administrative purposes. The network facilitated caravan trade and increased its volume throughout the empire. The Royal Road that went from Susa across the Tigris below Arbella, passed by Harran and ended at Sardis, whence it was extended to Ephesus. One thousand six hundred and seventy-seven miles long, it was divided into one hundred and eleven post stations, each

Below left: The Royal Road.
To maintain contact with the widely separated centres of his empire Darius created a network of arterial roads. Their total length was 1677 miles, and the system was divided into 111 post stations, at each of which fresh horses awaited the King's envoys. The whole network could thus be traversed by his messengers in a week. Caravans, on the other hand, took ninety days to complete the journey.

Below right: Statuette of an Iranian horseman (5th–4th centuries BC), from a drawing. The way in which the horse's mane is cropped was peculiar to the Achaemenians.

Right: Darius's code of ethics, from a tablet found at Susa which reproduces, with some variations, an inscription from his tomb at Naqsh-i-Rustam.

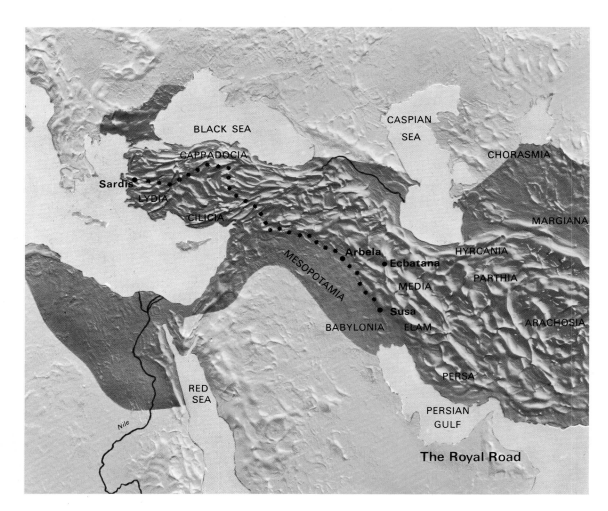

The Royal Road

with relays of fresh horses for the royal couriers. According to the ancient historians, the caravans took ninety days to travel this road from end to end, while the royal envoys covered it in a week. The old route that linked Babylon with Egypt via Carchemish was improved and connected with another leading from Babylon to Holwan, Bisutun and Hamadan. This road was extended to the valley of the upper Kabul, whence, following the river, it reached the valley of the Indus. Inside the country, other roads, lesser in length but equally indispensable, were built, such as the road joining Susa and Persepolis, of which part of the stone-paved surface can still be seen near Bebahan. These roads were not only a part of the imperial structure of the Achaemenians, but were also their legacy to the ancient east, since they were used for many centuries after the passing away of the Achaemenian universal state.

Darius knew that an empire could not be constructed without a legal framework. Scholars who have studied the numerous texts left by Darius in many places at Bisutun and Persepolis, at Susa and Naqsh-i Rustam, have recognised a number of parallels between his writings and the ancient code of Hammurabi. These official texts, copied on stelae, tablets or papyrus, were sent to all the main provincial centres of the empire. Thus fragments of the Bisutun inscriptions have been found written in Aramaic on a papyrus at Elephantine, and in Babylonian at Babylon. A tablet found at Susa reproduces, with some variations, the inscription that Darius had engraved on his tomb at Naqsh-i Rustam. It is useful to quote it at some length (see the extract on the opposite page) because it gives a graphic picture of the universal state built by Cyrus and Darius, and the code of ethics which governed it.

An exceptional feature of the judicial system established by Darius, and which was noted by Herodotus, laid it down that the royal judges, chosen from among the Persians, held office until their death, unless they were removed for miscarriage of justice. It was they who judged cases, interpreted national laws, and were appealed to in all disputes. The vanquished people who became members of the universal state retained their own legal system, as was decreed by Cyrus, side by side with that of Darius. Darius was a true law-giver and he always emphasised the virtues of truth and justice. This is to be seen in several of his inscriptions.

Another special trait of the philosophy which Darius evolved for the people of Iran is the spirit of nationalism, totally unknown in earlier ancient oriental empires. One of his inscriptions runs thus: 'Saith Darius the King: may Ahuramazda bear me aid, with the gods of the royal house; and may Ahuramazda protect this country from a [hostile] army, from famine, from the Lie! Upon this country may there not come an army, nor famine nor the Lie; this I pray as a boon from Ahuramazda, together with the gods of the royal house. This boon may Ahuramazda, together with the gods of the royal house give to me!'

This sentiment of nationalism did not exclude a preoccupation with the welfare of other countries whose destinies the Great King directed at the behest of his supreme god. The philosophy of the Great King was partly a reflection of the reality. The spirit of the Persian people was imbued with this love of country; this was remarked on by Herodotus, who emphasised that no Persian ever prayed to his god for a personal benefit. 'But he prays for the welfare of the king and of the whole Persian people, among whom he is of necessity included.

This patriotic ideal inspired and developed a national conscience in the fulfilment of the imperial task that was a part of the nation's destiny.'

A GREAT GOD IS AHURAMAZDA, WHO CREATED THIS EARTH, WHO CREATED YONDER SKY, WHO CREATED MAN, WHO CREATED HAPPINESS FOR MAN, WHO MADE DARIUS KING, ONE KING OF MANY, ONE LORD OF MANY.

I AM DARIUS THE GREAT KING, KING OF KINGS, KING OF COUNTRIES CONTAINING ALL KINDS OF MEN, KING IN THIS GREAT EARTH FAR AND WIDE, SON OF HYSTASPES, AN ACHAEMENIAN, A PERSIAN, SON OF A PERSIAN, AN ARYAN, HAVING ARYAN LINEAGE.

SAITH DARIUS THE KING: BY THE FAVOUR OF AHURAMAZDA THESE ARE THE COUNTRIES WHICH I SEIZED OUTSIDE PERSIA; I RULED OVER THEM; THEY BORE TRIBUTE TO ME; WHAT WAS SAID TO THEM BY ME, THAT THEY DID; MY LAW – THAT HELD THEM FIRM: MEDIA, ELAM, PARTHIA, ARIA, BACTRIA, SOGDIANA, CHORASMIA, DRANGIANA, ARACHOSIA, SATTAGYDIA, GANDARA, AMYRGIAN, SIND, SCYTHIANS, SCYTHIANS WITH POINTED CAPS, BABYLONIA, ASSYRIA, ARABIA, EGYPT, ARMENIA, CAPPADOCIA, SARDIS, IONIA, SCYTHIANS WHO ARE ACROSS THE SEA, SKUDRA, PETASOS-WEARING IONIANS, LIBYANS, ETHIOPIANS, MEN OF MAKA, CARIANS.

SAITH DARIUS THE KING: MUCH WHICH WAS ILL-DONE, THAT I MADE GOOD. PROVINCES WERE IN COMMOTION; ONE MAN WAS SMITING ANOTHER. THE FOLLOWING I BROUGHT ABOUT BY THE FAVOUR OF AHURAMAZDA, THAT THE ONE DOES NOT SMITE THE OTHER AT ALL, EACH ONE IS IN HIS PLACE. MY LAW — OF THAT THEY FEEL FEAR, SO THAT THE STRONGER DOES NOT SMITE NOR DESTROY THE WEAK.

SAITH DARIUS THE KING: BY THE FAVOUR OF AHURAMAZDA, MUCH HANDIWORK WHICH PREVIOUSLY HAD BEEN PUT OUT OF ITS PLACE, THAT I PUT IN ITS PLACE. A TOWN BY NAME . . . [ITS] WALL FALLEN FROM AGE, BEFORE THIS, UNREPAIRED — I BUILT ANOTHER WALL [TO SERVE] FROM THAT TIME INTO THE FUTURE.

SAITH DARIUS THE KING: MAY AHURAMAZDA, TOGETHER WITH THE GODS PROTECT ME AND MY ROYAL HOUSE, AND WHAT HAS BEEN INSCRIBED BY ME.

The Zoroastrian religion explained that the world was ruled by two principles, Good and Evil – the first being… Ahuramazda, the second a malevolent spirit, Ahriman… The struggle between Good and Evil was to end in the victory of Good.

The philosophical-religious basis of the Achaemenian civilisation was typically Persian, and finds few parallels in ancient civilisations. Ahuramazda was the Great God, the creator of all, the benefactor of every living creature. It was he who by his will directed the actions of the king on whom he had conferred power. The sword of the Achaemenian king was carried to other lands, not in his own name, but in that of Ahuramazda. The king was only fulfilling the divine commands. Persia of the Achaemenians was not a state founded on religion, as was the case with the Abbasid caliphs. Although Darius derived his power from the god himself, there was, in his case, no question of being bowed down under the weight of a doctrine which became a religion. There was no imperial cult, but the mere fact that the king had been placed on the throne by the will of Ahuramazda gave a sort of unity to the Persian world.

There were other gods besides Ahuramazda, such as the sun (Mithra), the moon (Mah), the earth (Zam), fire (Atar), water (Apam Napat), and wind (Vahyu). The inscriptions of Darius and his two successors make no mention of the name of any god apart from Ahuramazda, and it may be that under the first two Achaemenians a distinction should be made between the official religion and that of the rest of the people. Later, the official pantheon was enlarged by divinities who are mentioned with Ahuramazda in the texts, and these are Mithra, the sun god, god of justice and redemption, who was a very old Iranian deity, and Anahita, goddess of the waters, of fertility and procreation, who shows the influence of non-Iranian cults. We know of three temples belonging to the Achaemenian period: one at Pasargadae built by Cyrus, another at Naqsh-i Rustam in front of the tomb of Darius and, probably, built by him,

and a third at Susa, apparently dating from the time of Artaxerxes II. Each is in the form of a square tower enclosing a single room reached by a stairway, and here the Magi tended the sacred fire. It appears that religious ceremonies took place in the open, for all the altars known to us have been found in the open country some distance away from the temples. The Persians also made images of their gods. Statues of Anahita at Susa, Ecbatana and Babylon and other great centres of the empire were set up by Artaxerxes II. All the bas-reliefs above the Achaemenian tombs represent the prince sacrificing before an altar with the sacred fire, and above him is a winged disc, out of which arises the head and shoulders of Ahuramazda. The same figure is on the bas-reliefs of Bisutun and on certain of the monuments at Persepolis. The significance of this figure is believed to be as follows: the world was divided: Ahuramazda reigned in the sky and 'enfolds and protects with his wings the earth and its ruler', the Achaemenian king, his viceroy, who reigned upon the earth.

The Achaemenian religion was not yet monotheistic, but there was already a strong movement in that direction. The Mazdian religion reformed by Zoroaster began to spread through the empire during the reign of Darius. The date of Zoroaster, the prophet, is still in dispute. Believed to have been born in Media, but forced to go into exile, he is thought to have preached in eastern Iran, where he is known to have converted a certain Prince Hystaspes, thought by some authorities to be the father of Darius. The religion of Zoroaster spread from the east throughout the country. The Zoroastrian religion explained that the world was ruled by two principles, Good and Evil – the first being a kind of hypostasis of Ahuramazda, the second a malevolent spirit, Ahriman. Ahuramazda was assisted by divine spirits. The struggle between Good and Evil was to end in the victory of Good. Thus Zoroastrian dualism was only apparent, and the Zoroastrian religion was a kind of monotheism. The sociological explanation of the acceptance of this religion is interesting. Eastern Iran was constantly exposed to the attacks and depredations of the invading nomads, who were equated with Evil.

Once established as a national religion, its implications meant a code of ethics. Good thoughts, good words and good deeds, was the triad on which this code was based. Man had to be kind to animals, look after them and treat them well. Aryan sacrifices were forbidden, since the beast which fed and worked for man ought to be venerated. The

Above: Fire altars at Naqsh-i-Rustam, probably of the Sassanian period.

Right: The god Aharumazda, an impression from a cylinder seal. On each side of the altar stands a king in prayer.

intoxicating drink, Haoma, was also banned. Among the wicked were included the bad judge, the man who neglected his fields, and he who oppressed others. The good prince fought for his religion, defended his people, fed the poor and protected the weak. Finally, under this Zoroastrian code of ethics, the dead could neither be interred, nor burned or immersed for fear of defiling the three sacred elements of earth, fire and water. Zoroastrianism was almost contemporary with Buddhism, and both were protests against the crude practices and bloody rites of the old Aryan religions which were the products of their nomadic life. Zoroastrianism was the work of an aristocracy, while Buddhism expressed popular aspirations. This may perhaps explain why Buddhism spread and still has hundreds of millions of adherents, whereas Zoroastrianism is today confined to a small community which defends it fanatically.

The cultural life of the Achaemenian civilisation was rich and varied. The invention of cuneiform writing to express Old Persian probably goes back to Teispes, or was, perhaps, even inherited from the Medians. We have a clay tablet found at Susa; this would give us the idea that the Persians at the time of the kingdom in Fars probably wrote on clay tablets. Soon after the Achaemenians spread all over the ancient known world. The speed with which the empire was formed made it impossible to create an army of scribes capable of translating Persian into all the other languages. On the other hand, Aramaic had become very widespread since the beginning of the first millenium BC. It was used extensively in commerce and even in conversation under the Assyrians. By the Achaemenian period, Aramaic had become a true *lingua franca* in Asia, and was employed, particularly for state business, from Egypt to India. The result was that all the Persian chancelleries employed Aramaic. Nevertheless, the Persians must also have written their own language. The use of cuneiform writing was restricted to inscriptions on stone monuments, and, in the course of time, fell into disuse. The scribes who knew it became few and the inscriptions faulty. However, taking the period as a whole, all the evidence points to the fact that the Persians adopted Aramaic writing to express their own language.

The Achaemenians were magnificent builders of urban civilisations, and especially palaces. The austere conditions of the soldier-king changed with the expansion of the empire. Darius, once he became the powerful Great King, required capital cities and palaces that were larger

Below: Drawing of a decorative pillar, the capital being in the form of addorsed bulls, from the palace at Susa.

Right: A lion-griffin; a detail of a similar beast is shown on pages 46–7.

Centre: Plan of the palace.

Far right: A brick-work frieze of archers at Susa. These were the so-called Immortals, who, under the leadership of Darius, conquered Egypt and later helped him to regain his throne.

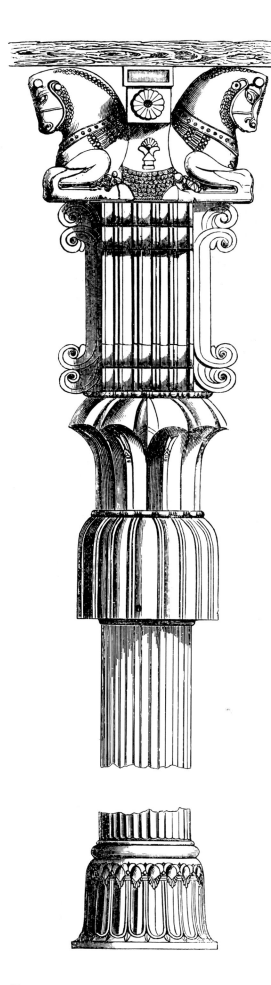

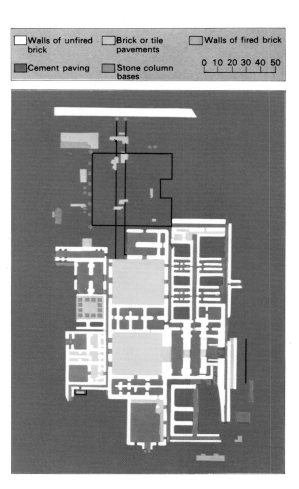

☐ Walls of unfired brick	☐ Brick or tile pavements	☐ Walls of fired brick
☐ Cement paving	☐ Stone column bases	0 10 20 30 40 50

and finer than those built by the Babylonian and Assyrian monarchs. In his time, architecture and ornament became measures of his power, his might, and the pomp of his Court. He moved his capital from Babylon to Susa, probably in 521 BC. Here, on the acropolis, he constructed a strong citadel. On a neighbouring mound he built his palace and the apadana, the hypostyle throne room. Further to the east, and separated from the palace by a broad avenue, lay the city proper. The whole complex was surrounded by a strong wall, flanked with projecting towers. At the foot of the wall he dug a large moat, which surrounded the town and made it an impregnable island. As capital of the world, connected with the sea by four rivers and thronged with kings, princes, ambassadors, doctors, men of letters and artists, Susa had to be worthy of the role assigned to it by the Great King. Darius left for posterity an inscription which not only tells us today how he carried out this work, but which is also one of the finest examples of Achaemenian official literature. It is useful to quote the essential passages of this historic document which has been described as the 'charter of the Palace of Susa'.

'This is the palace which I built at Susa. From afar its ornamentation was brought.

Downward the earth was dug until I reached rock in the earth. When the excavation was made, then rubble was packed down, one part forty cubits in depth, another [part] twenty cubits in depth. On that rubble the palace was built.

'And that the earth was dug downward, and that the rubble was packed down, and that the sun-dried brick was moulded, the Babylonian people it did [these tasks]. The cedarwood this – a mountain by name Lebanon – from there was brought; the Assyrian people, it brought it to Babylon; from Babylon the Carians and the Ionians brought it to Susa. The yakawood was

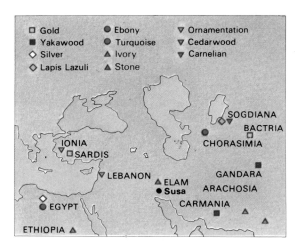

in Elam – from there were brought. The stone cutters who wrought the stone, these were Ionians and Sardians. The goldsmiths which wrought the gold, those were Medians and Egyptians. The men who wrought the baked brick, those were Babylonians. The men who adorned the wall, those were Medes and Egyptians'.

This text gives a faithful picture of the empire. The architecture of the palace was still considerably influenced by Elamite principles and the recently excavated ruins at Susa, which are of Elamite standard, prove that Darius employed Elamite architects.

Left: Regions from which were brought the materials – timber, metals, ivory and precious stones – used in the building of Darius's palace at Susa.

Above: A gold armlet with finials in the form of griffins, from the Oxus treasure (5th century BC).

Lower right: The Achaemenians often decorated their fabrics with gold ornaments such as these, which were sewn onto their clothes.

brought from Gandara and from Carmania. The gold was brought from Sardis and from Bactria, which here was wrought. The precious stone lapis lazuli and carnelian which were wrought here, this was brought from Sogdiana. The precious stone turquoise this was brought from Chorasimia, which was wrought here. The silver and the ebony was brought from Egypt. The ornamentation with which the wall was adorned, that from Ionia was brought. The ivory which was wrought here, was brought from Ethiopia and from Sind and from Arachosia. The stone columns which were here wrought – a village by name Abiradus,

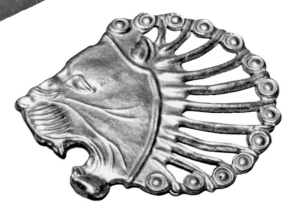

Below: A sword (5th century BC) from Hamadan with a golden hilt. The pommel is ornamented with lions' heads and the shoulder of the blade with the heads of ibexes. This form of decoration had been known in the Near East for centuries.

Below left: Part of a gold necklace decorated with animals' heads, from the grave of an Achaemenian princess (*c.* 345 BC); also beads carved from semi-precious stones, forming part of a necklace. Precious stones were unknown to the Achaemenians.

Below right: A gold earring of intricate design. The many finds of jewellery such as this suggest that much of it was mass-produced.

The Achaemenian empire unified the whole of western Asia, which enjoyed administration under central control, good means of transport and communication, and a perfectly balanced system of tax collection.

The palace at Susa had hardly been finished when Darius decided to build another residence at Persepolis in his native country of Fars. At Persepolis a great terrace with its back to the mountain was partly quarried out of the rock and partly constructed on large blocks of stone joined by iron clamps fixed with molten lead. This construction had already been adopted by his predecessors. A defensive wall of unbaked brick followed the contour of the terrace fairly high up on the hillside in order to protect the rear. A great staircase with a double turn gave access to the esplanade, whence two further flights led to the apadana. This was a replica of the one built at Susa, since the same artists who worked at Susa were brought to Persepolis. The cedar-wood ceiling was supported by seventy-two fluted columns, as in Susa. They were about sixty-five feet in height, and were surmounted by protomes of bulls, lions and horned lions. A long procession of Immortals sculptured in stone decorate, as in the palace at Susa, the sides of the staircase. They are followed by a line of

courtiers, both Medes and Persians. Finally, in two registers, is a procession of subject nations bringing gifts: some lead rare animals, others carry the products for which their countries were noted, jewellery, vessels and cloth. The principal aim of the Achaemenian art expressed here was to illustrate, on the one hand, the power of the king, and on the other, the diversity of people composing the empire. It was an art in the service of power and was, above all, decorative. In pursuit of this aim, the artists of the age excelled in animal portraiture. The style of the decoration achieved under Darius is marked by clarity, balance, power and firmness, and translates into stone the character of his career. Near the Apadana, at a slightly higher level, he built his own palace in the style of a Nordic house, which became the typical dwelling of the Iranians. At one side was a small building, the tripylon, with columns surmounted by human-headed capitals. Hard up against the mountain lay the Treasury, where two bas-reliefs depict identical scenes: the reception by Darius of a court official.

The 'foundation charter of the palace' quoted above, is not only valid for Susa, but must also apply to building work at Persepolis and Ecbatana. It gives a picture of the whole of official Achaemenian art. In the cosmopolitan capitals of the Great King, this art, so closely linked with the fortunes of the empire, also became, in itself, cosmopolitan. In truth, the Persians could not do otherwise than draw on the achievements of the older oriental civilisations, for they themselves had passed too rapidly from humble dwelling to palace. In this, did they not act as many other peoples had done before them? Did not the Urartians draw on the Assyrians as well as on the civilisations of Asia Minor or Mesopotamia? And were not the Assyrians heirs of Sumero-Akkadian, Hurrian and Hittite art? No other people, however, attained a splendour comparable with that of the Achaemenian art, even though there is an obvious lack of proportion between the column, the highest known to ancient architecture, and the procession of decorative figures at the base. The dynamics

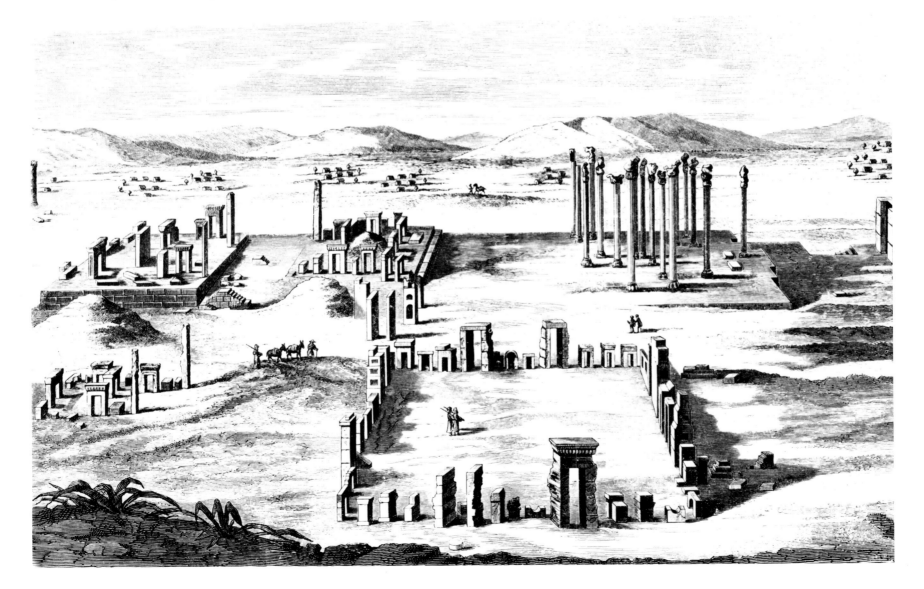

A reconstruction of Persepolis (5th century BC). Until it was destroyed in 331 BC, the palace, which was the religious and ceremonial centre of the Achaemenian kings, comprised a great audience chamber, the Hall of a Hundred Columns, anterooms, a treasury, stables and numerous other buildings.

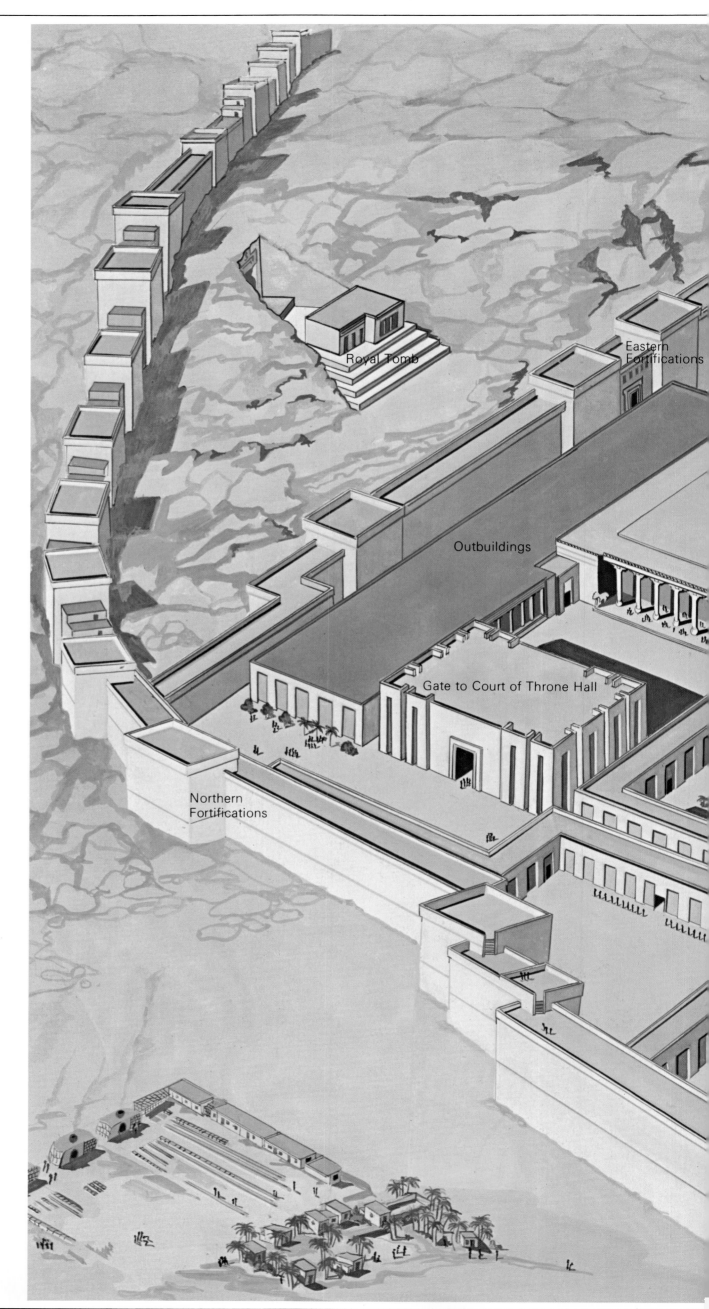

Royal Tomb

Eastern Fortifications

Outbuildings

Gate to Court of Throne Hall

Northern Fortifications

54

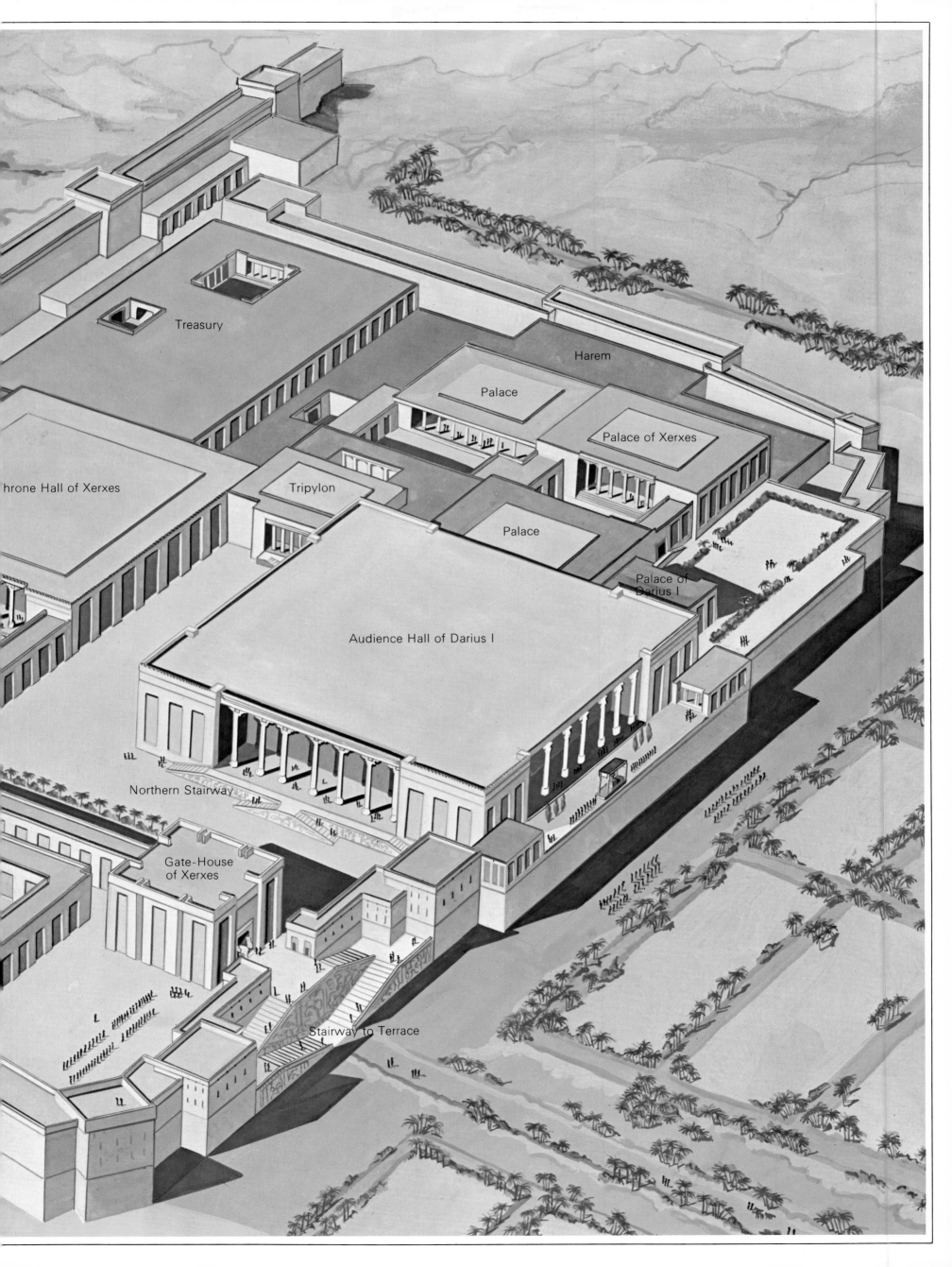

Treasury

Harem

Palace

Palace of Xerxes

Throne Hall of Xerxes

Tripylon

Palace

Palace of Darius I

Audience Hall of Darius I

Northern Stairway

Gate-House of Xerxes

Stairway to Terrace

Details from a bas-relief at Persepolis depicting the nations that came to pay tribute to Darius: *right:* a Syrian; *below:* Scythians; *far right:* a Persian.

Left: a Persian introducing a Mede; (*above*) a group of Syrians bearing gifts.

Below: a Persian dignatory leading Gandarans,
and (*below*) a Mede leading Bactrians;
lower left: Cilicians.

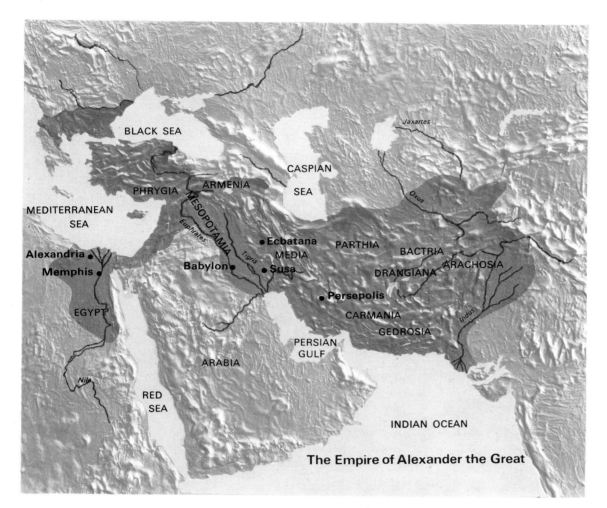

The Empire of Alexander the Great

should give him a certain authority with the Greek cities. He introduced the *proskynos*, or prostration, required by the etiquette of the Achaemenian Court from every Persian subject in the presence of the Great King.

The empire of which Alexander could only lay the foundations did not survive him. On his death, it broke up into three parts. Of Alexander's successors, Seleucus, more than any other was in sympathy with his ideas and best fitted to assimilate himself to the Iranian world. He had been made leader of the cavalry formations of Persian nobles after the capture of Susa, and had transformed them into a homogeneous body numbering several tens of thousands of warriors. Married to Apama, a noble Persian, he founded a dynasty in which Iranian and Macedonian blood was mingled in equal proportions. Satrap of Babylonia, he finally inherited the Achaemenian empire shorn of Egypt, Palestine, southern Syria and certain parts of the coast of Asia Minor. The only territory he himself ceded was on the eastern marches in Arachosia and Gedrosia. This was given to King Chandragupta of India in exchange for elephants which he needed for the protection of his western frontiers. But after his death his empire began to disintegrate, a process that continued, despite efforts of some of his successors, especially Antiochus I (280–261 BC), Antiochus III (223–187 BC) and Antiochus IV (175–169 BC), until its final fall.

The Seleucids were heirs of the Achaemenians in practically all their possessions, and very largely adopted the principles of the Achaemenian administration. They were compelled to strive for the unity of their state notwithstanding the diversity of its peoples and their heterogeneous civilisation. This was an aim their predecessors had only temporarily succeeded in realising, and they themselves were no more successful in the

an alliance with the Greek city states to fight the Persians. We may note in passing that Demosthenes violently opposed this Macedonian policy, seeing the salvation of his country in an alliance with the Great King. The dispute between Philip of Macedonia and the other Greek city states brought about the end of Greek independence in 338 BC. Alexander, son of Philip, began his career of conquest first with his own homeland, and ended it in Babylonia, after destroying the power of the Achaemenians. With this, came the first crisis in the annals of Iranian civilisation. A foreign conqueror with an alien culture came to power in Iran. The invasion of the Macedonians, a non-Greek people who had adopted Hellenism, meant a test for the vitality of the civilisation which the Aryans had built on the Plateau of Iran.

The Greek interlude, important as it was to prove, lasted for about two centuries of Iranian history. Alexander devoted the last months of his life to the organisation of his newly won empire. His measures were much influenced by the ideas of the great Achaemenian kings. He kept the division of the empire into satrapies and retained a number of Persian satraps at Babylon, Susa, Paraetakene, in Aria and in Media, the last being governed by Atropates, who gave his

name to Atropatene, known today as Azerbaijan. The Macedonian was aware of the weakness of the previous central governments that had often proved powerless to prevent the satraps from asserting their autonomy. He instituted a duality of power to remedy this by doubling the Persian satrap with a commander of Macedonian troops. All the means adopted by the Achaemenians to maintain the unity of Asia were known to him. The farther he went, the more he felt the need to rely on the conquered people. The Greeks and Macedonians could not understand how their King could place them on the same footing as the Iranians. Yet, the loyalty and the courage of these peoples won the sympathy of Alexander, and the opposition of which he was conscious among his companions and soldiers may have inclined him still further towards his new subjects. He desired to govern in their interests as much as in those of the Greeks and Macedonians. Having conquered Egypt where royalty was conceived of as divine, and Persia where the king was a kind of emanation of the god, Alexander, whom Zeus-Ammon had recognised as his son, introduced the deification of his person not with the aim of becoming the object of an official cult, but as a political measure that task. The first kings were faced with the fundamental task of unity. The Achaemenians relied for their support on the Iranian people, and Alexander on the Macedonians. The Seleucids, however, were not a national dynasty. The solution which commended itself to them was to extract from this diversity some kind of union which might remain loyal to them. They began to populate the land with Greeks and Macedonians. This ambitious project was furthered because Greece at that time was over-populated and suffering from great poverty. Throughout the third century BC an almost limitless stream of peoples from south-eastern Europe poured into Syria, Babylonia and Iran. To provide for their settlement a vast scheme of urban development was drawn up and put into execution. Military and non-military colonies were created. The Greek language began to spread in Iran. Marriages between Iranian women and Macedonians, first encouraged by Alexander as a policy in the founding of these colonies, increased commerce, improved administration and justice, helped to make the Greek language the *lingua franca*, making a large part of the population bi-lingual. These Greek influences, or Hellenisation, were officially sponsored. On the other hand, they became less effective because of the penetration of the Iranian element into the political and administrative life of the empire. The Hellenisation of the Iranians was a part of the process which led to the Iranisation of the Greeks, and thus came into existence the mixed society which prevailed in the cities.

It would be wrong to believe that Iran was Hellenised during the rule of the Seleucids. The great mass of the Iranians, the rural population, remained untouched by Hellenisation. It is, of course, difficult to assess the extent of Greek penetration even in the urban areas, and equally difficult to determine how rapidly and how completely the Greeks fell under Iranian influence. As regards the outward and material aspects of civilisation, Hellenism undoubtedly made far-reaching and relatively rapid progress. At the same time, it had far less influence on the spiritual and religious life of the people. A comparison with modern times is instructive, for it shows that the external and material features of a foreign culture are adopted far more quickly than the spiritual, and that there is, moreover, a marked contrast in the reaction of town and country. In general, Hellenism may be said to have suffered a defeat in Iran; its leaders could never escape from a political, social

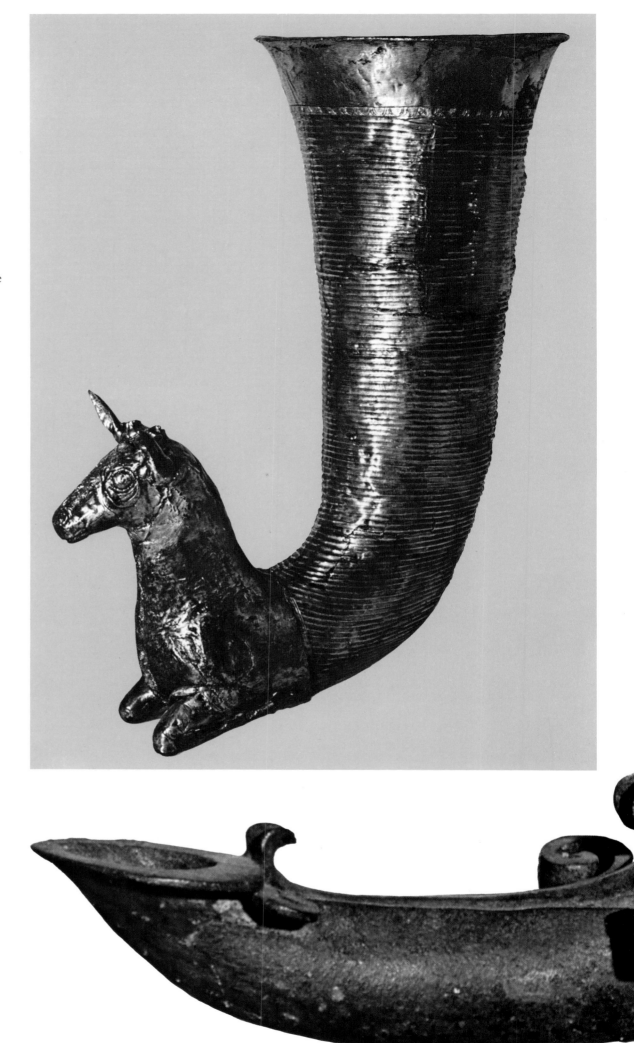

Left: A Seleucid silver rhyton in the shape of an animal, possibly a kid.

Below: A bronze oil-lamp found by Professor Ghirshman at Susa. The cover is surmounted by the figure of a monkey, symbol of intelligence, holding a book.

Lower right: A find from the Bakhtiari mountains (2nd–1st centuries BC). This draped torso, carved in alabaster, shows a distinctly Hellenistic influence and may have represented a Greek goddess.

and economic antinomy. There was a constant conflict between the eastern and the western way of life, between the city state and oriental monarchy, and between an economic system based on private enterprise and controlled oriental economy. Hellenism was unable to solve these and other problems inherent in such a mixed society. In the end, the civilisation which the Iranians built under Cyrus and Darius, triumphed over the values which Alexander tried to sow in Iranian soil. The Macedonians and Greeks whom he made citizens of Iran ultimately ceased to be what they originally were. The temporarily vanquished people of Iran conquered them so completely that posterity was never to recognise them as the Macedonians and Greeks of Alexander or the short-lived dynasty of the Seleucids.

Mithridates II made Iran into a world power, and its relations with Rome in the west and China in the east show the importance of the position it occupied in the political and economic life of the contemporary world.

A reaction set in against the penetration of Hellenism and its imposition on a foreign sub-stratum; in the east sprang up the Parthians and the Kushans, and in the west Carthage and Rome. All were on the fringes of the Hellenistic world and were, to a greater or lesser extent, affected by Hellenism. Nevertheless, they had preserved their individual and national characters. The last century of the pre-Christian and the first centuries of the Christian era witnessed the greatest expansion of the Iranian world. Under the Parthians, Iran advanced to the frontiers of Egypt; the Kushan empire occupied the whole of north India, Russian Turkestan and part of Chinese Turkestan; the Sarmatians, who swarmed over the Eurasian steppes, became masters of a great part of the northern shore of the Black Sea, reached the borders of the Danubian world and spread into central Asia. The Iranian world took its revenge on the Greeks by attacking its two eastern outposts. The Graeco-Baktrian kingdom disappeared under the onslaught of the Yueh-chih, the later Kushans, and the Greek settlements on the Black Sea coast were over-run by the Sarmatians. Iran maintained its pressure against the Romans when they appeared in Asia. The wars of Mithridates of Pontus represent the resistance of the Asians under Iranian leadership. From this titanic duel Iran under the Parthians emerged victorious over the dying Seleucid empire.

Such information as we possess about the origin of the Parthians indicates that they belonged to the Parni tribe. They were horsemen and warriors for whom, according to the ancient writers, to die fighting was the supreme happiness, and death from natural causes ignominious and shameful. The penetration of the Parni into Iranian territory may be regarded as the precursor of the vast movement of Scythian tribes, whose invasion a century later overthrew the Iranian state and put an end to the Graeco-Baktrian kingdom. It is thought that about 250 BC two brothers, Arsaces and Tiridates, with their forces under the command of five other chiefs, occupied the district of upper Tejen. Arsaces was to become the first king of the Arsacid or Parthian dynasty.

This was the period when Seleucus II was just about to consolidate his empire. The Parthians continued to challenge the Greek imperial authority, particularly as the Seleucids faced revolts in their empire and a challenge from Rome. Almost a century after the first Parthian claim to possess an independent kingdom, Mithridates I

founded their empire between the years 160 and 140 BC. Mithridates I annexed Media, Elymais, Persia, Characene, Babylonia and Assyria in the west and Gedrosia and possibly Herat and Seistan in the east. Seleucia, on the Tigris, was the largest city in this part of Asia at that time. It was a rich commercial centre, ruled by a Graeco-Semitic aristocracy. The Parthians did not annex Seleucia, but built a vast military camp facing the city on the left bank of the Tigris. This later became the Parthian capital of Ctesiphon. The Seleucid, Demetrius II, set out to reconquer the eastern part of his empire. He lost his battle

against the Parthian cavalry and fell into the hands of Mithridates I. The Parthian king treated him with great magnanimity, installing him in Hyrcania, and gave him his daughter in marriage. Mithridates I has been mentioned as being many admirable qualities – virtuous, brave and a good legislator. He was, in fact, the restorer of the old Achaemenian empire, and took the title of the 'Great King'. The part he played in the revival of the Iranian state may be compared to that of Cyrus the Great, whom in some ways, he resembled in character. He died in 137 BC.

Twelve years later, the Seleucid empire really passed away in 129 BC in a battle between Antiochus VII Sidetes and the Parthians. The Greeks were defeated. This was a fateful day for Hellenism. It never again recovered and the Seleucid kingdom, though it survived for several more decades, lay prostrate before triumphant Iran. The frontier of Europe, extended by Alexander to the banks of the Indus, was now thrown back to the Euphrates. Six years later Mithridates II took charge of the Parthian empire. It was he who guarded Iran in the east. After restoring order in the west, he pushed the frontiers of his empire as far back as the Oxus, re-occupied the eastern provinces of the Parthian empire and dammed back the flood of the nomads. His

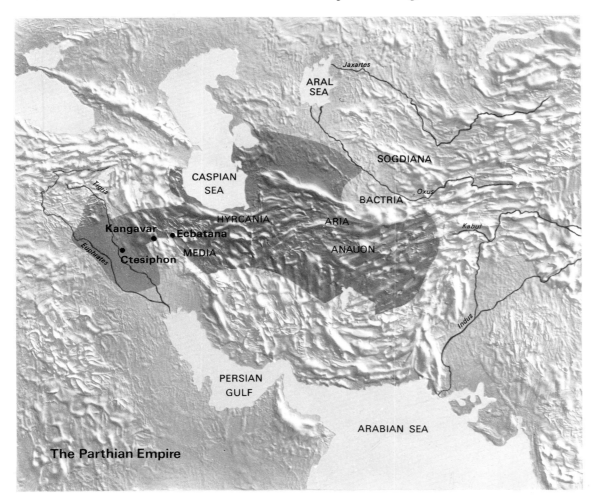

The Parthian Empire

success was of the first importance, for it saved the western world from the menace of the Sakae. In this the Parthian king revived the historic role of Iran of protecting the civilisation of western Asia. The greatness of Mithridates II can be judged from the attitude of the other great empires towards him. About 115 BC he received an embassy from the Emperor of China and the two rulers concluded a treaty designed to facilitate the movement of international commerce, in which Iran, as a transit state, formed a vitally important link. He also brought Armenia within the Iranian sphere of influence. The parts played by Mithridates I and Mithridates II in the Parthian empire may be likened respectively to those of Cyrus and Darius. The former ruler was responsible for its territorial expansion, while the latter consolidated and organised what had been won. Mithridates II made Iran into a world power, and its relations with Rome in the west and China in the east show the importance of the position it occupied in the political and economic life of the contemporary world. Mithridates II gave formal expression to the increase in his power by assuming the title of 'King of Kings'.

The Parthians were not keen to take up arms against Rome. In fact, they entered

into negotiations with Rome and accepted to be neutral in the Roman wars against Armenia. However, the Romans, in their pride and ignorance, continued to show little regard for the Parthians, who had kept their pledges scrupulously. Pompey violated the Roman-Parthian peace treaty, seized the western provinces of Parthia, intrigued with its vassal princes and insulted the Parthian emperor, Phraates II when he protested. The Romans behaved unscrupulously and without shame. For example, when after the death of Phraates II, Mithridates III wanted to seize the Parthian throne from Orodes II, Gabinius agreed to

assist him in return for a large sum of money. However, he turned against him because he accepted the offer of a larger amount of money from another pretender. The greed of the Roman leaders reached its apogee when Crassus was made pro-consul of Syria. It is true that the Roman senate had no desire for a war with Parthia. Crassus, on the other hand, believed that the conquest of Iran would be an easy victory and would yield a rich booty. Thus was joined the battle between the Romans and the Parthians.

The Parthian heavy cavalry commanded by Surena smashed the Roman army and killed or captured three-quarters of the forces of Crassus. Crassus himself paid for the disaster with his own life and that of his son. In this battle, fought at Carrhae in 53 BC, the combined Parthian forces of heavy cavalry and mounted bowmen carried the day and proved superior to the Roman army, which had no mounted formations. The Battle of Carrhae forced Rome to introduce cavalry into its army, just as nearly a thousand years earlier the first Iranians to reach the plateau had induced the Assyrians to introduce a similar reform. The shock of the Parthian victory opened the eyes of Rome to the real strength of Parthia – a power whose policy was defensive rather than offensive. The Parthians carried away the Roman eagles of the legions of Crassus, and these remained only in the Parthian temples. Once again Iran had forcibly thrown back from its frontiers the Hellenism to which the Romans claimed to be heirs. The consequence was that for a whole century the Parthian frontiers on the Euphrates remained inviolate, and not only the Iranians, but the western Semites, such as the Jews of Palestine, the Nabateans of Damascus, the Arabs of the desert, and the inhabitants of Palmyra, looked with hope to

Parthia where the Parthians appeared as
true successors of the Achaemenians. They
felt that they were to have their revenge on
the Romans through the Parthian horsemen,
whose coming to defeat the Roman beast
was foretold in the Apocalypse.

The Romans made repeated attempts to
conquer what was known as 'the Roman
east' back from the Parthians. During the
reign of Phraates IV (c.37 BC) Antony
mounted a major invasion of the territories
of the Parthian empire. His failure led
Augustus to adopt a policy of compromise.
The consequent agreement with Parthia led
to the return of the eagles of the legions of

with the reversal of the Roman policy of compromise and adjustment. Trajan reversed the ideas of Augustus and decided that the Romans must conquer Armenia, converting it into a Roman province, and that Parthia must be reduced to vassalage, to be governed by a puppet king. In AD 114 Trajan began his campaign and started conquering the lands of the Caucasus and areas around the Black Sea. He invaded Armenia and even conquered the Parthian capital, Ctesiphon. He went further south, up to the Persian Gulf. The Parthians had remained mysteriously quiet; they waited for the inevitable, which was the revolt of

retained its hold on the popular, and also probably on the official, religion, under the Parthians. Though there are no texts to confirm this in Iran, there is written evidence of its existence in Armenia, where the ancient historians refer to cult-places with three altars dedicated to these three divinities. This evidence, combined with that from the Achaemenian period, suggests that the two open-air altars found at Naqsh-i Rustam and Pasargadae, as well as the third standing near the temple tower were also dedicated to this triad. Worship of the three divinities is also indicated on the coins of the princes of Persia and the

Crassus to Rome. This period coincided with the slow decay of the House of Mithridates, and its replacement by another Parthian dynasty. The change helped the revival of Iran, since the new dynasty helped the country to become more Iranian and national in character.

The first signs of the new Iranian renaissance appeared under Vologases I; on the reverse of his coinage is depicted a fire altar with a sacrificing priest. For the first time, Iranian money bore letters of the Pahlavi-Arsacid alphabet. According to a later tradition, the text of the Avesta was compiled in his reign. This revival coincided

the conquered peoples against the Romans. The Jews of Cyrenaica, Egypt and Cyprus rose in rebellion, and the revolt spread to Palestine, Syria, northern Mesopotamia and eventually to the entire Semitic world. It was at this time that the Parthians struck. The result was that the great victories of Rome turned to defeat.

With the accession of Vologases II (AD 148–92) the Iranian retribution began to be exacted from the Romans. The wars continued for decades; cities changed hands and territories were conquered and lost by both parties. In the end the Romans were defeated. The Parthian, Artabanus V, was twice victorious over the Emperor Macrinus and imposed a heavy tribute on Rome. Thus, after two and a half centuries, Roman attempts to reduce Iran to vassalage ended in failure. The contest between Rome and Parthia, from the point of view of Iran, was essentially defensive in nature. The Parthians had opportunities to march on to Rome, but they did not do so on purpose. They were satisfied with their vast empire, within which, according to the classical writers, there were eighteen vassal states.

Iranian society retained its ancient traditions under the Parthians. The triad Ahuramazda-Mithra-Anahita, worshipped under the Achaemenians, seems to have

vassals of the Parthians. These coins depicted three fires burning on three altars over the roof of a temple tower. Of the Iranian triad, it was Anahita who enjoyed most popularity beyond the western frontiers of Iran. Her cult spread to Lydia, where she was called 'the lady of Bactria', to Pontus, Cappadocia and Armenia. It was probably even more popular than that of Mithra, which the pirates captured by Pompey took to Rome, whence it was carried by the Roman armies as far as the Rhine and Danube.

The Parthian Arsacids, who, like the Kushans, sprang from the nomadic Iranian peoples of Central Asia, were very tolerant of foreign religions. In Mesopotamia, they adopted the cults of the country they conquered, though they modified them and gave them a slightly different aspect. They considered that the foreign gods of the western regions of the empire were benevolent and protected them. They do not seem to have encouraged proselytising among the conquered peoples. Among the many sanctuaries excavated at Dura-Europos, which long remained an advance post of the Parthian empire, not a single fire temple was discovered, although there was an important Iranian colony in this trading centre. The tolerance of the Parthians was

particularly evident in their relations with the Jews. Having been oppressed by the Seleucids and the Romans, they believed that Iran was the only great power capable of delivering them from the foreign yoke, as it had done once before in the Achaemenian period. The Parthians' role in the liberation of the Jews gave rise to the well-known saying: 'When you see a Parthian charger tied up to a tomb-stone in Palestine, the hour of the Messiah will be near.'

The true character of the Parthians and of Iran over which they ruled for nearly five centuries, is gradually emerging as a result of research into its history, religion and civilisation. At first it was no more than a conquest by a small and insignificant outlying province of the Seleucid empire. Gradually the Parthians eliminated the traces of dying Hellenism. The Parthian advance to the west had its counterpart in that of Rome to the east. Eventually the two peoples, Iranian and Roman, who had divided between them the material and spiritual heritage of Hellenism, came face to face on opposite banks of the Euphrates. The former, claiming to be heir to the Achaemenians and Seleucids, aspired to restore the ancient empire with its outlets on the Mediterranean. The latter, under the Caesars, claimed to be heir to Alexander and aspired to the dominion of the whole of Asia, including India. For nearly three centuries, Iran stood on the defensive against Rome, all of whose sallies, apart from certain ephemeral successes, were doomed to failure. Iran emerged victorious from the long struggle with the formidable Roman empire. This struggle proved to the Iranians that they possessed resources capable of resisting the assault of the west and that they could maintain their country's independence and their integrity. A national consciousness was slowly reborn. This gradual awakening was probably encouraged by the emergence of a new dynasty, and was reflected in the political, religious and economic life of the nation.

In addition to this struggle with Rome, Parthian Iran had to face the onslaught of nomadic invasions, some of which came from the north-east steppes and others through the Caucasian passes. By resisting these attacks, Iran made a great contribution to the world, since it defended, and perhaps saved from destruction, the ancient civilisation of western Asia. By their revival of the Iranian spirit and their successful foreign policy, the Parthians prepared the way for the Sassanians, who were enabled to achieve a national unity and a civilisation that was more exclusively Iranian than it had ever been before.

The long encounter between Iran and Rome soon assumed a new aspect. The Roman emperor, Constantine the Great, and Armenia were both converted to Christianity, and this led to closer ties between Armenia and Byzantium.

Five and a half centuries separated the end of the Achaemenian empire and the beginning of the Sassanian dynasty. Throughout this long stretch of years, Iran suffered from the onslaught of the two worlds between whom it acted as a connecting influence. The Greek advance from the west was matched by that of the Parthians coming from the eastern steppes. During these centuries opposing elements and contrasting peoples were fused together as it were in a gigantic crucible. Western influence left a permanent impression on the Iranian spirit and gave rise to oriental forms that have come to the fore in the

present century. Thus the Sassanian dynasty which was rooted in the old Irano-oriental culture, came to power at a propitious moment for the flowering of Iranian civilisation.

According to tradition, Sassan, the ancestor of the Sassanian kings, was a high dignitary in the temple of Anahita at Stakhr. His son, Papak, who succeeded him in this office, married the daughter of a local prince, from whom he seized power by a *coup d'état*. He was believed, by later tradition, to be the real founder of the dynasty, and his accession in AD 208 was the starting point for a new era. His suzerain, the Parthian king, refused to recognise the legality of his action and withheld his consent when Papak wished to secure the succession for his elder son, who died in an accident. His younger son, Ardashir, proclaimed himself king of Persia. Ardashir quickly reduced to submission all the small kingdoms in the province of Fars, succeeded in uniting the province under his rule, and extended his suzerainty beyond its borders to Isfahan and Kerman. His sudden rise to increasing power worried the Parthian king, who ordered the king of Ahwaz to march against him. This king was defeated and shortly afterwards Ardashir routed the army of the Parthian

king in three successive battles, in the last of which, at Susiana in AD 224, he was killed. The way to Ctesiphon lay open and two years later Ardashir was crowned king. Five and a half centuries after the fall of the Achaemenians, the Persian people had regained power, and the new dynasty, as the legitimate successor of the Achaemenians, ensured the continuity of Iranian civilisation.

Ardashir had still to face enemies before he could re-establish the frontiers of the former empire. A powerful coalition was formed against him by the king of Armenia, the Scythians and the king of the Kushans, which the Romans seemed to support. He fought this formidable coalition in a series of battles, and partly by diplomacy and partly by valour, he defeated all the partners of the coalition. This victory made him master of an empire extending from the Euphrates to Merv, Herat and Seistan. Having won at home, he started the consolidation of his frontiers. Conflict with Rome became inevitable. It ended with the Persians regaining two important fortresses – Nisibis and Carrhae. The wars continued during Ardashir's reign of nearly fifteen years. He overcame one enemy after another and succeeded in building up a new Iranian empire. His greatest achievement was to forge the army into a powerful instrument that made possible the realisation of his policy. He associated his son, Shapur, in his rule, and, according to tradition, handed over the crown to him and retired from active life a few years before his death.

Shapur inherited from his father an empire which still needed to be firmly established. In the context of the age, this meant further wars. He fought against the Kushans in the east and Rome in the west. He has left a long inscription on the walls of the fire temple at Naqsh-i Rustam recording his success: his victorious armies seized Peshawar, the winter capital of the Kushan king, occupied the Indus valley, and pushing north, cross the Hindu Kush, conquered Bactria, crossed over the Oxus, and entered Samarkand and Tashkent. The Kushan dynasty founded by the great Kaniksha was deposed and in its place were put the princes who recognised Persian suzerainty. As an heir of the Achaemenians, and following the ambitions of his father, whose war with Rome took place to recover the eastern provinces of the Persian empire, lost since the conquests of Alexander the Great, Shapur attacked the western power and scored three brilliant victories over the Roman armies. Three times, Antioch, the oriental capital of the Roman empire, fell into the hands of the Persians. This struggle came to a culmination with the battle of

Left: Drawing of Shapur I (*detail*), from a statue at Bishapur (late 3rd century BC).

Lower left: The triple triumph of Shapur I, from a monumental relief at Bishapur. The King's three enemies, rulers of Rome with whom he fought for twenty-five years, are shown as his captives. Behind him, his hand clasped by the King's, stands the Emperor Valerian; kneeling before the King on one knee is Philip the Arab, and beneath the feet of the King's horse lies the body of Gordian III.

Below: At Naqsh-i-Rustam is this relief (early 4th century AD) showing the victory of Hormizd II over an enemy, dismounted by the impetus of the King's furious charge. Compared with carvings of the previous century, it is crude in design and execution.

Lower right: The Sassanian Empire. Five and a half centuries after the fall of the Achaemenians, the Sassanians came to power as their legitimate successors and established a highly civilised empire.

Following pages: The investiture of Ardeshir I (3rd century AD) by Ahuramazda. The god and the King are both mounted on horses. In his left hand Ahuramazda holds a *barsom* or bundle of sacred twigs symbolising priesthood; the King is crowned with a *korymbos*, a spherical adornment of hair wrapped in silken gauze. Their horses are trampling underfoot Ahriman, the evil spirit, who is the enemy of the god, and the King's Parthian adversary, Artebanus V.

Edessa in which the Emperor Valerian, with seventy thousand of his legionnaires, was taken prisoner by the victorious King of Kings. These legionnaires were exiled to Iran and they provided the empire with specialists, architects, engineers and technicians who were employed on large scale public works, notably the building of bridges, barrages and roads which conferred great benefits on the rich province of Khuzistan. Some of their remains are still in use. To commemorate these victories, Shapur had five bas-reliefs sculptured on the rocks and cliffs of Fars, in one of which the Roman emperor is shown prostrate at his feet. Shapur was not only a great military leader, he was possessed of wide interests and an inquiring mind. He commissioned the translation of numerous Greek and Indian works dealing with such varied subjects as medicine, astronomy and philosophy. He took an interest in Mani and extended his protection to this founder of a 'universal' religion, whose ideas, borrowed from Zoroastrianism, Buddhism and Christianity, gained adherents in western Asia among the followers of these great religions. Shapur died in AD 272. He was succeeded by his two sons, Hormizd I and Vahram I, of whose reigns little is known. A war with Rome marked the reign of Vahram II, who ruled

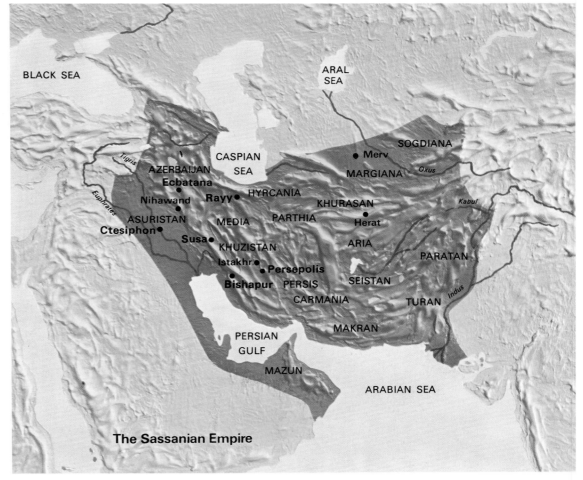

The Sassanian Empire

A horse's head, cast in silver, the bridle being silver-gilt, which probably formed part of a Sassanian throne; from the Kerman region (4th century AD). The technique of applying silver-gilt ornamentation to silver objects was a speciality of the Iranians.

78

from AD 276–93, and was followed by Vahram III, Narsah and Hormizd II.

The real successor of the two founders of the Sassanian empire and civilisation was Shapur II. He ascended the throne as a minor after the death of Hormizd II, and his long reign of seventy years (AD 309–79) proved worthy of those of the first two princes of the line. During his minority, the Kushans had encroached upon the territories of the Sassanians, and the first task which Shapur II undertook on reaching adulthood was to begin his operations against these invaders. In this he was following in the footsteps of Shapur I who had brought the Kushans under Sassanian domination. Shapur II smashed the Kushan empire and annexed its territory to Iran as a new province governed by kings chosen from among the Sassanian princes who resided at Balkh. It was here that the kingdom of the Ephthalites was founded later. It took advantage of Iranian weakness towards the beginning of the fifth century and expanded on both sides of the Hindu Kush, threatening Iran as well as India. Cultural expansion followed on political success, and Sassanian art spread to the east. It reached the distant towns of Chinese Turkestan and even penetrated into China.

Shapur II inherited the disgrace of the two agreements concluded with the Romans by Vahram II and Narsah which had led to the loss of the greater part of the western provinces of the empire. Having removed the threat to his security in the east, Shapur II resumed the war in the west with a view to wiping out this disgrace. These operations proved protracted. At one stage the Romans tried to negotiate a settlement, but this was rejected since, unlike the Parthians, the Sassanians were not willing to be always on the defensive. The most brilliant feat of arms on this campaign was the capture of Amida by the Sassanian army. The Romans counter-attacked and threatened Ctesiphon. It was at this stage that the Roman emperor, Julian, was killed in battle and the Roman army withdrew. The subsequent peace restored the disputed provinces to Shapur II. Armenia too was recovered. However the Romans continued to intrigue to place a Roman prince in power in Armenia and compelled Shapur II to reduce it to a Persian province and governed by a *marzban*, or commander of the frontier marches.

The long encounter between Iran and Rome soon assumed a new aspect. The Roman emperor, Constantine the Great, and Armenia were both converted to Christianity, and this led to closer ties between Armenia and Byzantium. Armenia, which had long been the cockpit of the Irano-Roman wars, was now torn between two factions of its population. The newly converted Christians were pro-Roman, and opposed to them was a powerful section of Armenian nobility which sought to maintain the old connection with Iran whose civilisation had so profoundly infuenced their country. When Christianity became the official religion of the Roman empire, the Chrisitian subjects of the King of Kings inevitably became political suspects in the eyes of the Iranian authorities, and repression against them became inevitable

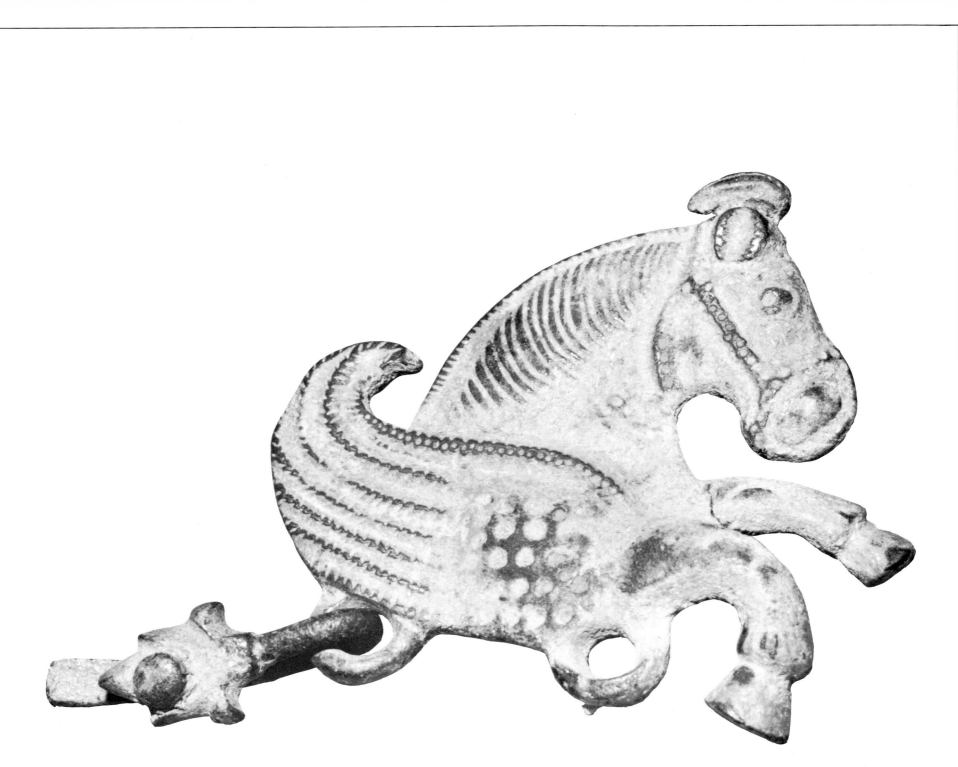

during the rest of the long reign of Shapur II. His death was followed by half a century of decline in the power of the kings, opposed by the nobility which had grown from the days of Ardashir. This struggle continued until the emergence of Vahram V, known as the most famous of the Sassanian emperors.

Vahram V (AD 421–38) was compelled to curb the expansionist ambitions of the Ephthalites. After success over them, he fought a short war with Byzantium. The main cause for this clash with Rome did not lie in any territorial disputes. The difference arose on the question of the treatment of the Christians in the Sassanian empire. The war

ended in agreement because Vahram V did not believe in oppressing the Christians. The new entente between Rome and Iran led to freedom of worship for the Christians. The Christians of Iran, however, were not a united force. Their internecine quarrels were ultimately resolved by a synod, which decided to make the Christian church of Iran independent of that of Byzantium. Thus the suspicion against the Christian Iranians who had, in the past, been accused of intriguing with the Romans was brought to an end. As a consequence of the entente, a joint arrangement between the Romans and the Sassanians was made for the defence of the northern areas against the incessant attacks of the nomadic tribes. Vahram V, however, won renown more as a hunter, poet and musician. He was immortalised in many legends which tell of his prowess and was a favourite subject of Iranian artists for centuries, even after the fall of the empire. After the death of Vahram V, another century of internal upheaval shook the Sassanian empire, especially under Peroz (AD 459–84), whose reign and death marked the start of a period lasting almost half a century, during which Iran, under Balash (AD 484–88), the two reigns of Kavad (AD 488–96 and 499–531), and Djamasp (AD 497–99), was heavily

devastated by an epidemic of plague and social disorders. She was also forced to pay tribute to the Ephthalites.

The next great Sassanian king, Chosroes I, came to the throne in AD 531 after a long struggle between the aristocracy and the other sections of the people. His emergence as the new monarch gave him an exceptional position. His authority was recognised by all the classes, including the priesthood. He spent the earlier years of his life in the re-establishment of a settled society and in wiping out the consequences of Mazdakite excesses perpetrated during the rule of Kavad. During this period he took urgent measures to save the countryside; villages were rebuilt, roads and bridges restored, neglected canals cleaned out and lost cattle replaced. His government introduced legislation that reformed the fiscal organisation of the empire. A survey was made of all land, taxes were fixed according to yield, situation and type of crop. The tax on the individual was based on the category and class of person. All these reforms were the desire of the Crown to introduce more equity into its demands, on which depended the state revenues and the conduct of internal administration and foreign wars. Reforms were also introduced in the army. Four commanders were appointed for the

four divisions of the empire in place of the single commander-in-chief. Peasant soldiers were created by the introduction of compulsory military service. Subject tribes were settled in the frontier districts in order to improve the defences of the empire. Strong fortifications were erected in the Derband pass to hold the road against nomadic invaders, and a wall, several miles long, built near the south-east corner of the Caspian Sea to protect the plain of Gurgan, the gap in the mountain armour of Iran.

Nine years after he came to the throne, Chosroes I began his military campaigns in the west with the invasion of Syria in AD 540. Antioch was captured and burned, and its inhabitants transplanted to a new town built on the same plan near Ctesiphon. Byzantium was willing to conclude peace. In return for increased tribute, Chosroes I was willing to leave the western frontier unchanged. The war in the east was renewed twenty years later when, in alliance with the western Turks, Chosroes I smashed the renewed Ephthalite power: its possessions were partitioned between the allies, and the eastern frontier of Iran was re-established on the Oxus. In the north, he successfully resisted attacks by the Huns, and annexed Yemen in the south. This territorial expansion of Iran resulting

from its growing strength and military success raised in Byzantium the fear of a new conflict with its old adversary. Rome, therefore, engaged its energies in large-scale diplomatic activity with the object of forming an anti-Iranian coalition that would virtually encircle the enemy. This attempt, however, proved abortive, disturbances in Armenia provided further proof of Iranian military superiority; Mesopotamia was invaded and devastated by the forces of the King of Kings. While peace negotiations were taking place, the old king died, after a reign of nearly half a century. He was idealised by oriental tradition as a defender of the people, a lover of justice and a stern, yet benevolent ruler. His reign may be considered as the most brilliant period of the Sassanian age, both for its military and diplomatic triumphs and for the achievements of Iranian civilisation in art, science and literature.

The last great king of the Sassanians was Chosroes II (AD 590–628) who was the grandson of Chosroes I. He came to the throne in a difficult situation. During the rule of his father, Hormizd IV, a revolt had taken place against the Sassanian monarchy. This was led by Vahram Chobin, one of the outstanding military figures of the day. Vahram Chobin, with the support of the

nobles, had dethroned Hormizd IV, and thereafter, with the support of the army, had seized the capital and declared himself king – a crime of lese-majesty, since he was not a member of the Sassanian family. Chosroes II was powerless in the face of this *coup d'état* and was compelled to take refuge with the Emperor Maurice, from whom he obtained troops. However, Byzantium exacted a heavy price for this assistance and Persia lost practically all Armenia, and the Greek frontier was extended to Lake Van and Tiflis.

Chosroes II waited for some years to organise his power. The murder of the Emperor Maurice gave him the pretext which he required to attack Byzantium. The Persian army regained Armenia, south Edessa, marched across Cappadocia to Caesarea, and reached the Bosphorus near Scutari (AD 610). The following year it captured Antioch, Damascus, and finally Jerusalem. In AD 616 the army captured Gaza and invaded Egypt. It took Babylon (old Cairo) and Alexandria, and then marched up the Nile to the borders of Ethiopia. Iran thus regained frontiers that it had not held since the time of the Achaemenians. In Asia Minor, the Persians captured Ancyra (Ankara) and besieged Constantinople. This coincided with victories against the Ephthalite vassals of the Turks on the eastern front. These successes were unparalleled in the history of the empire, which had never appeared more formidable. Never had the Roman empire seemed so near to disaster. However, the Romans now attacked, and in the battle for Ctesiphon, Chosroes II was assassinated. This marked the beginning of the end of the Sassanian empire. The last Sassanian king, Yezdegerd III, died in the neighbourhood of Merv in AD 651. The empire which has resisted and fought back the enemies in the west and the east to preserve its Achaemenian character had fallen at the hands of victorious Arabs.

81

Sassanian cameo carved in sardonyx (4th century AD), depicting the seizure of the Emperor Valerian by Shapur I. According to legend this incident occurred while the two monarchs were engaged in single combat.

A general idea of Iranian social structure may be obtained from original sources that date from the beginning of the Sassanian period. It was a rigid pyramid, at the apex of which stood the head of the state, the King of Kings. The Sassanian administration formed another pyramid, at the head of which stood the Grand Vizier, or Prime Minister, who, in practice, held the reins of power which he exercised under the control of the sovereign. This high dignitary deputised for the king during his absence, and was responsible for political and diplomatic affairs, signing treaties and conventions. He was sometimes given the high command of the army in the field. He was also the head of the 'ministries' or *divans*, directed by 'secretaries' highly skilled in drawing up reports, diplomatic treaties and official correspondence. The administrative sphere of the 'secretariat' in the *divans* included the offices of the chancellery, appointments and honours, justice, war and finance. The last office was of particular importance; it was under the director of taxes, who had at his disposal an army of accountants, tax collectors and agents. The bulk of the revenue in an

agricultural country like Iran was furnished by dues levied on the land, augmented by individual taxes. The Sassanian kings made frequent attempts to alleviate the conditions of the masses, who were the main tax payers, by cancelling outstanding debts or improving the system of payment. The Sassanians in general, and some of their kings in particular, were famous for the administration of justice. The king was the supreme judge, and those of his subjects who failed to obtain justice had the right of appeal to the Crown. The Iranian people always set great store by the right of justice, and an upright judge was highly esteemed.

The internal administration of the country under the Sassanians continued to be based on the division into provinces or satrapies, which were governed by high dignitaries chosen from the members of the royal family and nobility, or, towards the end, from among the military leaders. The boundaries of the provinces were not always fixed. The provinces were dived into districts under governors, and subdivided into cantons. This administrative machinery remained practically intact after the Arab conquest, and its traces may still be found today. The

main features of the system went back to the Parthian period, when the feudal aristocracy had already begun to share in the administration. The great achievement of the Sassanians in the administrative field was the creation of a stable bureaucracy, which provided the link between the provinces and the central authority to which it was responsible. The Sassanian empire had been faced at the outset with a country that had split up into a multitude of petty kingdoms. The centralisation which it introduced was the foundation of its greatness.

During the first three centuries of Sassanian rule, the organisation and command of the army was in the hands of a commander-in-chief, an hereditary office always held by a member of the royal family. Two high military officers – the adjutant-general and the commander of the cavalry – acted under his orders, and these posts were filled from the great families of the empire. Chosroes I radically altered the system and suppressed the office of commander-in-chief. He entrusted command of the army to four leaders, each with a deputy. As under the Parthians, the Sassanian army was based on the heavy armoured cavalry furnished by the Iranian nobility. This was protected by the light cavalry of archers formed by the petty nobility. Behind these shock troops came elephants, which the Parthians had never used. The rearguard was provided by the infantry – a mass of peasants. Of greater importance were the auxiliary formations of the different vassal peoples on the borders of the empire who, since the time of the first Achaemenians had furnished a cavalry that was famous for its fighting qualities. The army was divided into corps, formed of divisions, which, in turn, comprised small units. Siege warfare had hardly been developed under the Parthians, but received a great impetus under the Sassanians, and in this science they were the equal of the Romans. Frontier defence was provided for by military colonies, composed of war-like subject tribes who had been moved from their homes. Chosroes I was particularly associated with this policy and the empire was thus surrounded by a girdle of true defence, furnished by its vassals behind whom stood the regular Iranian army. There seems to have been a rich technical literature devoted to military science. These were treatises dealing with the organisation of the army in war and peace and on the use of cavalry and the care of horses, how to draw the bow and on victualling troops. There were chapters dealing with tactics, the treatment of the enemy, the choice of time and place for battle, etc. On the whole,

Iranian military science at this period was in no way inferior to that of the Romans.

Zoroastrianism, according to a late tradition, had been preserved in its original form in the province of Fars, and was made the official state religion by Ardashir Papakan. Modern research into Sassanian religion, however, has discredited this account, which seems to be at variance with historical truth as it emerges from texts, inscriptions and archeological evidence. Undoubtedly the traditional religion was preserved in Fars, but it was the ancient Mazdian faith, and seems to have been unaffected by the reforms of Zoroaster. When the Sassanian dynasty came to power the province of Fars was a centre of the cult of Anahita and of Ahuramazda. The cult of Anahita was officially introduced by Artaxerxes, the successor of Darius, with the intention of introducing a religion that would be common to all the peoples of his empire. The traditional association of the Sassanian royal family with the cult of Anahita continued under Shapur I, who founded a temple in the city of Bishapur. The striking feature of this building is an installation for bringing water several hundred yards and making it flow round the central chamber. This suggests that the cult of water, of which Anahita was the personification, may have been associated with that of fire. Such was the religious position in south-west Iran. In the north-east, the ancient Iranian faith was centred round the great sanctuary of Shiz, where the ancient fraternity of the Magi or *mobads,* while preserving the tradition of the priestly cast, had adopted Zoroastrian ideas.

The problem of an imperial religion must have arisen under Shapur I at a time when the young empire was winning success in foreign policy and needed to mobilise all its national forces for the struggle with Rome. This may account for the sympathetic interest shown by Shapur in the teachings of Mani, of whom he made a companion. The prophet Mani was of noble birth, and, like Zoroaster, the Buddha and Jesus, claimed to have been sent by God to fulfil what had been previously revealed. He preached a new universal religion which, like Christianity, embraced all races and conditions of men. His doctrines were derived from the cults of Babylonia and Iran and were influenced by Buddhism and Christianity. Shapur I conferred great favours on Mani and allowed him complete freedom to preach and make converts. It is possible that the king intended ultimately to

Below: A silver parcel-gilt dish, of the Sassanian period, (6th–7th centuries) decorated with a mythical animal, part wolf and part tiger.

Lower left: The palace at Firuzabad, built of rubble and plaster, a mixture in common use as building material during the Sassanian period; from a drawing.

Right: Cameo bust, possibly of King Kavad (5th–6th centuries AD).

belief must have proved a valuable defensive weapon in the hands of the *mobads*. They took over the traditions of the south-west and, since they could not abolish the old gods, such as Anahita and Mithra, they relegated them to second place. In order not to be outdone by the Mediterranean custom of the people of the Book, it became essential for them to have a similar weapon and to fix the sacred traditions in writing. This was done in the *Avesta*, which was a collection of oral traditions, some of them very ancient. Certain scholars maintain that this work was compiled in the fourth century, whereas others date it not earlier than the sixth century. It is not known to what extent the Magi, in addition to performing their political functions, also sought to enlighten the new religion by considering philosophy and science. Religious unity followed on political unity. With the support of the temporal power, Zoroastrianism drove out Manicheism and held Christianity in check on the line of the Euphrates, and Buddhism on the Helmand. Just as in the Hellenistic period Iran had been hostile to the cosmopolitanism of the Greek civilisation, so now there was a revival of nationalism, an intense opposition to the international world represented by Rome and its new Christian religion. Zoroastrianism, which had been given the status of an official cult, supported the state in its struggle with Rome and placed the spiritual forces of the nation at its disposal for the defence of the Orient.

Sassanian art is not the expression of a sudden renaissance, nor is it a delayed manifestation of Greek art. Neither is it the reappearance of old oriental traditions purged of western influence. It represents the last phase of an oriental art that had been in existence for four millenia. It was a direct successor of the last phase of Parthian art, which was essentially Iranian in character. It was responsive to foreign influences, but it adapted them to the tradition of its native land, and as the art of a world empire, it spread into far-distant countries. A blaze of strong western influence, as much in sculpture as in rupestral art, and even in town-planning, is noticeable under Shapur I. The reason for this can be easily explained. A quarter of a century of victorious wars against Rome; prolonged occupation by the Persians of the eastern provinces of the Roman Empire, Syria and Antioch in particular; the sojourn of the Great King in the conquered regions, and the presence of thousands of Roman prisoners in diverse regions of Iran where they had been exiled and settled – these facts explain the penetration of western

make the Manichaen faith the state religion. He may also have believed that, having established a strong empire, it was the mission of the new dynasty to endow Iran with new spiritual riches and to encourage a religion, moreover, which owing to its tolerant syncretism could adapt itself to contemporary trends of thought. The Manichaen faith might have fulfilled Shapur's expectations, but after his death there was a violent reaction on the part of the Mazidan priesthood, especially among the northern Magi, whose leader, Kartir, played an important part in the affairs of the state under Shapur's successors. Shortly

after the death of Shapur, Mani was tried, condemned and executed. His followers fled abroad, some to the east where their teachings flourished in central Asia, others to Syria and Egypt. Ultimately Mazdaism was reinstated and strengthened the alliance with the throne by the subordination of the spiritual to the temporal.

How far had Zoroastrianism been preserved by the Magi and what part did it play in state religion? Ahuramazda was still worshipped and the dogmas, with their emphasis on a single divinity, were upheld at a period when the influence of the great monotheistic religions was spreading. This

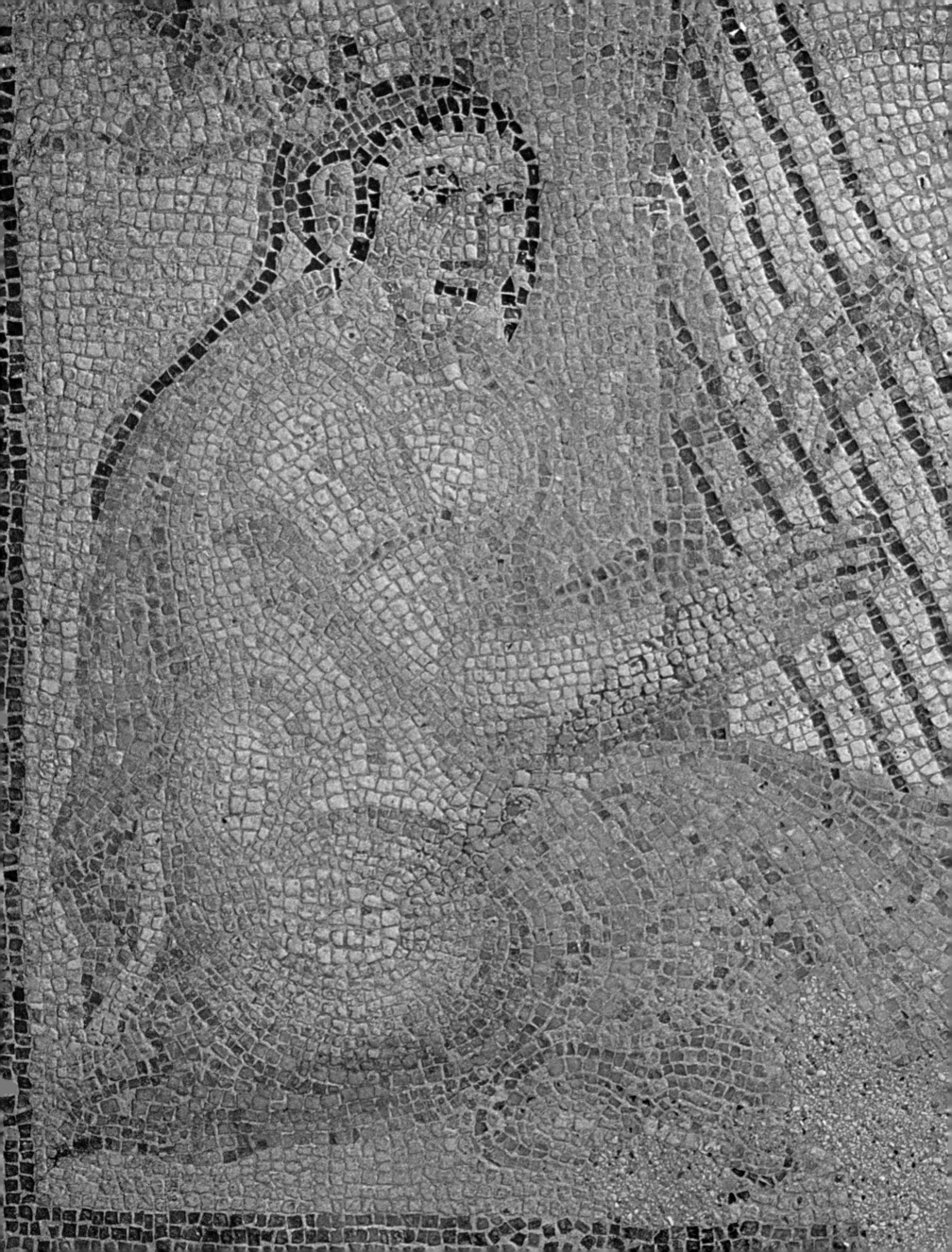

influence in Sassanian art under Shapur I. The Sassanians were great builders of towns, and the historical sources record urban development is most reigns. Sassanian architecture, reflecting this truth, was strongly influenced by national traditions, and carried on those of the Parthians. Buildings of well-dressed stone remained in fashion up to the end of the third century AD, and one of the palaces at Bishapur was built in this time. We learn from the historical records that Sassanian palaces had painted decoration and that at Ctesiphon there was a fresco representing the capture of Antioch. None of these ornaments has so far been recovered, but the recent discovery by the writer of a mosaic pavement in the *iwan* of the Bishapur palace partly fills the gap, since the mosaicists are known to have worked from painted cartoons. Some of the mosaic panels represent portraits, and out of twenty-two of these, no two are alike – proof that at this period the artist sought to convey individual likenesses. With the exception of a few heads in profile, all are shown three-quarter face; this seems to have been the most popular position in Sassanian art, and may have been due to Syrio-Roman influences. Alternating with portraits are larger panels on which we may see a great lady fanning herself, courtesans with long robes and crowns of flowers, holding bouquets, or a naked musician playing a stringed instrument.

The Sassanian kings encouraged the tradition of rock bas-relief, known in Iran from the third millenium BC. More than thirty of the reliefs are sculptured on the rock of the Plateau, the majority in Fars, the native province of the dynasty. None is religious in character; the subjects include the investiture, triumphs, victory over the enemy, the chase, and the king with members of his Court or family, and illustrate the many influences that affected Sassanian monumental art during the four centuries of its existence. The earliest phase is known from the bas-relief at Firuzabad, which represents the victory of Ardashir over Artabanus V. This still shows Parthian influence and has the same flat relief and rendering of detail by incision. A little later in the same reign, the modelling shows greater depth. This is particularly noticeable in the investiture scene of the king and Ahuramazda, the composition of which is in the traditional heraldic style of the East. The art of Sassanian bas-relief reached its highest point under Vahram I, and his scene of investiture at Bishapur is the most lively and expressive work achieved by Iranian artists. The standards remained high under Vahram II, but from the fourth

century the modelling became flat and uninspired and detail was again rendered by incision. Sassanian toreutic is better represented by a considerable number of decorated plates, cups and bottles, the favourite subject of the design being the royal hunt. The prince is shown mounted on horseback and clad in rich garments and an elaborate crown. He pursues his quarry at the gallop, and shoots the animal with arrows. The scene is treated in a conventional manner and is similar in conception to those of the rock reliefs. That this is not an actual hunt is shown by the dress of the prince and the number of animals surrounding the hunter. It is a picture with a hidden meaning, which, by a kind of magic, secures success for the king in his hunting exploits and gives him courage to meet lion, tiger or boar. It is a representation of the 'royal huntsman'.

Rock crystal, a stone that had been highly prized from earliest antiquity, remained popular with the Sassanian artists. Few objects of this material have survived, and it is probable that it was being replaced by products of the glass industry. The most famous object of rock crystal is the centre medallion of the gold cup from the Treasury of St Denis, now in the Cabinet des Medailles in Paris. This represents a Sassanian prince

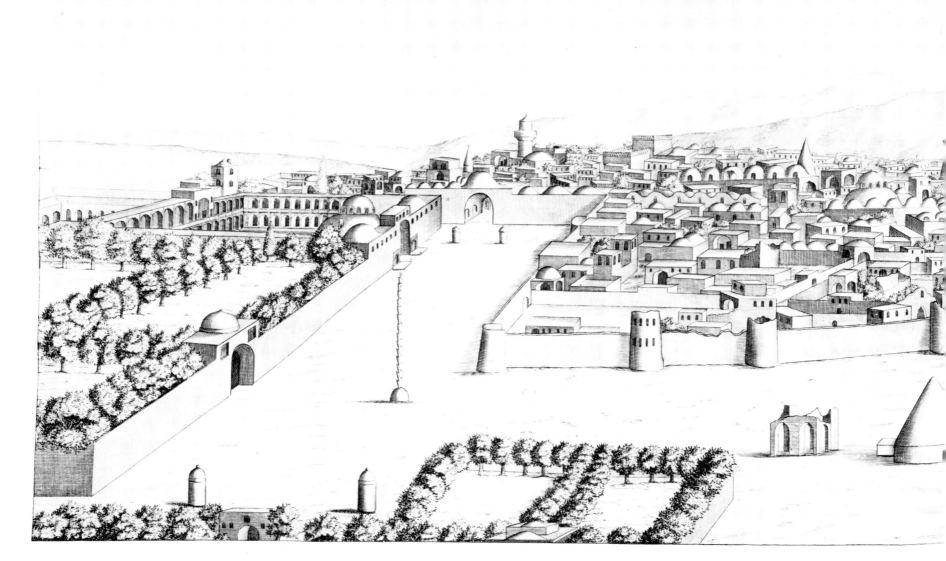

Only a few sporadic and isolated revolts show that some national feeling survived in this subjugated people, and the number of uprisings increased under the 'Abbasid Caliphate. Whatever purpose Abu Muslim may have nurtured in secret, other heretical leaders were later to avail themselves of him as a kind of precursor. Khorasan was aroused by a highly successful campaign against the legitimate Caliphs, and soon after the execution of Abu Muslim by order of his ungrateful masters, Sunbadh 'the Magician' arose. He marched from Nishapur with a following of Zoroastrians, Mazdakites, Shi'ites and others to revenge Abu Muslim's death, but after a short struggle he was defeated. Another of Abu Muslim's companions, Ishaq, nicknamed 'the Turk', also preached that Abu Muslim was still alive and was a prophet sent by Zoroaster. Later, between 777 and 780, a native of Merv, familiarly known as al-Muqanna', 'the Veiled One', threw the country into confusion with his claim to be an incarnation of God, and gave rise to a new heresy whose adherents dressed themselves in white (al-mubaiyida).

Worst of all was the revolt of Babak in Azerbaijan, north of Ardabil, threatening as it did communications between the caliphate and the Eastern Caucasus, which was inhabited by turbulent populations. Babak allied himself with the neighbouring Armenians across the Araxes and tried to obtain support from the Emperor Theophilus.

The revolt lasted twenty-two years (816–838) and caused the Caliphate great losses in men and money. The essence of Babak's heresy is obscure, but it is known that his Khurramis (or al-muhammara) the 'red-shirts', were of non-Arab race ('uluj) and belonged to the peasantry. Babak caused such disorder in the government of the north-western provinces of Persia that even the energetic princes of the Sajid dynasty (889–929), who at first served the Caliphate, eventually proved disloyal; their fall was followed by the rise of several autonomous and independent principalities.

The 'Abbasid empire, rent by rivalry and discord, began to fall apart, not only in the West but in the East also, where the decline of imperial authority can be divided into periods associated with the dynasties of the Tahirids (821–78); the Saffarids (867–902); the Samanids (892–999); the Buyids (932–1055), the Musafirids (919–83), and others. The origins of these dynasties were diverse: though different social groups were involved, they shared the same purely political objectives, which were devoid of any religious considerations.

It should be added, however, that there was to be seen through them the revival by stages of the Persian national sentiment. The rise of these political dynasties and their gradual assertion of semi-independent and independent status away from the aegis of the Caliphs was part of a wider renaissance of Persia, represented by the re-emergence

of the Persian language once again as not only the language of the ordinary people which, in fact, it had never ceased to be, but also as the language of literature and scholarship, replacing Arabic.

The poets Rudaki (d. 940), Daqiqi (d. 975) and, above all, Firdausi (d. 1040), the author of the Persian national epic Shahnameh (Book of Kings), began the use of modern Persian (Farsi) as we know it today. In the Shahnameh, a work which is longer than Homer's Iliad, Firdausi rarely resorts to the use of an Arabic word. After a thousand years it remains unsurpassed as the greatest and most popular work in Farsi literature. The story it relates purports to cover the whole course of Persian history from the beginning of time up to the end of the Sassanian empire. It tells of kings and heroes and of their deeds.

Side by side with this great literary renaissance among Persian men of letters, Persian scientists, who had written great works of science and philosophy in Arabic, on the basis of knowledge derived from Greek and Roman sources and of the Arabic language itself, started to use the Persian language for their works. Ibn Sina (980–1037) known in the West as Avicenna, one of the greatest names in Islamic medicine and philosophy began his work in Samanid times in Bokhara and later continued it at Gorgan and Isphahan at the courts of the contemporary Persian princes. He wrote the first Persian work of philosophy, called the

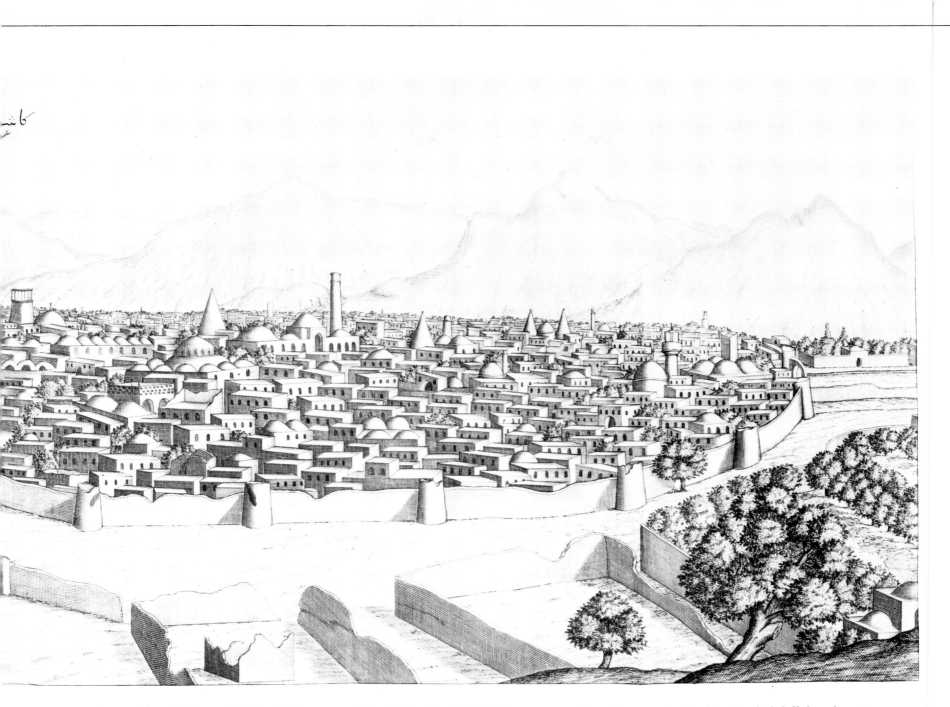

Danishnameh (*Book of Knowledge*) *Ala'i*, dedicated to the Persian Prince of Isphahan, Ala ad-Daula, at whose court he spent the last fruitful years of his life, renowned as one of the most famous physicians of Islam and the world. His *Canon of Medicine* was translated into various European languages and was used as a textbook at European universities. It remained as the standard source of medical knowledge in Europe for some four centuries.

The founder of the Tahirid dynasty, Tahir ibn Husain, came from a Persian family related to the Yemenite Arab governor of Sistan. Tahir's grandfather had taken part in Abu Muslim's struggle and had been elected governor of Pushang (now Ghuriyan on the southern shore of the Herat River). The family had, however, continued to live on its own lands and during the struggles between the son of Harun al-Rashid, Tahir, after rapidly distinguishing himself, had been appointed governor of his native Khorasan. Two years later, in 822, he started to omit the name of al-Ma'mun from the Friday *khutba* or sermon. A few days after this strange incident, which marked the point of departure for further developments, Tahir died. As his successor, al-Ma'mun elected Tahir's son and from that time onwards the governorship became hereditary, the first step towards independence. The exceptional administrative gifts of 'Abdallah ibn Tahir (828–44) consolidated the dynasty's power. In the east, the Samanid lords were still to a certain extent subject to 'Abdallah, whose troops operated against the Turks through their territory. In the west, the Tahirids occupied Rayy for some time and extended their power to the Caspian provinces, where they met with resistance from the 'Alids, who were established in Dailam. On the whole, the Tahirids remained faithful to the Caliphs until their end in 893, and showed no sign of nationalistic aims.

In origin and policy, the Saffarids were the antithesis of the Tahirids. Their native land, Sistan, was a remote area separated by deserts and inhospitable wastelands from the other Persian provinces and lying on the threshold of the Indian world of 'unbelievers'. Such a province was a natural refuge for religious dissenters and bandits who assumed

Above: Kashan, from a 17th-century drawing. 'Kashan is a large and populous city; it is situated in a fertile plain . . . and contains several well-built mosques and caravanserais. The market place is well furnished with . . . the common manufactures of Persia . . . silk and cotton stuffs, carpets, besides some other articles which make this a place of considerable trade.' John Bell, *Travels in Asia*, 1715–18.

Left: Courtyard of the Tarik Khaneh mosque at Damghan. It is the oldest mosque of this type in Persia, dating from the 8th century.

the mantle of 'defenders of the faith'. There were large bodies of men known as *'aiyar*, who may have originated in the *futuvva* (chivalry) organisations, who were always ready to seize any opportunity for causing riots and havoc. In 858, Ya'qub ibn Laith, a coppersmith (*saffar*), who was himself an *'aiyar*, took part in a revolt against the Tahirid governor and in 861 was proclaimed lord of Sistan. By 867, he had occupied Herat and Pushang, and the Tahirids signed a peace treaty by which his authority over the whole of southern Persia, including Kerman and Fars, was recognised. This led to a conflict with the Caliphal governor of Fars, but the Caliph al-Mu'tamid, who was himself involved in the civil strife raging in the country, recognised Ya'qub as the legal governor. Shortly afterwards, he waged war against Ghazna, Kabul and Balkh and defeated the Kharijite anti-caliph, afterwards sending his severed head to Baghdad and enrolling his men in his own army without regard to their beliefs. In 873, he marched against his Tahirid sovereign and captured him at Nishapur. He managed to thrust forward to the Caspian provinces, but there his advance was halted by forests and rice fields. The Caliph expressed his displeasure at the destruction of the Tahirids, but Ya'qub took up the challenge and in 876

marched against Baghdad. Having been deserted without warning by some of his officers, Ya'qub was forced to capitulate, and withdrew to Khuzistan, where he died three years later (879). Even though his attempt ended in failure, this bold gesture by a feudal adventurer provided the first warning that the Caliphate's authority was threatened. Ya'qub owed all his success to his own energies. He was a tough warrior, yet out of humility during military parades he used to report in person to the commanding officer to receive his pay.

Ya'qub was succeeded by his no less famous brother, 'Amr, who took over not only the titles but also the position of honorary governor of Baghdad and of the holy places. In Khorasan he was opposed by a Khuzistan chief, who was killed in 882 during the suppression of a revolt of which he was the leader. Shortly after a rebellion of negro slaves (Zanj) in Lower Mesopotamia had been put down in 883, the Caliph's brother, al-Muwaffaq, decided to enforce a strong policy in Persia. The Caliph announced to Khorasan pilgrims that 'Amr had been deposed, whereupon al-Muwaffaq threw him back as far as his native Sistan. Just at this time, however, the army of the North African Tulunid Dynasty threatened Damascus and the operations in the east had to be abandoned. 'Amr was restored as governor of Kerman, Fars and Khorasan on condition that an annual tribute of ten million *dirham* was paid. For a time, everything seemed to have returned to normal, but in 890 'Amr's brother allied himself with a Khorasan rebel. 'Amr, once again in disgrace with the court of Baghdad, managed to extricate himself from his difficulties, removed the name of al-Muwaffaq from the *khutba* and marched on Khuzistan. The Caliph, growing alarmed, replaced 'Amr's name on the flags and ordered it to be included in the Friday sermon, read in Mecca. Finally, 'Amr went to war with the Samanids, and the new Caliph granted him a

charter as governor of Transoxiana in the hope that this would mark his end. 'Amr was in fact captured by Isma'il, taken to Baghdad, and later murdered in prison (902).

Under 'Amr's descendants, the Saffarid state quickly disintegrated. Struggles began with other pretenders and in 911 Samanid troops occupied Sistan. Some time later, the rulers of Bokhara assigned Sistan to a distant relation of the Saffarids, Abu Ja'far Ahmad (923–63). At a still later date, the maliks of Sistan were to boast of their descent from this outstanding man and great patron of the arts.

However rough and rude were Ya'qub, the coppersmith and his brother 'Amr, the muleteer, the resurgence of Persia dates from their time. It is odd that it was due to Ya'qub's ignorance that Persian poetry was born: his secretary, Muhammad ibn Wasif, was forced to write in Persian, and his verses – now preserved in the *History of Sistan* – may be regarded as some of the oldest poems in Neo-Persian literature.

The Samanid dynasty originally came from the village of Saman in the province of Balkh in what is now Afghanistan. The founder, Saman-Khudat, embraced Islam only at the beginning of the eighth century. The Caliph al-Ma'mun appointed his four grandsons as governors of the eastern provinces: Samarkand, Farghana, Shash (now Tashkent) and Herat. In 842, al-Mu'tamid granted the governorship of the whole of Transoxiana to the head of the family, Ahmad ibn As'ad ibn Saman-Khudat. This vast region, in fact, formed part of the external Iran, since it lay outside the boundaries of the old Sassanid state, but under the Samanids Transoxiana and Khorasan were united both in politics and culture, and the Samanids played a conspicuous role in the resurgence of Persia. The languages spoken in Transoxiana (Sogdian and Khwarezmian) differed markedly from Persian, but Persian was introduced into the region by settlers, merchants and

religious communities. Under the Samanids, therefore, Bokhara and Samarkand became the melting pot from which modern Persia was produced, and later it was to acquire the dignity of being the administrative and cultural language. The Samanids were munificent, orthodox, and generous patrons; they set an example to their successors both in Central Asia and in Persia and for more than a century shielded the Iranian race and civilisation from the Turkish tribes massed against the eastern frontiers.

The first great Samanid sovereign, Isma'il ibn Ahmad (892–903), who governed Bokhara until 874, conquered Khorasan in a victory over the Saffarid 'Amr. In about 902 he led his troops into Zanjan, on the south-eastern frontier of Azerbaijan, which he held for some time, while his successes against the Turks took him as far as Taraz, east of the Jaxartes. These rapid conquests forced him to incorporate a good many restless vassals in his state, the most turbulent being the ambitious Muhtajids of Chaghaniyan on the southern bank of the Oxus river opposite Balkh. Later, the Simjurids of Quhistan, south of Khorasan, gave him considerable trouble because of their intrigues. To deal with this situation, the Samanids tried to set up a guard that was under no obligation to the local vassals, but as this guard was stationed at Bokhara it also became gradually drawn into factional struggles. Most of the guards were Turkish slaves who, though excellent soldiers, could not forget their origin and often remained faithful to their captains.

The great historian of Turkestan, V. Barthold, has called both the Tahirid and the Samanid governments 'enlightened despotisms', these undoubtedly conservative dynasties being much concerned with the needs of the people and opposed to abuses of political power. The difference between the two lay in the fact that the Tahirids were

always part of the imperial organisation of the Caliphate, while the Samanids became in practice independent after the turbulent period of Saffarid dominion. Furthermore, after 920, the Dailam warriors occupying central Persia cut the lines of communication between Khorasan and Baghdad, and from that time on contacts with the central government became difficult.

The fundamental weakness of the state arose mainly from the opposition of the land-owners to any attempt at centralisation of power. The priesthood, too, was closely associated with the major land-owners, and the Samanids were unable to obtain its co-operation in critical times. The Samanids were mostly orthodox Sunnis, but towards the end of the rule of Nasr II (914–43), the propaganda of the 'Alids obtained some success in Bokhara with the masses, and it appears that even the prince was converted to the Fatimid faith. The clerical hierarchy conspired with the Turkish guards and although Nuh ibn Nasr (943–54) managed to suppress these intrigues, the influential ruler of Chaghaniyan, 'Abu 'Ali, was the real power behind the throne during Nuh's reign. Later, there was fighting in the west against the Buyids, and the Turkish general Fa'iq became the highest personage in Bokhara. During the reign of Nuh II (976–97), his prime minister, 'Utbi, attempted to counter the influence of the Turkish *amir*, but he was assassinated by one of Fa'iq's agents. The Turks joined in the struggle for the distribution of feuds and a new power suddenly appeared on the scene in the person of Bughra-Khan Harun, leader of the independent Turks.

Called in by the landowners, who wished to be left to live in peace, the *ilig-khan* occupied Samarkand and entered Bokhara in 992. The Samanids were abandoned, but illness forced the new Turkish master to return to his native land and on 17 August of that year Nuh returned to his capital. However, he became involved in so many intrigues that he was soon obliged to seek help and protection from his Ghaznavid vassals, who restored him to the throne. During the reign of Nuh's young son, al-Mansur II (997–99), a treacherous prime minister called back the Ilig Khan and this time Mahmud of Ghazna, in an attempt to arrest the westward advance of the new rivals, captured Khorasan, so that the khan and the Turk, Mahmud, became neighbours on the banks of the Oxus.

The adventures of the last Samanid, al-Muntasir (999–1004), read like an epic poem. He even tried to launch the Turkmens against their brothers in Central Asia, who formed the Ilig Khan's armies. Though he

was unable to change the course of history, at least his death provided a fitting end to the saga of his family.

The role played by the court at Bokhara in the resurgence of national literature, still in its purest form uncontaminated by the pessimism and spirit of renunciation that were to prevail in later times, was of immense importance in the history of the Persian nation. It was like a national banner which guided the Persian people throughout the vicissitudes of their existence.

Unlike the turbulent *'aiyar* of Sistan, who were greatly concerned by the events taking place in their province, the inhabitants of

Transoxiana, who were educated in passive obedience to the authorities, readily submitted to the new leaders, while the doctors of Islamic law exhorted the people not to risk their lives in the struggle between two rulers, both of them Moslems. This conflict was considered from the opportunistic point of view, not as a conflict between Iranians and Turks. The problem was how to quash the intrigues and end the minor wars and achieve a more stable regime. In the long run, the substitution of the Iranians by the Turks fundamentally changed the race, appearance, character and language of the people of Transoxiana.

While the Persians were shaking off the Arab yoke, new clouds were gathering in the east

Until a few years ago, the importance of the western dynasties in the resurgence of Persia was not fully recognised. Moslem authors considered the slow contraction of the 'Abbasid empire as a cause of regret, and it has been mainly as a result of the publication of Miskawaih's *History* (begun by Caetani and completed by Amedroz and Margoliouth) that we have been able to look at the situation from the national Persian point of view.

The southern shore of the Caspian sea, separated from the central uplands by the immense Elburz chain, with its sub-tropical climate, and crossed only by paths winding through forests and rice paddies, maintained an existence of its own for many years, being incorporated into the central government system only in the sixteenth century. The part of the coastal region farthest to the west is Gilan and the mountainous areas to the south and to the other side of Gilan are called Dailam. This territory has a moderate, dry climate, but is far less rich and fertile than the lowlands. It is the soil of a strong race which was unable to wrest a living from the area and even in ancient times provided many mercenaries. In the beginning of the tenth century, these tribes played a role in Persia and Mesopotamia similar to that of the Normans in Europe. Many soldiers of fortune leading bands of their compatriots, men of Dailam and Gilan, appeared on the central uplands and, profiting from the weakness of the Caliphate, began the conquest of territories to the west of the areas held by the Samanids.

Before they made their entrance into the pages of Persian history, these groups consisted merely of isolated adventurers, but they were soon followed by the more important Ziyarids, who united and ruled a substantial part of southern and central Persia. Mardavij ibn Ziyar (928–35), who reigned in Rayy, seized Isphahan (934) and made an audacious attack on the Caliph's troops, entering Azerbaijan, reaching Hamadan, and penetrating even as far as Hulwan on the threshold of Mesopotamia. Mardavij came from the Arghish tribe, and his native land – never conquered by the Caliph – continued to live on memories of the past glory of the Sassanid empire. Mardavij himself dreamed of thrones, golden crowns, and the pomp and ceremony of the courts of yore. He was mentally unbalanced and frequently ill-treated and humiliated his Turkish guards, one of whom eventually assassinated him.

His brother and successor, Vushmagir (the 'quail-catcher'), established himself at Rayy, but was overthrown by the Buyids in 943. After this, the fortunes of the Ziyarids

Left: A miniature from the *Shahnameh* (*c.* 1440), painted for Mohammed Prince Juki.

Below: Astrolabe of inlaid brass (12th century). The Persians were highly skilled in the designing and making of such intricate instruments.

115

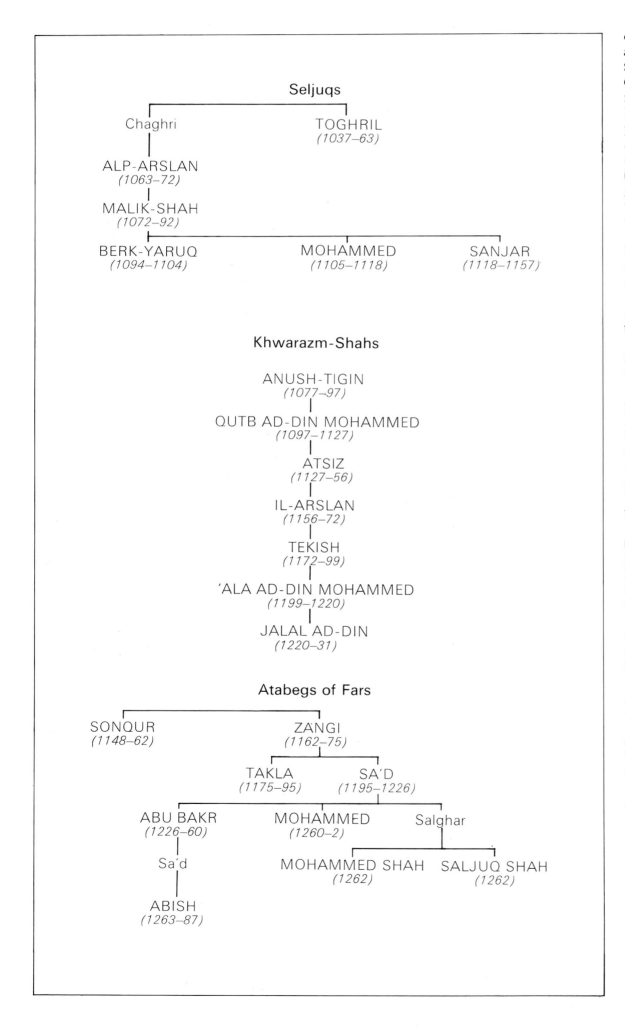

Seljuqs

Chaghri   TOGHRIL
(1037–63)

ALP-ARSLAN
(1063–72)

MALIK-SHAH
(1072–92)

BERK-YARUQ   MOHAMMED   SANJAR
(1094–1104)   *(1105–1118)*   *(1118–1157)*

Khwarazm-Shahs

ANUSH-TIGIN
(1077–97)

QUTB AD-DIN MOHAMMED
(1097–1127)

ATSIZ
(1127–56)

IL-ARSLAN
(1156–72)

TEKISH
(1172–99)

'ALA AD-DIN MOHAMMED
(1199–1220)

JALAL AD-DIN
(1220–31)

Atabegs of Fars

SONQUR   ZANGI
(1148–62)   *(1162–75)*

TAKLA   SA'D
(1175–95)   *(1195–1226)*

ABU BAKR   MOHAMMED   Salghar
(1226–60)   *(1260–2)*

Sa'd

MOHAMMED SHAH   SALJUQ SHAH
(1262)   *(1262)*

ABISH
(1263–87)

continued to be closely linked with Gurgan at the south-eastern region of the Caspian Sea. Vushmagir was succeeded by his son, Qabus (976–1012), known by the Arabic nickname of 'the Sun of High Concepts' because of his literary abilities and his patronage of the great scholars of his time. Al-Beruni dedicated his first works to him and the philosopher Abu 'Ali ibn Sina, (Avicenna), went to his court. Despite his generosity towards his friends, he was harsh to those in his service and was highly vindictive. His courtiers deposed him in 1012 and his son, Manuchihr, submitted himself to Mahmud of Ghazna, whose daughter he married. From then onwards the Ziyarids were only of local importance, but they maintained their cultural traditions at a high level. Qabus's grandson, who bore the same name, wrote the famous *Mirror for Princes* or *Qabusnameh* in 1082, when the Seljuqs were the overlords of Persia and the Ziyarids had lost all political power.

Of far greater importance was the rise to power of the Buyids (or Buwayhids in Arabic), around whose activities the Dailamite period may be said to have revolved. Their family (*Shir-dil* or 'lion-heart') could boast no special marks of distinction. The three brothers in the family began their careers as soldiers of fortune in the service of the Dailami generals and under Mardavij. The eldest of the three, 'Ali ('Imad ad-Daula), was appointed provincial governor in Karaj (between Arak and Burujird, not to be confused with the modern town to the west of Tehran), and soon afterwards occupied Isphahan without warning while it was still governed by the Caliph's representative. Threatened by Mardavij, however, 'Ali withdrew to Shiraz (934), of which the weak Caliph recognised him as the official governor. In the following year, ibn Ra'iq installed the first of a series of commanders-in-chief (*amir al-umara*), who transformed the Caliphs into puppets and rendered their prime ministers impotent. Thus the way was prepared for the advent of the Buyids, who, on the death of Mardavij, became the masters of the Iranian plateau and gradually established relations with the Caliph. In 946, Ahmad ibn Buya entered Baghdad and swore an oath of loyalty to the Caliph, despite the fact that the Buyids, like the rest of the population of Dailam, were firm supporters of the Shi'ites. Not unnaturally, complications arose, and twelve days after the swearing of the oath Ahmad (Mu'izz ad-Daula) arrested the Caliph al-Mustakfi and appointed a new Caliph, giving him the title of 'Obedient to God' (al-Muti'lillah). Thus began the era of the Buyids' unbroken supremacy, and the

loss of all vestiges of the Caliphate's power. It was a memorable event in the history of Persia, as the whole country was now under the rule of Iranian princes.

In 947, Basra was wrenched from the hands of the Baridites, and by this act was formed the third side of the triangle administered by the Buyids, which extended to Rayy, Shiraz and Baghdad; each of these three cities was governed by one of the three brothers, whose ties of blood kept them loyal to each other. At first the head of the family was 'Imad ad-Daula of Fars; upon his death he was replaced by Rukn ad-Daula, of Rayy, whose authority was strengthened by the fact that his son, 'Adud ad-Daula, had succeeded 'Imad as prince of Shiraz.

The extent to which the Buyids allowed themselves to be guided by practical considerations in their administration is shown by the fact that despite their Shi'ite faith they did not abolish the Caliphate, but used the influence of their protégés on the Sunni rulers for their own ends, the rulers still requiring 'Abbasid investiture. The Buyids did not submit to the Fatimids, the true 'Alid anti-caliphs of the west, and were on terms of open hostility with the Qarmati extremists in Bahrein. Even the 'Alids of Gilan had to conceal their intentions from the Buyids. The Shi'ite formula, for instance, did not appear on Buyid coins. On the practical side, however, the Buyids supported the 'Alids of Baghdad and developed the popular Dailami custom of mourning the dead, organising complex funeral ceremonies, and singing chants in honour of the 'Alid martyrs.

The vicissitudes of Mesopotamia cannot be adequately dealt with in so short a summary as this. In Persia, Rukn ad-Daula fought for many years against the Samanids and the Ziyarids, but neglected the north-western areas where the influence of the Musafirids was consolidated.

The country's internal administration was affected by the 'Abbasids and their dignitaries possessed vast holdings that were confiscated by the new overlords. Money was scarce, and to appease their turbulent companions, the Buyids introduced a system of allocation (*iqta'*) of the confiscated or uncultivated lands. Although this system appeared to be reasonable, it had its drawbacks; those receiving such lands knew nothing of farming and neglected their possessions in the hope of receiving further allocations. The distribution of feudal lands, especially in Fars and Kerman, created a complex situation and only during the reign of 'Adud ad-Duala was the position to some extent remedied.

The Dailamites were rough mountain folk, who scraped a poor living for themselves. They were armed with javelins and shields under the protection of which they advanced or beat off attacks. Apart from the fact that they were too few in number to defend a large state, extending from Khorasan to Mesopotamia, they had no cavalry, and for this they had to rely on Turkish mercenaries and slaves, an arrangement that led to continuous strife between the Dailamites and the Turks and consequently to the weakening of the former.

The first leaders were without experience of government or administration; Mu'izz, although his democratic ways made him popular with the poor, was fierce and irascible; his brother Rukn, was chivalrous and faithful, but his hasty decisions often placed his advisers in difficult situations and especially did this apply to his famous vizir, the learned ibn al-'Amid.

In 976, after a reign that had lasted forty-four years, Rukn died and was succeeded by his son, 'Adud, the most illustrious of the dynasty, who extended his dominions from Fars to Mesopotamia. He ruled at Fars from 949, and from Mesopotamia from 978 to 983. A disciple of ibn al-'Amid, he was familiar with the cultural developments of his times and patronised poets, including the Arab

Below: Esfandiyar slays Arjasp in the iron fortress, from the *Shahnameh* painted in Herat *c.* 1440.

Far right: Brass ewer inlaid with silver, *c.* 1200. The technique of inlaying metals such as bronze and brass was already known in the Sassanian period; the art was perfected, however, at Herat in the 12th century.

al-Mutanabbi, and was also an outstanding builder. However, 'Adud's reign saw the beginning of rivalry within the family. Pursued by his brother Mu'aiyad, of Isphahan and Rayy, 'Adud's other brother, Fakhr of Hamadan, was forced to take refuge with his father-in-law, Qabus the Ziyarid, and later to flee the country with Qabus to seek the protection of the Samanids. After his brothers' death, Fakhr returned to Rayy and attempted unsuccessfully to occupy Baghdad. On his death in 997, his able widow, a Tabaristan princess, became regent on behalf of her sons, but they soon rebelled against her. The pride of Mu'aiyad's and Fakhr's reigns was the vizir, Isma'il ibn al-'Abbad, 'as-Sahib' (938–95), who guided the ship of state for the Buyids in Rayy. His literary circle attracted many learned Persians and Arabs and under his protection contemporary Persian poets flourished.

Besides exercising extensive political power over widespread dominions, the Shi'ite Buyid princes were patrons of learning. Rukn ud-Daula (932–36), of Rayy, maintained a court whose members included a number of famous figures, among them the scientist abu-Jafar al-Khazin of Khorasan, who ascertained the obliquity of the ecliptic and solved a problem posed by Archimedes which results in a cubic equation. At Rayy, too, at this time there was a great library with so many manuscripts in it that the catalogue extended to ten volumes. The library founded in Shiraz by 'Adud ad-Daula (997–82) was manned by a regular staff who supervised the arrangement of the books and the keeping of the catalogues. One of the greatest of Persian historians, Miskawayh, whose name stands beside that of al-Tabari and al-Baladhuri, two more of Persia's foremost historians, who wrote in Arabic, compiled a universal history and held the office of Treasurer at Adud's court. The Buyid princes built several observatories, notably one established by Sharaf ud-Daula in his palace at Baghdad. Abd ar-Rahman as-Sufi (d. 986), the author of *al-Kawakib al Thabitah*, an astronomical classic on the fixed stars, worked in this observatory, as did other astronomers of the time, such as Ahmed as-Saghani (d. 990) and abu al-Wafa (d. 997).

The third generation of Buyids initiated a period of strife and disorder. In 994, there was even a rebellion in the army owing to the debased coinage with which the soldiers were paid.

The three branches of the Buyid family were swept away by Turkish invasions. In Rayy, Majd foolishly appealed for help to Mahmud of Ghazna, who entered the town in 1029, deposed Majd, took possession of

the treasure, hanged the heretics, Mu'tazilites and Batinis (or Isma'ilis), and burned their books. Malik ar-Rahim of Baghdad, a later and lesser member of the family, was taken prisoner by Toghril in 1055, and in 1062 the dynasty that had dominated Fars came to an end when Shiraz was captured by the Seljuq Qavurd.

The Dailamite movement had a profound effect on the renaissance of Khorasan, spreading as it did to the heart of the Persian territory, placing the Iranian 'uluj (non-Arabs) in power in Baghdad, and giving them tutelage of the Caliph himself. It was this 'Iranian intermezzo' between the Arab occupation and the Turkish invasion which ended the sequence of foreign conquests. Had this interlude not taken place, the Persian nation would probably never have been resurrected. The liberating role of the Dailamites is best shown by the number of minor Persian dynasties which followed in their wake.

The Kakuyids may be regarded as an extension of the Buyids in Rayy. The founder of the dynasty, which flourished only for a few years in the period between the Ghaznavids and the Seljuks, was 'Ala ad-Daula, whose father is thought to have been the son of a maternal uncle (kaku) of the famous Sayyida, the mother of Majd ad-Daula. 'Ala ad-Daula was, in fact, from Mazandaran, and not from Dailam. In about 1007, Sayyida appointed him governor of Isphahan and he extended his rule to Hamadan and even to parts of Kurdistan and Luristan. He spent the period of the Ghaznavid invasion (1029–30) in exile, but afterwards returned to take over the Buyid succession. Although his reign was bedevilled by incessant strife, he continued the Iranian tradition and ensured his own fame by welcoming ibn Sina (Avicenna) as his counsellor. His son recognised the new Seljuq invaders, receiving from them the distant regions of Yazd and Abarquh, where his successors survived with the title of ata-beg until the fourteenth century.

During the period of the last of the Buyids, the semi-nomadic tribes in south-eastern Fars, known as Shaban-Kareh, set up an independent territory embracing Ij, Darabgird, and other places where their dynasty survived until 1363.

The vast north-western area of Persia, embracing Azerbaijan, was taken over by another Dailamite family, the Musafirids (or Kangarids). Dailam had its own dynasty which from 805 until 928 stayed in the mountains and never left them, ruling through subsequent generations until 1042. Its subjects, the Musafirids, showed more initiative. They appeared first of all in

Tarum, an inaccessible area on the Safid-rud. Muhammad ibn Musafir, who was married to a royal princess of Dailam, began his rise to power when Yusuf, the last governor of Azerbaijan appointed by Baghdad, was disgraced (919). One of his sons remained in Tarum while the other, Marzuban (nicknamed Sallar) went out to conquer Azerbaijan, then occupied by the Kurd Daisam, a former general of Yusuf's. Marzuban was a Batini, that is probably a follower of the Fatimids, and this encouraged him to embark on even more bitter struggles against the Kharijite Daisam. From his new capital, Ardabil, Marzuban crossed the Araxes and entered Transcaucasia, where he exacted tribute from many Armenian principalities. In 943, he fought against the Russians, who had sailed their ships across the Caspian Sea and up the river Kur to Barda'a (Partav). From there, Marzuban attacked the Hamdanids and finally marched on Rayy. There he was captured by the Buyid Rukn and held as a prisoner in Fars, but he managed to escape and once again achieved power. He died in 957, leaving his domains to his brother, who started a lengthy struggle against other pretenders. The Tarum branch survived until the Seljuq invasion, and the Azerbaijan branch was deposed in 983.

The Musafirids were duly succeeded in Azerbaijan by the Rawwadids, a family that was originally Arab, but whose line had in course of time become Kurdicised. Their capital was Tabriz and their chief supporters were the Kurdish tribal chiefs (*Hadhbani*). They appeared on the scene early in 956 and in about 983 unified Azerbaijan under their rule. They repelled the first attacks by Turkish hordes, but were scattered by the Seljuqs in 1070. The Maragha branch was to survive for many decades and took part in the wars against the Crusaders.

The Kurdish Shaddadids were originally soldiers of fortune, who took advantage of the imprisonment of Marzuban, the Musafirid (984–953), to conquer Dvin, the capital of Armenia, north of the Araxes. They stood for a further expansion of the Iranian movement into an area bordering the country. The most famous of the Shaddadids, Abul Asvar Shavur, fought the Armenians, the Georgians, and even the Byzantines, who had advanced into Transcaucasia. Abul Asvar set up his court at Dvin (1022–49), but later (1049–67) he transferred it to Ganja on the Kur river. Under Seljuq protection, the last of the Shaddadids occupied the Armenian capital, Ani, where he reigned until about 1199.

The Iranian influence on the princes of

Shirvan (an area north of the Kur), who were descendents of the Arab Shaibanids, can be considered to be an indirect result of the Iranian reawakening.

Further south, along the lines leading from Hamadan to Mesopotamia, the Hasanuyids of the Kurdish tribe of the Barzikans founded a very large principality. Badr ibn Hasanuya (980–1014) was a prince renowned for the buildings that he inspired and for his generosity. The famous Sayyida, widow of the Buyid Fakhr, who had been expelled by her son, found refuge with Badr, who restored her to power in Rayy. The Hasanuyid principality resulted from a mingling of Kurdish nomadic tribes grouped around fortified castles.

Despite their Arab name, the 'Annazids (first half of the eleventh century) were also Kurds from the Shadanjan tribe. Their sphere of operations was the vast area lying to the west of the Hasanuyid territory, near Hulwan on the threshold of Mesopotamia. They took part in the struggles of the Arab tribes and were swept away by the Seljuqs.

Even further to the west, in the Diyarbekr and Mayyafariqin region, the Kurd Badh, who died in 990, united the Humaidi and Bashnaui tribes in a single principality. Under his successors, known as the Marwanids (990–1085), this principality grew to considerable dimensions. In the west it extended to the borders of Syria and in the east it held the Hamdanids in check. Only in 1085 did the Seljuqs succeed in annexing their territory to the *ata-beg* possessions of Mosul.

This, then, was the long chain of Iranian states that was forged after the rise of the Buyids in Persia and their expansion to Mesopotamia. Their importance in the history of Persia has yet to be fully appreciated.

While the Persians were shaking off the Arab yoke, new clouds were gathering in the east. The Turks, who until this time had visited the west in small groups as servants or mercenaries, had organised themselves as new principalities and were moving towards the west *en masse*. There were three such waves. The Ilig Khans, more frequently called the Qarakhanids, had become masters of the Samanid states. They belonged to a noble family and their native land was between Kashghar and the river basin near Lake Issyk-Kul. Their supporters were mainly recruited from the Qarluq tribes. There is no doubt that they inherited the cultural achievements of the Samanids, but since their slow territorial expansion was halted at the Oxus (Amu-darya) by the Ghaznavids, their story does not form part of the history of Persia itself.

The Persians did not come into contact with the compact masses of the Turks until the first half of the eleventh century

The origins of the powerful Ghaznavids lay in the secession of a Turkish general from the service of the Samanids in 962. At first the emirs had come to power on the basis of merit. The hereditary principle was introduced only after the death of Sultan Mahmud's father, Sabuk (Sebuk)-Tegin. Whatever the tribes to which these emirs belonged, their organisation was far from tribal in nature. Their troops included contingents widely different in origin, among them Dailamites, Kurds and Afghan mountain peoples. Civil administration remained in Iranian hands, but the generals and governors were Turks. The Ghaznavids' ventures were aimed mainly in a southward direction towards India, an inexhaustible source of slaves and booty, and their expansion on the Iranian plateau was brief. In 1030, a year after removing the Buyids of Rayy from their throne, Sultan Mahmud died and his heir, Mas'ud, hurriedly returned to Afghanistan, so that the Kakuyids could win back the lands dominated by the Buyids. Only the more remote eastern provinces, such as Sistan, underwent any lasting influence from the Ghaznavids. From the Persian point of view, the importance of the group of scholars who collected at the court of Mahmud was considerable, although we read of the feeling of disillusionment with which Firdausi left the court. It was typical of the patriotic feelings that inspired him that he wished to withdraw the dedication of the *Shahnameh* to Mahmud and re-dedicate this work, in which all the national and legendary traditions of Persia are enshrined, to a local Mazandarani ruler of pure Iranian stock. The fact that the works of many other Persian poets in Ghazna were lost to posterity shows how Ghazna was isolated from the mainstream of Iranian culture.

The impact of the Oghuz invasion from east to west was very different; this was guided, though only partly controlled, by the dynasty descending from Seljuq. The Persians did not come into contact with the compact masses of the Turks until the first half of the eleventh century. The Oghuz group, to which the forerunners of the Seljuqs belonged, lived along the lower course of the Syr-darya. After its conversion to Islam, the Seljuq tribe was in dispute with its leader and broke away, withdrawing to the area near Samarkand, where it placed itself in the service of the Samanids. Obstacles arose in Sultan Mahmud's reign when the newcomers declared that they had insufficient lands and asked for permission to emigrate to Khorasan. Against the advice of the local governor, Mahmud allowed four thousand families to enter the region which now constitutes the

Soviet Republic's territory of Turkmenistan. After Mahmud's death in 1030, the Oghuz grew progressively stronger, and finally laid waste the city of Merv and its surroundings (1034). In 1038 Nishapur was occupied by Toghril, and his name was read out in the public sermon (*khutba*). Two years later Sultan Mas'ud was routed by the Seljuqs at Dandanaqan, and the whole territory to the west of the Oxus thus passed into the hands of the Seljuqs: their road to Central Persia was now open. In 1055 after the fall of Rayy and Isphahan, Toghril appeared in Baghdad and, as a loyal representative of orthodoxy, expelled the last scion of the Shi'ah Buyids. After Toghril's death in 1063, his nephew, Alp Arslan (1063–72), defeated the Byzantine emperor (1071), thus extending his domains from the Oxus (Amu-darya) to Syria. The new Islamic empire reached its greatest splendour under his son, Malik-Shah (1072–92). His name and reign are immortalised by the Maliki or Jalali Era. In 1074 a group of astronomers, including the famous Omar Khayyam (better known in the West for his *Rubaiyat*) devised a reformation of the calendar more accurate than that of Pope Gregory, although 500 years earlier.

Following these conquests, Persia was included in the vast territory controlled by the new Seljuq masters, but Isphahan was

their more or less permanent capital and the centres from which the empire was governed were always in Persia. Thus great opportunities were afforded to the Persian class of functionaries who had retained their knowledge of finance and administrative methods from the time of the Sassanids, and which they had perfected under the Arabs. From the beginning they collaborated with the Seljuqs. Their most typical representative was Nizam al-Mulk (1019–92), the greatest organiser of the Seljuq empire. He was an enlightened conservative, whose ideal was an administration combining the efficiency of the Sassanid and the Caliphs' clerical class and backed by the strength of the inexpert Turks. He aimed to achieve order and centralisation, and wished to see every class retaining its own position, while reinforcing the machinery of government and abolishing administrative irregularities.

His task was difficult because his subtle methods were not appreciated. He wanted to set up a regular postal service and also to organise a system of espionage, but his master, Alp Arslan, declared that secret reports upset his peace of mind. Though Nizam defended orthodoxy, he wished at the same time to control the supreme head of Islam through the latter's vizier, ibn Jahir, who was devoted to Nizam. He hated

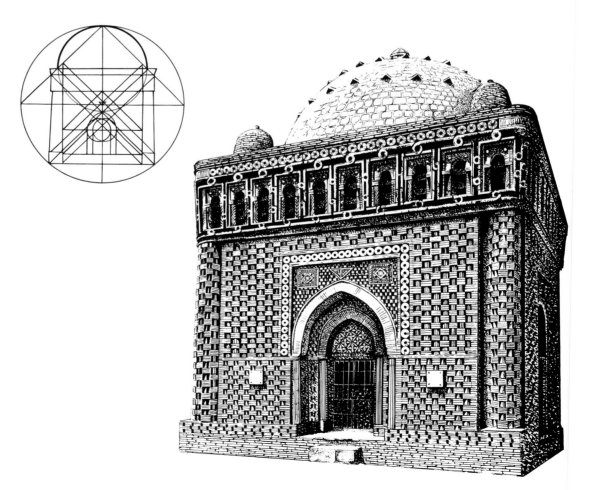

Left: A miniature from the *Shahnameh* (*c.* 1440): the combat between Lahhak and Giv, the sword against the lance.

Below: Minai pottery bowl from Rayy, 12–13th century.

Right: The return of Shapur to Khosro, by Mirak, from the manuscript of the *Khamsa* of Nizami, 1539–43.

disorder, and especially heresies, in which – as always in the Islamic world – the forces of political and social opposition found expression. Nizam al-Mulk's predecessor, Kunduri, had introduced the practise of publicly cursing the Shi'ites and Ash'arites in the mosque. In his famous memorandum on administration (Siyasat-nameh), Nizam al-Mulk tried to arouse his master by accusations against the Isma'ilites, whom he compared to all the heretics from Mazdak's time onwards.

Gradually the former Iranian princes were replaced by Seljuq princes and emirs. At first there was a deep-rooted sense of discipline within the royal family, although quite soon after coming to power Toghril was forced to condemn to death his rebel half-brother, Ibrahim Yinal, and Malik Shah defeated and put to death his ambitious uncle, Qavurd, the head of the Kerman branch of the dynasty.

The system of land distribution (*iqta'*) which should in theory have been a temporary measure, the land being granted on certain conditions. was widely practised even under the Buyids, but the Seljuqs made use of it on a far larger scale. Some major land-owners retained their possessions, but many weaker owners had to be eliminated by the Turks.

The Turkish yoke weighed particularly heavily on the peasants, as the Turkish nomads, following their own peculiar style of life, trespassed on cultivated lands and tried to transform the farmers into providers of food for their tribes. In his book, Nizam al-Mulk quotes the words of Alp Arslan, who warned the Turks against accepting Jews, Christians, Zoroastrians or Shi'ites in their service: 'We are foreign to them', said the Sultan, 'we are all pure Mohammedans and these inhabitants of [Persian] Iraq are of evil faith and partisans of the Dailamites'. The Isma'ilite resistance from their fortified castles during the Seljuq period was

undoubtedly due to the help of the peasants. Shi'ism, especially in its more extreme form, stood for opposition both to the authoritarian aspects of the regime of Nizam al-Mulk and to the arbitrary system of the Turks.

Nizam al-Mulk was murdered by one of his Isma'ilite enemies and his ruler, Malik Shah, died in that same year, 1092. Thus, after some fifty years of peace and stability, wars of succession began within the royal family and the country had to submit to incursions of cavalry, such as the invasion of Tutush from Syria to the confines of Rayy, and to innumerable bloody battles between Berk-yaruq (1092–1104) and his brother Muhammad.

The authority of the last great Seljuq, Sanjar (1118–57), was still respected within the royal family, but his feudal domain of Merv was far distant from Persia and his three years of imprisonment by the Oghuz rebels (1153–56) was a sad foretaste of the collapse of the empire. In central Persia, other members of the family continued to quarrel among themselves; Sanjar himself favoured Malik Shah's grandson, Toghril II, as his successor. After his death in 1134, the great empire was no longer united, the Seljuq family being divided into two branches, the branch of Persian Iraq, with its capitals at Isphahan and Hamadan, and the Kerman branch. The importance of the latter was purely local. It survived until 1187, when an Oghuz rebel chief named Dinar seized Kerman.

The Persian Iraq branch, on the other hand, continued to represent the central government of Persia.

The Turkish practice of appointing grand emirs as Atabeg, or tutors, to young princes was an additional factor in the collapse of the state, since each Atabeg protected his own pupil and resisted all the central government's attempts to exercise control over his domain.

The major feudal domain of this type was Azerbaijan, which was governed by the emir Eldiguz or Ildegiz. After the death of his patron, Toghril II, he proclaimed his pupil, Arslan, as the successor and married Toghril's widow, who bore him sons, and the position of Arslan and especially of Arslan's son, Toghril III, became increasingly difficult owing to the opposition of his Eldiguzid relations. Toghril III (1177–94), an energetic and courageous young man, defeated his Eldiguzid rival, Qutlugh-Inanch. However, the latter sought help from the rising star, Tekish, the Khwarazm-Shah, and at the battle of Rayy (1194) Toghril, the last of the Seljuqs, was killed.

Left: The tomb tower of Qabus, one of the most talented of all the Ziyarid princes. This is the earliest tower of its kind in Persia (*c.* 1006). It is built entirely of brick and is 167 feet high. A narrow door facing towards the east is the only means of access. The height of the tower is emphasised by the mount on which it stands, so that it is a landmark for miles around.

Below: The tomb tower (detail) of Pir-i-Alander (1021) at Damghan.

Right: At Varamin stands the great brick tower, 85 feet high, of Ala ad-Din Muhammad, who in his day was one of the most powerful representatives of the Islamic world. Some fifty similar towers, built over a period of 700 years and varying in size and design, have been found in various parts of Persia.

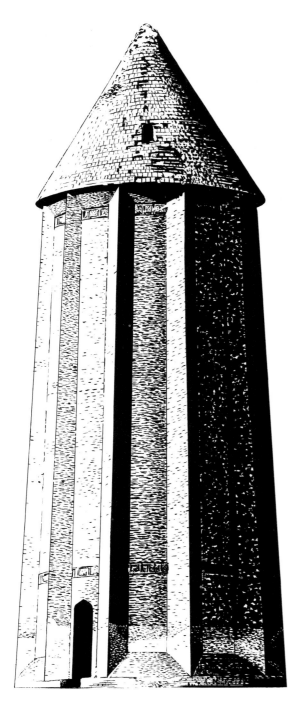

(1172–1200), the Khwarazmians occupied Khorasan, Rayy, and Isphahan, and Tekish's son, 'Ala ad-Din Muhammad (1200–1220) attempted to emulate the great Seljuqs. He occupied most of Persia and dreamed of installing a Caliph of 'Alid origin in Baghdad instead of relying on the energetic Caliph, Nasir (1180–1225), who had sent his governors to the south-western provinces of Persia. 'Ala ad-Din's relations with his neighbours in Central Asia, the Ghurids of Afghanistan, the Qarakhanids of Bokhara, the Qara Khitai (Liao) chiefs in Yeti-su (Semirechye in Russian) and their successor, Kuchlug of the Naiman tribe, were settled in a more or less satisfactory manner, but in the struggle against Genghis Khan, 'Ala ad-Din lost his kingdom piece by piece. When he died, a fugitive on an island in the south-eastern region of the Caspian Sea, his son, Jalal ad-Din, was still fighting rearguard actions in Afghanistan against the pursuing Mongols. At a critical moment, he managed to flee to the left bank of the Indus river and to gather together what remained of his armies. From there he returned to Persia from the south-east, and, pursued by Mongol forward detachments, reached the opposite end of the country. After a clash with the Caliph's army, he entered Azerbaijan, where he deposed the weak Eldiguzid Oz-beg and married his wife (1225). From Tabriz he attacked the Christian kingdom of Georgia in the Caucasus, and after a forced march to Kerman lasting seventeen days and covering a distance of 1250 miles, he fought a battle with the Ayyubids of Akhlat. Supported by forces of the Seljuqs from Asia Minor, the Ayyubids became the victors, and eventually in 1231, Jalal ad-Din, pursued relentlessly by the Mongols, died in the mountains of Kurdistan. Thus ended the life of the man who had swept through the history of Persia like a meteor and whom poets and historians alike had at first hailed as the saviour of Islam from the Mongol infidels.

A number of other dynasties arose from the ruins of that of the Seljuqs. Among these were the Qutlugh-Shahs of Kerman, who were of Far Eastern origin, from Qara Khitai, Liao, and had arrived in Persia with the Khwarazmians (1222–1302) and later submitted to the Mongols. The founder of the dynasty was 'ill-disposed towards the Persians and men of letters', but his descendants, both male and female, became poets in the Persian language. Marco Polo passed through Kerman during the reign of Princess Qutlugh-Terken.

There were also the Atabegs of Fars, from the Turkmen tribe of the Salghurids

(1148–1281), who were vassals of the Seljuqs, the Khwarazm-Shahs and the Mongols in turn. They enjoyed a good measure of independence and administered their domains peacefully. The great Persian poet Sa'di, who graced their court, glorified the works of this dynasty in dedicating to the Atabeg Abu Bakr (1226–60) his celebrated *Bustan* (*Orchard*), a collection of ethical tales and reflections in beautiful verse, also his similar and even more celebrated *Gulistan* (*Rose Garden*), in mingled prose and verse, both of which have been translated into all the main languages of the East and the West.

The Atabegs of Yazd, descendents of the Kakuyids, continued to govern in their feudal domain, and the Shaban-Kare emirs continued to resist their neighbours.

The two dynasties of Luristan, the Atabegs of the Greater Lur in the south (1155–1423), whose capital was Idhag (Malamir), and the Atabegs of the Lesser Lur, who reigned in the north (1184–1597), were of Iranian origin and helped to save Luristan, the south-western region of Persia, from the invaders.

The Caspian provinces, governed by the ancient dynasties of the Bavandids (Mazandaran), the Paduspanids (Ruyan) and other princely families of lesser note, still formed an independent and inconquerable oasis. Protected by their mountains, these minor dynasties jealously guarded their ancient customs and traditions.

The most important of the purely political parties of Seljuq times was the omnipresent order of the Isma'ilis, or Assassins, which was under the leadership of the Grand Masters of Alamut. Although, for political reasons, the Buyids did not recognise the Fatimids, Fatimid propaganda had penetrated deep into Persia and even into Transoxiana. The schism between the Isma'ilites occurred after the death of the eighth Fatimid Caliph in 1094, who was succeeded by his son, al-Musta'li, while a

The Eldiguzids were thus left in control of Azerbaijan, while Persia passed to the new contenders to dominion over the Islamic world, the Khwarazm-Shahs. (Khwarazm was a remote oasis, and one of the oldest of Iranian lands.) In 995, the last of the Khwarazm-Shahs, the twenty-second, was killed by a member of the neighbouring Ma'munid family, who came from the left bank of the river Oxus. The fall of the Ma'munids was to follow soon after, in 1017, when Sultan Mahmud replaced them with his own Turkish slaves. The best-known dynasty of Khwarazm was founded by another Turk, appointed by the Seljuq Malik Shah in 1077, and it lasted until 1231. By that time the oasis had been overrun by the Turkish invaders, although we now know that the ancient Khwarazmian language was still being spoken there in the fourteenth century.

Under the Khwarazm-Shah, Tekish

strong group of the faithful supported the rights of the Caliph's eldest son, Nizar. A member of this group was Hasan ibn as-Sabbah, a Persian who was a native of Qum, who had been converted when only a boy by Isma'ili preachers. In 1078, he went to Egypt, but received none too warm a welcome by the partisans of al-Musta'li because of his loyalty to Nizar. His estrangement from official circles probably gave him greater freedom of action when he returned to Isphahan in 1081.

The secret doctrines of the Isma'ilites went far further than the problem of the imam's rights of succession. The sect had

novelty of this organisational structure, however, lay in the fact that the fortresses belonged to no recognised system of government, but formed an extraneous and rival factor within the territory of the state. Another characteristic of this system was that the sect's leaders trained fanatically devoted agents who were ready to sacrifice their own lives for the cause (*fida'i*), and regarded terrorism and political assassination as legitimate means of attaining their objectives. Their monopoly of these means was tacitly recognised even by certain men of state, who frequently used the *fida'is* to destroy their enemies.

absorbed many non-Islamic beliefs that had survived in the Near and Middle East and had formulated a subtle theory of reincarnation by which a series of emanations were said to come into the world in hierarchical order. A noteworthy innovation was the system of different degrees of initiation during which various doctrines were taught, ranging from the grossest superstition to pure philosophical concepts. In this way, the sect could attract different levels of society and organise the faithful in a single bloc. The organisation of the sect, which was violently opposed to the official state and its representatives, was based on the existence of a series of isolated fortresses which protected the rural population and was in turn protected by them. The theory advanced by V. Barthold that these fortresses restored a Sassanid type of feudalism may be true up to a point; the

Upon the peoples of Islam the Mongol invasion had the paralysing effect of some great national disaster.

Below left: An amulet case made to contain a miniature copy of the Koran and probably worn as a necklace (*c.* 12th century).

Right: Dervish's bowl, dated 1279, carved from a double coconut shell decorated with an incised inscription and a pattern of animals and flowers.

The rise of Isma'ili power dates from the capture of Alamut by Hasan ibn as-Sabbah in 1090. This fortress, built by the ancient kings of Dailam in 860, was situated in the land of the Shi'ite Buyids, who about 150 years before had left it to conquer Persia and Baghdad.

In 1092, during Malik Shah's reign an expedition was sent against Alamut and another fortress, as a result of which Nizam al-Mulk, Malik Shah's famous Vizier, was assassinated by the *fida'i*. The struggle continued for years, but the Sultan Sanjar, cowed by the *fida'is'* threats, quickly established a *modus vivendi* with the followers of the sect. Hasan ibn as-Sabbah, a severe man, had condemned both his sons to death for their weakness of character, and after his death in 1124 power passed into the hands of the local chief, Buzurg-Ummid, under whose grandson, Hasan (1162–66),

great changes were introduced in Alamut. In 1164, the new leader proclaimed himself a direct descendant of Nizar, in other words not a representative of the imam, but the imam in person.

Hasan was assassinated by his brother-in-law, a distant descendant of the Buyid family. His grandson, Jalal ad-Din Hasan (1166–1210), submitted to the Caliph, restored orthodox Sunni faith, and attempted to restore friendly relations with his neighbours. The policy of the 'New Muslim', as he was called, was not consistent, and as soon as Genghis Khan crossed the Oxus, Jalal ad-Din Hasan sent messengers to pay him homage. During the childhood of his son, 'Ala ad-Din (1210–55), the former heresy (*ie*, Isma'ilism) gained ground within the organisation. 'Ala ad-Din's son, Rukn ad-Din, returned to Islam, but reigned only for a year. Since Hulegu

was marching from Mongolia with orders to destroy the lawless sect of the Assassins, Rukn ad-Din immediately surrendered to the conqueror (1256). He was taken to Mongolia, where he was murdered, while Alamut and forty other fortresses were occupied and sacked. The Isma'ili population surrendered and after being dispersed among the various Mongol camps was exterminated. During the whole of the period from 1090 to 1256, the masters of Alamut, who adopted means of political conduct which by normal standards would be considered as criminal, played a very important part in those times in many parts of Persia. Their doctrines, which incorporated popular beliefs (Messianism, tangibility of divine power, and so forth) attracted adherents and were of comfort to them. They held the Seljuqs and their governors in check, defied orthodoxy and the government apparatus, and in a certain sense acted as a corrective to the ills of that primitive epoch. They numbered many supporters among the people and the rural classes, and it was due to the latter's help that the organisation lasted so long. The Isma'ilites left not a few traces in the traditions and customs of later generations.

The impact of the Mongol hordes was the hardest trial borne by Persia. Even if only superficially, the Turks were Muslim and common ground could always be found with them. The Mongols were pagans, barbarians, and nobody could understand their language.

Upon the peoples of Islam the Mongol invasion had the paralysing effect of some great natural disaster. The famous Arab historian ibn al-Athir (*d.* 1234) remarks that for some years he was averse from mentioning this event, deeming it so horrible that he shrank from discussing it. 'The greatest catastrophe and the most dire calamity' that had ever overtaken mankind was how he described it. He refers in particular to the great and systematic massacres which characterised the conquest of north-eastern Persia, massacres which are described in detail by the Persian historian Juvaini (1226–1283). Time and again Juvaini relates that after the capture of a city the population was slaughtered, each Mongol soldier being made responsible for the execution of several hundred persons. The total figures are incredible: according to ibn al-Athir, 90,000 people were killed at Merv alone. Juvaini records that a Moslem divine, 'together with some other persons, passed thirteen days and nights in counting the people slain within the town. Taking into account only those that were plain to see and leaving aside those that had been

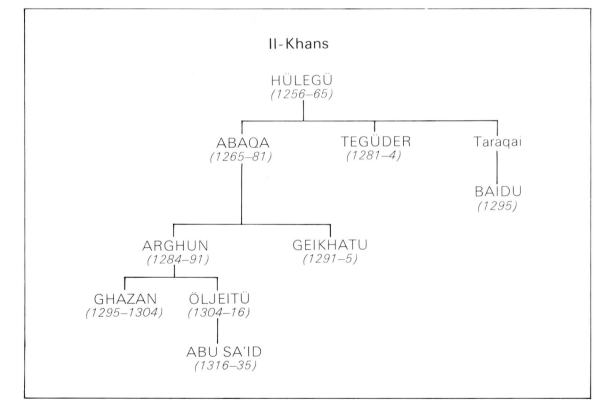

Il-Khans

HÜLEGÜ
(1256–65)

ABAQA
(1265–81)

TEGÜDER
(1281–4)

Taraqai

BAIDU
(1295)

ARGHUN
(1284–91)

GEIKHATU
(1291–5)

GHAZAN
(1295–1304)

ÖLJEITÜ
(1304–16)

ABU SA'ID
(1316–35)

killed in holes and cavities and in the villages and deserts, they arrived at a figure of more than one million, three hundred thousand.' Even higher figures are given of those killed at Herat. At Nishapur, where a son-in-law of Genghis Khan had fallen in the fighting, it was ordered 'that the town should be laid waste in such a manner that the site could be ploughed upon; and that in the exaction of vengeance not even cats and dogs should be left alive'. Except for 400 craftsmen reserved for transportation to Mongolia as slaves, the whole population was put to death. The heads of the slain were severed from their bodies and piled in heaps, those of the men being separate from those of the women and children. The question arose of how the population of such great cities could passively submit to being slaughtered like sheep, and the blame has been placed on Sufism for undermining their will to resist. It is clear, however, that these strange warriors, seemingly from another world, did inspire a paralysing kind of fear in all who encountered them.

In the time of Genghis Khan, his son Tolui invaded Khorasan. Then in 1220–21, the generals, Jebe and Subetei, reconnoitred the area round the Caspian Sea. In 1230, Chormaghan managed to put an end to the adventures of the Khwarazm-Shah, Jalal ad-Din. His successor, Baiju (1242–56) completed the Mongol conquests, pushing on deep into Asia Minor. Immediately after the conquest, the Mongol administrators arrived, most of them Turkish Uighurs and others who were familiar with the Chinese methods of government and who attempted to rebuild the cities and establish some kind of order. As in the times of the Seljuqs, Persian

functionaries again collaborated with the Mongols and helped them to restore order in the country. In about 1232, ten years after the invasion, the father of Juvaini, the historian, received the insignia of office of *Sahib-divan* from the Khan, and Juvaini himself (*b*. 1226) was employed in the service of the able administrator, Arghun Agha, whom he accompanied on his travels in Mongolia. His able brother, Shams ad-Din, served the Mongols for twenty-two years. Although this form of collaboration was in some respects dishonest, men such as these managed to place some restraint on the barbarity of the Mongols and there is no doubt that they contributed to the process by which the Persian nation finally managed to absorb and Iranicise its conquerors.

In this early period, the Moslems smarted under the humiliation of being governed by pagans, who of course made no distinction between Moslems, Jews or Christians. There was some consolation, however, in the continued presence of the Caliph in Baghdad. Even more intolerable were the changes in the ownership of land, the confiscation of cattle, offences against their women, and the Mongols' repulsive habits.

At a grand council (*quriltai*) held in Mongolia in 1251, it was decided that a brother of the Great Khan, Qubilai, should go to China and another, Hulegu, to Persia, as imperial lieutenants in those countries. Only in 1256, however, did Hulegu cross the Oxus and take possession of his domains. Destroying the Isma'ili fortresses on his way, he reached Azerbaijan, and from thence he marched on Baghdad. In 1258, the mainstay of Muslim orthodoxy, the Abbasid Caliph, was captured and ignominiously put to death. Nobody could have imagined a

more atrocious offence in the eyes of the Moslems. However, by destroying Isma'ilite power at one blow, a great thorn was removed from the flesh of the body politic of Islam, and, strange to relate, one of Hulegu's sons, Ahmad Tegude (1282–84), was converted to Islam.

Hulegu set up his residence at Maragha in Azerbaijan (the capital was later transferred to Tabriz), and within a short period of time merchants and citizens began to realise the advantages of safe lines of communication, and to appreciate the riches that flowed to the centres of a new and great state. In matters of religion the Mongols were still indifferent and the Moslems were able to live their community lives in peace, even though they had lost their former privileges. The peasants suffered most, as increasing hordes pitched their tents on cultivated ground, but soon even the Mongols began to appreciate the importance of respecting villages and of taking part in trade, with the result that the country people they were supposed to protect found themselves leading a slightly less uncertain existence.

The Uighur language and script were used in administration and Uighur was learnt by a few enterprising Persians, but on the whole, both Persian and Arabic put up a successful resistance to the alien tongue. The language which stands for national unity showed scarcely any effects of the Mongol incursion; indeed, it continued to develop through the works of historians and other writers of the time.

The most outstanding ruler to succeed Hulegu was Ghazan Khan, son of Arghun (1295–1304). He was a highly gifted man, who spoke many languages and was familiar with many forms of art. Although not

physically strong, he became by dint of exercise a good soldier. Though the reforms he introduced were recommended by his vizier, Rashid ad-Din, they showed his interest in his subjects' welfare.

Ghazan was the fourth generation of the Il-Khanids of Persia. At that time the ranks of the Mongols – who even at the beginning had not been so numerous as the Oghuz before them – had been thinned out considerably by the various campaigns, especially the wars against invincible Egypt. The effects of these defeats began to be felt, but there was no hope of further reinforcements from Mongolia, from which

Persia was divided by the *yurt* or lands belonging to other branches of the family which were somewhat hostile to Hulegu's grandsons. It was impossible, therefore, to dominate the compact mass of the Moslem peoples with the help of an exhausted Mongol army and occasional Christian detachments recruited from the Caucasus. These considerations persuaded Ghazan to accept his emir Nauruz's advice.

Nauruz, the son of the pagan Arghun Agha, was a zealous convert to Islam. He persuaded Ghazan that the Moslems would 'be faithful to his cause', once they were raised from the degradation into which they

had fallen at the hands of the Mongols. In 1295, Ghazan and his army were solemnly converted to Islam and, with the support of the Moslems, Ghazan – or Mahmud, as he was called from then on – gained the advantage over his rivals. At the same time, the conquerors and the conquered began to coalesce. Gradually the Mongols forgot their own language and finally became by intermarriage completely merged with the rest of the population.

The most able of the viziers who collaborated with Ghazan was Rashid ad-Din, a member of a family of physicians (apparently Jewish) and an enlightened

statesman, who wrote a famous universal history. He became one of the richest land owners of his day in the service of the Mongols, but nevertheless he showed some understanding of the needs of the poorer classes. The first part of his historical work, inspired by the Il-Khan Ghazan, deals with the history of the Mongols down to Ghazan's own time.

In the second part, commissioned by Ghazan's brother and successor, Oljeitu (1304–16), Rashid was set the formidable task of compiling a general history of all the Eurasian peoples, with whom the Mongols had come into contact. It is, in fact, the first universal history in the full sense. His writings provide a very interesting picture of the administrative disorder and despotism that existed under the Mongols, as well as explaining Ghazan's systematic reforms. An economic census was carried out to establish the basis for an improved system of taxation. The amount of taxes payable having been decided, the amount was made public, so as to put an end to the system of arbitrary collection. Improvements were encouraged by tax concessions, and thirty-year regulations were introduced to prevent the submitting of false documents and forged claims to the possession of land.

The great courtyard of the Masjid-i-Shah, the King's Mosque, at Isphahan, one of the largest and most splendid buildings in Persia. It was begun on the orders of Shah 'Abbas I in 1612, but was not completed until 1638. The walls of the courtyard are completely covered with multi-coloured tiles instead of the traditional mosaics of an earlier period.

The military feudal domains were also reorganised. Mongol finances had been very badly affected by the disastrous attempt to introduce paper money (under the Chinese name of *chao*) during the reign of Keikhatu (1291–95), so the imperial treasury was placed under the stringent control of specially selected officials. In accordance with the precepts of the Koran, the lending of money at interest was prohibited in order to restrict usury. Movements by official travellers (*elchi*), whose food and mounts were provided by the population, were strictly curtailed.

Ghazan's brother and successor, Oljeitu, was converted to Islam under his wife's influence, and showed a particular leaning towards Shi'ism, as the faith best fitted to the interests of a hereditary king. Ghazan's plans of conquest over Gilan failed, and his decision to found a new capital at Sultaniya was of brief duration. On the whole, however, he was faithful to Ghazan's tradition. The reign of his son, Abu Sa'id (1316–34), was more troubled. Abu Sa'id's violent passions showed a marked lack of balance in his character. His reign was disgraced by the execution of the old Rashid ad-Din and many other great emirs. Abu Sa'id died without heirs and was the last of the Il-Khanids.

The Mongol domination over Persia, which lasted one hundred and forty years, seventy-five of which were under pagan government, could not fail to leave a deep imprint on the Persian way of life. The Mongol administration gradually improved and the *pax Mongolica* proved beneficial to every class of society. Trading routes were opened to all parts of the Mongol empire and Persia's horizons widened as her knowledge was enriched by the arts and sciences of the Far East. Tabriz became one of the leading centres of the world and here all faiths were treated without prejudice. In due course, this state of affairs led to relations with Europe and the Popes exchanged ambassadors with the Il-Khanids in the hope of winning their support against the Moslem preponderance in the Near East. After Ghazan's conversion, the international situation changed in some degree, although his rule was one of the most beneficial for Persia. The death of Abu Sa'id ushered in a period of dismemberment and feudal strife.

Abu Sa'id was succeeded by distant relations of the Il-Khanids, who included women as well as various pretenders (1334–41), and gradually the state fell to pieces and passed into new hands. Two Mongol houses, now completely Iranicised, were competing for the succession to the Il-Khanids. At first, the Sulduz occupied the

throne; these were descendants of the great emir Choban. They were eliminated in 1335 by the Khan of the Golden Horde, to whom a *mulla* had carried the complaints of the population.

Next came the Jalayirids, a more important dynasty, who reigned over a curious combination of territories extending from Tabriz to Baghdad and including parts of Transcaucasia and Khuzistan. The Jalayirids (1340–1411) to some extent maintained the prestige of the Il-Khanids and were accepted by the population as their legitimate successors. Some of the Jalayirids were great patrons of Persian

poetry and they even composed many poems themselves.

In the south-east these immediate successors to the Mongols bordered on the lands of the Muzaffarids (1113–93), who had become governors of Fars under the last of the Mongols. The Muzaffarids expelled the ephemeral dynasty of the Inju'ids (so called because they had formerly served as keepers of the private property, or *inju*, of the Il-Khanids in Fars), and took possession of Yazd, Kerman and Isphahan. At times they even managed to occupy Tabriz and to push on into Kurdistan. It seems that the Muzaffarids were of pure Iranian origin.

They were split into many branches which were perpetually at odds with each other. This, however, did not prevent them from fostering architecture and other arts: Hafiz, Persia's great lyric poet, was their panegyrist. At first their relations with Timur were good, but later he replaced them by his own sons.

There is a well-known story that on the occasion of his first invasion of Fars Timur summoned Hafiz and reproached him for the famous lines in which he says: 'If that Shirazi Turk will take my heart in her hand, I will give Samarkand and Bokhara for the black mole on her cheek.'

'With the blows of my lustrous sword,' said Timur, 'I have subjugated most of the habitable globe and laid waste thousands of towns and countries to embellish Samarkand and Bokhara, my native towns and the seats of my government; and you, miserable wretch that you are, would sell them both for the black mole of a Turk of Shiraz!' 'Sire,' replied Hafiz, 'it is through such prodigality that I have fallen on such evil days'.

In Khorasan, the oppression of Mongol tax collectors had led to a revolt among the local population. From 1337 onwards the rebels were led by a former functionary of Persian origin, called 'Abd ar-Razzaq. This energetic man founded a strange popular republic governed by elected dictators, twelve of whose names, from the period 1337–1387, are known to us. As was usual in Persia, this democratic movement was associated with the 'Alid sect. Most of its leaders, who came to be known by the derisive nickname of Sar-ba-dari or 'gallows-birds', were able men who had risen from the people. From their centre at Sabzavar, in Khorasan, they spread out to Nishapur and Mazandaran.

To the east of the Sar-ba-dari in Herat, reigned the Karts (1245–1389), who were related to the earlier Ghurids (1148–1215), although their field of action was more circumscribed.

To the north of the Sar-ba-dari, in the Gurgan region, a distant branch of the house of Genghis Khan in the person of Togha-Temur, was proclaimed king in 1337 and took part, unsuccessfully, in the struggle for the Il-Khanid succession. In this he was supported by the descendants of Nauruz, whose feudal domain embraced Nishapur and Tus. Togha-Temur's successor was his son-in-law, Amir Vali, but his descendants are recorded only up to 1409.

The irresistible invasions of Timur swept away all these minor dynasties and resulted in a redistribution of the provinces among new rulers.

Below: The entrance to the caravanserai at Aminabad (c. 1500–36).

Below right: Aminabad, from a drawing in Flandin and Coste's Voyage en Perse pendant les années 1846 et 1842 (Paris, 1843–54).

It is not correct to think of Timur (1336–1405) as a Mongol, for he belonged to the Barlas tribe, which had become Turkish and had settled in Transoxiana, the western part of the *ulus* originally allocated to Chagatay, the third son of Genghis Khan. Timur never claimed to be a Khan, but merely a *gurkan*, that is the son-in-law of a nominal khan, who led a shadowy life in Timur's domains.

Timur's rise dated from about 1360, the year in which he was appointed emir of Qarshi (Shahr-i-Sabz, to the south-west of Bokhara). Ten years later he was master of Transoxiana. Not until 1381 did he lead his first expedition into Khorasan, and the following year he reached Shiraz. In 1384–5, he conquered northern Persia up to Sultaniya. His Luristan campaign dated from 1386, and he drove Sultan Ahmad Jalayir from Tabriz. In 1387 he occupied the country to the west of Lake Urmia. During the 'five-year campaign', particularly between 1392 and 1395, he made many incursions into various regions of Persia, annihilating the Muzaffarids of Fars and capturing Baghdad from Sultan Ahmad. After certain expeditions which had forced him to turn his attention to southern Russia and India, Timur returned to Persia in 1399. During the 'seven-year campaign' which was to take him to Syria and Smyrna, he defeated the Ottoman sultan, Bayezid at Ankara (1402), and was submitted to by the sultan of Egypt, Nasir Faraj (1403). Timur died in 1405 whilst marching against China.

His military genius was unquestionable, but there are no grounds for idealising his attempts to govern Persia. There he created nothing, but devastated the country by his continuous campaigns and punitive expeditions. In Isphahan alone seven thousand men were massacred by his troops (1387). He was not even able to ensure peace in the Middle and Near East; as soon as his back was turned rebellion broke out. His domination cannot be compared to that of the Mongols, whose viziers did at least attempt a permanent improvement of the conditions under which the population was living. Timur merely swept from one encampment to the next, halting his marches only to greet his women, who came to visit him in his winter quarters. He created a brilliant capital at Samarkand, but he did so at the expense of Persia, which he despoiled of its architects and artisans.

It is virtually impossible to discern any constructive plan in his conquests. Indeed, almost the only sign of consistency was the regularity with which he appointed his intimates as his lieutenants. Immediately after his death, they fell out with each other and eventually his fourth son, Shah-Rukh,

triumphed over his brothers to enjoy a long and fortunate reign (1405–47). In temperament he was the opposite of his father – calm and peaceful, although at times he could show the same strength. He was a good example of a pious Moslem sovereign. Under Timur the separate administrations of the 'Mongols' and the 'Tajiks' had been welded together on the basis of a theoretical recognition of the equality of all Moslems, but Shah-Rukh took upon himself the task of erasing the surviving traces of paganism from his father's court, (wine festivals, the existence of *bakhshi* or Turkish sages, and so on). In

place of remote Samarkand, Shah-Rukh chose to set up his residence at Herat. The city was transformed into a splendid capital with magnificent mosques, palaces and bazaars, filled with men of learning, poets, miniaturists and artisans. However, there was a danger to the Persian language in the establishment of a parallel literature in Chagatyi Turkish.

During Shah-Rukh's reign, ideas about the rights of the ruler had undergone a profound change. Under Timur, the idea that all power belonged to the descendants of Genghis Khan was deep rooted. Timur himself, as we have seen, never aspired to

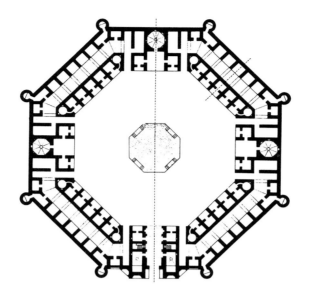

Right: Ground plan of the octagonal caravanserai, at Aminabad, between Shiraz and Isphahan. In times of prosperity such places were built all over Persia to provide shelter, food, and security for the caravans of merchants. Little was included in the way of furniture, travellers bringing with them most of the things they needed. The arcaded lodgings, which faced the courtyard, included separate apartments for women, and there were also stables for the animals, for which forage could be bought.

the rank of Khan. Under Shah-Rukh a new theory became current. To the concept of political power in the hands of the sovereign, therefore, was added the concept of divine investiture. According to the *khutba* drawn up by the court of Shah-Rukh for a sultan of India, he was to say, 'May God render eternal the reign and the sultanate [of Shah-Rukh] in the caliphate upon earth'.

Herat, being in a country that was still Iranian, was more suitable as a centre from which to exercise control over Persia, but the Timurids, who were established as governors of the various provinces, were involved in continuous disputes about the redistribution of their possessions. The most serious problems arose in Azerbaijan, from which Timur's eldest son, Miranshah, and his sons were expelled by the combined forces of Sultan Ahmad Jalayir and his supporters from the Qara-qoyunlu. Three times Shah-Rukh led his troops against these Turkmens, but finally he had to resign himself to their domination over Azerbaijan.

Little information has survived about the internal situation of Persia under the Timurids, except that the internecine wars bore heavily on the population. There were renewed disturbances during the time of

of Egypt. His faithful companion in exile had been Qara Yusuf, head of the federation of the Turkmen tribes of the Qara-qoyunlu. On the death of Timur they both fled from Damascus and with the help of Qara Yusuf and his Turkmens, Sultan Ahmad regained the throne. Sultan Ahmad allowed the Qara-qoyunlu to govern Tabriz, where in 1408 Qara Yusuf proclaimed his son, who had been adopted by Sultan Jalayir while he was in exile, as prince. To forestall imminent complications, Ahmad moved against his vassals at Tabriz, but was defeated and killed in 1410.

Thus we come to a fresh turning point in Persian history. The Turkmens extended their rule throughout almost the whole of the fifteenth century, at first only in the north-western part, Azerbaijan, and then

Turkoman tribes, giving them once again an organised form.

The Qara-qoyunlu had their centre on the Armenian plateau, close to the north-eastern curve of Lake Van. Their chiefs, who belonged to the Barani or Baharlu family, seem to have come originally from the vicinity of Hamadan, where there had once existed a strong Turkoman principality centred on the township of Bahar.

The Aq-qoyunlu occupied the territory to the south-west of the Qara-qoyunlu, in the region of Diyarbekir and Mardin. The two federations were rivals as well as being vassals of different kings. The Qara-qoyunlu were hostile to the Timurids and in general tended to establish good relations with the Ottomans and Egypt, while the Aq-qoyunlu looked to Timur for aid against both the Qara-qoyunlu and the Ottomans. Religion was also a decisive factor, for whereas the Aq-qoyunlu were orthodox Sunnites, the Qara-qoyunlu had been converted to the Shiah faith.

As successor to the Jalayir at Tabriz in 1410, Qara Yusuf took up a hostile attitude towards Shah-Rukh. He died in 1420 while on the march against Shah-Rukh's army. His son Eskandar (1420–37) was a man of unusual daring, but a brutal tyrant. Twice Shah-Rukh was compelled to punish him for

Timur, when the new Hurufi sect, afterwards to spread to Turkey and develop among the Bektashi dervishes, preached a fresh cabalistic interpretation of the Koran. The founder of this heresy, Fadl Allah of Astarabad, was brutally put to death by Miranshah. However, behind the mystical speculations on numbers there was very real discontent, as is shown by the fact that an attempt was made on Shah-Rukh's life in 1427 by a man of the Hurufi sect. Sultan Ahmad Jalayir had been expelled three times by Timur from his domains of Tabriz and Baghdad, and each time he had retreated into Asia Minor or the territories

throughout the country. Unlike the preceding invasions, which were mounted from the east, that of the Turkmens came from the west. Their clan must have come with the great migration of the Ghuzz under the Seljuks, but they penetrated further west than their colleagues from Persia, or may have been driven there by the Mongols. The designations of Qara-qoyunlu – 'those of the black sheep' – and Aq-qoyunlu – 'those of the white sheep', were unknown before the fourteenth century, and this shows that the two federations were of recent foundation. Some energetic chiefs had assumed the leadership of the scattered

his misdeeds and won the friendship of Eskandar's brother, Jahan-shah, whom he helped to place on the throne. Jahan-shah (1437–67) was shrewd in politics and fortunate in war. His troops occupied Persia right up to the Persian Gulf, and for a short time in 1458 he himself took Herat, the capital of the Timurids, though before long he had to return it to the Timurid Abu Sa'id and to agree to Simnan as a firm demarcation line between the domains of the Qara-qoyunlu and the Timurids. Charges of heresy and viciousness have been laid against Jahan-shah by Ottoman and Sunnite authorities. Certainly he had Shi'ite beliefs, and he was most probably an extremist, as his poetic compositions in Persian and Turkish bear witness; however this may be, contemporary writers had a high opinion of him as a ruler. The famous 'Blue Mosque' in Tabriz is proof of his artistic taste. Jahan-shah was killed in Armenia during an expedition against Uzun Hasan (1467) and his successor, a man of small ability and weak intellect, was robbed of the kingdom by the Aq-qoyunlu.

The new dynasty extended its hold gradually but steadily in the Armenian plateau, that is the territory lying between the Ottomans and the Qara-qoyunlu. By 1457 Uzun Hasan had occupied Erzinjan and the next year he married the niece of the Emperor of Trebizond. The defeat of Jahan-shah suddenly opened to him the way to the east. The ambitious Timurid Abu-Sa'id made an attempt to gain the succession of the Qara-qoyunlu and set out towards Azerbaijan with a powerful army. But the severe winter of 1468 caused grave hardship among his troops and he was compelled to withdraw to Mughan on the Araxes, which had a milder climate. There his camp was besieged by Uzun Hasan; men and horses died of hunger and in February 1469 Abu Sa'id was captured and executed. The whole of Persia was in the hands of Uzun Hasan, and in 1470 he sent troops to Herat to place his protégé, the Timurid pretender Yadigar Mirza, on the throne. This second victory made Uzun Hasan the most powerful king threatening the Ottoman rear. The republic of Venice dispatched several embassies to his court, including that of Zeno, who was a nephew of Uzun Hasan's Byzantine wife. The Republic tried to reinforce its Turkoman ally by sending a large number of bombards, culverins and matchlocks via Alexandretta.

In 1461 Uzun Hasan had already suffered the humiliation of seeing the dying empire of Trebizond, the defence of whose interests he had undertaken, occupied by Sultan Muhammad. When, emboldened by his victory over Abu-Sa'id, he ordered a raid to be made into Asia Minor, the Ottomans suddenly sent an army into Armenia and in 1475 Uzun Hasan was defeated at the battle of Terjan. Thus there vanished at a stroke the dream of conquering Constantinople which had been used by the Venetians as a trump card, and Uzun Hasan sought consolation in a fresh incursion into Christian Georgia. On returning from this enterprise he died. His successor, Ya'qub (1478–90), was a leading figure in the world of Islam. Like his father, he embellished the capital, Tabriz, and attracted writers and poets to his court.

Little information exists concerning life in Persia under the Qara-qoyunlu, but we know that under the Aq-qoyunlu there was still a dual administration. The Turks, whose numbers had been greatly swollen by the arrival of numerous tribes from the west, formed a military caste which was superimposed upon the agricultural populace, while civil administration remained entirely in the hands of Persian civil servants. On the orders of Uzun Hasan a new register of land was made, seemingly on equitable lines because subsequent references to this are found both in Turkey and in Persia. One of the biggest financial problems arose from the excessive allowances given to all pensioners and Moslem dignitaries. Under Ya'qub one vizier lost not only his position but also his life through an attempt to introduce reforms.

After Ya'qub's reign struggles began for the succession. Uzun Hasan's last descendants, ousted by Shah Isma'il, ended their days in the region of Diyarbekir (Alvand in 1504 and Murad in 1514).

The rise of the dynasty to which the origins of present-day Persia as an organised nation can be traced is a unique story. It has been said that by making Shi'ism their state religion, the Safavids isolated themselves from the body of Islam; but it might also be argued that thanks to this Persia was able to retain and renew its national characteristics instead of being absorbed by its neighbours.

The ancestors of the Safavids, descended from the prophet, are said to have come originally from Fars. The family had been settled for a long time in Ardabil; the eponym of the dynasty, Safi ad-Din (1252–1334), was a highly-esteemed orthodox Shaikh, to whom the famous vizier Rashid ad-Din was in the habit of sending gifts. From references in poems of the first Safavids it appears that they were fond of using the local Iranian dialect spoken around Ardabil, and that they also knew Turkish. They had many supporters among the Turkish tribes of Asia Minor and Syria. The attitude of the shaikhs of Ardabil underwent a far-reaching change

under Junaid (1447–60), the paternal grandfather of Shah Isma'il; Shi'ite extremism, probably resulting from contacts with the Qara-qoyunlu dynasty, had found its way into the family, bringing with it a desire for power and a hankering after adventure. This militant spirit gave a completely new political character to the organisation of the Safavids. At the request of Jahan-shah, who probably did not wish to see himself surrounded by rivals, Junaid was constrained to leave Ardabil and he passed several years wandering about Anatolia and Syria among his Turkmen adherents. After an unsuccessful attempt to capture Trebizond, he made common cause with Uzun Hasan in Diyarbekir, where he spent three years and eventually married the sister of the Aq-qoyunlu. At the head of his dervish (Sufi) followers, Junaid tried to force his way back to Ardabil; finding this impossible, he turned northwards and organised a Muslim raid into Daghestan against the infidels of the Caucasus. There followed an encounter with the prince of the

Left: At Sultaniyeh is the shell of the enormous mausoleum of the Mongol ruler, Oljeitu Khodabandeh (14th century). Of the eight minarets that encircled the huge dome, 80 feet in diameter and 117 feet high, and of the turquoise blue tiles that covered it, only fragments remain.

Shirvan and in 1460 Junaid was killed. His son Haidar was consumed with a desire to avenge his father. Haidar's uncle, Uzun Hasan, who meanwhile had overcome his enemies, gave him in marriage his own daughter Maria, otherwise known as Halima, brought to him by the princess of Trebizond. Returning in his father's footsteps, Haidar marched against the Caucasian infidels in 1483, and returned loaded with booty; but when he attempted to repeat this undertaking, the prince of the Shirvan, fearing Haidar's growing power, persuaded the Aq-qoyunlu King Ya'qub to send troops against the young Shaikh. Haidar fell in battle in 1488 and his sons were imprisoned. The eldest son took part in the battles of the Aq-qoyunlu adherents and himself died in combat in 1494, while Isma'il sought refuge in Gilan. Little by little Haidar's Sufis regrouped themselves around Isma'il and in 1499 he went to war, although being then only fifteen years old, to avenge his ancestors and to found a new kingdom. He occupied Shirvan in 1502 and met and defeated the Aq-qoyunlu at Sharur to the south of Erivan on the Araxes.

Isma'il was placed on the throne by the enthusiasm of his faithful Turkmen dervishes and the tribes which they represented. The new Safavid doctrine was based on a belief in the continuous reincarnation of deified 'Alid Imams – so much so that according to many sources Isma'il's followers looked on him as a living god. He himself, in the hymns which he composed for the edification of his followers, clearly shows that he aspired to divine rights. The faithful were known as Shahi-seven (lovers of the Shah): in this instance 'Shah' has a double meaning, that by adoring their king, his subjects were worshipping in him an incarnation of 'Ali deified, the acknowledged 'king of holiness' (*Shah-i vilayat*). It is generally assumed that the Shahi-seven tribes numbered seven; in fact, the Safavids had followers in several Turkmen tribes, but they were all rigidly organised as though within a single 'party'. Many of the Shahi-seven came from the old Qara-qoyunlu federation and to a certain extent the Aq-qoyunlu as well; it is interesting to find among them the groups called Rumlu and Shamlu, which indicate origins in Asia Minor and Syria respectively.

In 1500 Iran was still a Sunnite country, with the exception of some Shi'ite enclaves as at Qum, Rayy, and the provinces of the Caspian Sea, so that Ismail, at the head of his Turkmen followers, had to undertake the reconversion of the country by terror and the sword, according to Italian

observers of the time. A large number of learned Sunnites consequently emigrated to Turkey or Central Asia and as a result of this purge the number of Sunnites in Iran today is very small.

Azerbaijan and Central Iran were incorporated into the new kingdom in 1504, but its frontiers still remained undefined. Bold with success, Isma'il wanted to reap the twin inheritance of the Aq-qoyunlu to the west and the Timurids to the east. His emirs waged war in the region of Diyarbekir and Mardin and in 1507 they conquered the Prince of Dhu'l-Qadar, 'Ala ad-Daula, lord of Malatya and Elbistan. In 1508 Isma'il entered Baghdad in person. In the east he defeated the Uzbeks (who had meanwhile succeeded the Timurids), whose leader, Sheibani Khan, fell at the battle of Merv. However, the situation remained fluid and in 1512 Isma'il's general suffered the same fate at Bokhara. Isma'il's activities to the west, and above all the widespread relations which the Safavids enjoyed with the tribes of Asia Minor, alarmed the Ottoman Sultan Selim. At Chaldiran to the west of Khoi on August 22, 1514, the Sultan's army gained a great victory over the Shah's troops, whose valour and devotion could not prevail over the enemy's artillery and hand-guns, weapons with which they themselves were not equipped and which, indeed, they regarded as unmanly and cowardly. As a result of this victory Selim was for a time in occupation of Isma'il's capital at Tabriz. The Turks also took away the territories he had won in Mesopotamia. These disasters so affected Isma'il that for the last ten years of his reign (1514–24) he remained inactive.

Isma'il's son and successor, Tahmasp (1524–76), was not only a bigot, but was avaricious and lacking in initiative. The Pretorian Shahi-seven whom Isma'il had known how to curb, started to quarrel among themselves and eventually rebelled against the Shah, so that Tahmasp was forced to disperse some of the tribes, among them the Afshar and the Tekke. Meanwhile war continued on both fronts, against the Ottomans and the Uzbek. In 1534 and 1543 the Turks reoccupied Tabriz, forcing Tahmasp to move his capital further eastward to Qazvin. However, the Shah succeeded in strengthening his own power in the main provinces of Iran, even annexing Qandahar, in exchange for assistance rendered to the Moghul Emperor Humayun, who had sought refuge with him.

Under his immediate successors the situation worsened considerably. The attempt by Isma'il II, who was weakminded, to return to the *sunna* failed, and the Shahi-sevens'

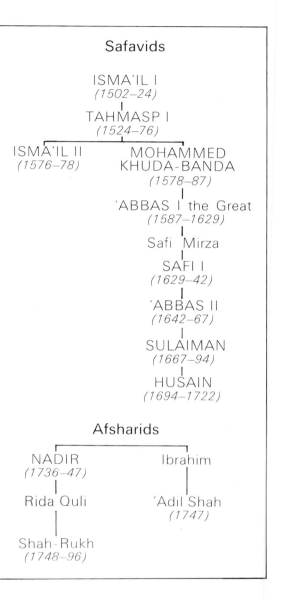

Safavids

ISMA'IL I
(1502–24)

TAHMASP I
(1524–76)

ISMA'IL II
(1576–78)

MOHAMMED KHUDA-BANDA
(1578–87)

'ABBAS I the Great
(1587–1629)

Safi Mirza

SAFI I
(1629–42)

'ABBAS II
(1642–67)

SULAIMAN
(1667–94)

HUSAIN
(1694–1722)

Afsharids

NADIR
(1736–47)

Ibrahim

Rida Quli

'Adil Shah
(1747)

Shah-Rukh
(1748–96)

turbulence and rivalries became intolerable.

The kingdom was saved by Shah 'Abbas, the greatest sovereign of the Safavid dynasty. He was born in 1571, but had already been proclaimed king by certain leading tribes in 1581, though it was not until 1587 that he actually mounted the throne. His reign lasted until his death in 1629. He found the country torn asunder by struggles and revolts and had to reconquer it. In 1596 he incorporated Mazandaran into the central administration and in the following year he annihilated the Lesser Lur dynasty. However, the struggle against foreign enemies was to continue for some time to come.

At the end of a war that lasted for thirteen years the Turks found themselves in possession of north-west Iran and Transcaucasia and in 1590 'Abbas had to sign a treaty by which these territories were handed over to the enemy. Meanwhile, the Uzbek penetration of Iran was proving so successful that the capital was constantly being moved further south, until in 1597 it became Isphahan. It was 1593 before

Below: The tomb of Imam Reza at Meshed, one of the most celebrated shrines in Persia. Three doors lead into the tomb chamber, one is of silver and two are of gold, one being studded with precious stones.

Right: It is estimated that more than a million Islamic pilgrims come each year to the Gawhar Shad Mosque at Meshed, of which the Imam's tomb forms a part. Since the 9th century this edifice, one of the most imposing and ornate in Persia, has been restored many times, notably by Shah-Rukh, the son of Tamerlaine (Timur), in the 15th century and by Shah 'Abbas I in the 16th century.

'Abbas succeeded in chasing the Uzbeks out of Khorasan. In 1601 he resumed hostilities against the Ottomans and in 1603 succeeded in expelling them from Iran and Transcaucasia and even managed temporarily to reoccupy Baghdad. Under the treaties of 1612 and 1618 the Turks renounced their conquests.

According to Pietro della Valle, military reforms were carried out in 1617, but this date only indicates the completion of a radical reorganisation which was a gradual process. It was a question of reducing the influence of the turbulent Turkmen, who, having been paid with concessions of land, were turning their possessions into self-governing territories. The number of *qizil-bash* or 'red heads', thus named from the colour of their turbans, which originally signified that they belonged to the Shahi-seven, was reduced from 70,000 to 30,000. Their place was taken by a cavalry corps of 'slaves' (*qul, ghulam*), armed with muskets instead of lances, a new corps of musketeers

on foot, and a corps of artillery. It is interesting to note that the infantry was recruited from the sturdy Persian peasants, while the 'slaves' were young converts, mostly Caucasians from Georgia and Armenia, who were similar to the Ottoman janissaries. These new troops received their pay direct from the Shah's treasury and had no tribal bonds of allegiance. They were also admitted to the higher levels of administrations, managing in time to counterbalance and finally to eliminate the old Pretorians. According to Turkish sources, those partisans of Shah 'Abbas who were resident in Turkey continued to look on him as an incarnation of divinity, but the new reforms were radically changing the character of theocracy as conceived by Shah Isma'il.

Following the discovery of the sea route round Africa, Iran became accessible to trade with Europe which did not require to go through Ottoman territory. On the other hand, the Moscow Company had been

founded (1555) in England, and the English were endeavouring to divert the silk trade – silk being Persia's main export – towards the Caspian Sea and the Volga. The Shah himself was by no means averse to trade being carried on on his behalf by his Armenian subjects. The news of the foundation of a strong Persian kingdom on Turkey's doorstep was welcomed by the courts of Europe, who lived under the Ottoman threat. And so Isphahan became flooded with diplomats, merchants, and even missionaries, while Iran welcomed the appearance of European arts. Shah 'Abbas maintained a friendly attitude towards the countries of the West, with the exception of Portugal, which had set up a kind of cordon across the maritime routes with Iran and monopolised trade from their colony on the island of Hormuz. In 1622, after enlisting the help of English ships in the Persian Gulf, the Shah occupied the island and transferred its trade to Persian ports situated on that stretch of the coast directly adjoining Isphahan.

The Qajar dynasty...witnessed the emergence of Persia as a modern state

Shah 'Abbas and his successors were great builders. Isphahan was the first eastern capital to benefit from town-planning. The other Safavid centres – the shrine of Ardebil, and the Safavids' first capital, Tabriz – benefited from their passion for building, but it was here at Isphahan that Safavid architecture reached its peak. It was characterised not by structural innovations, but by rich, magnificently coloured and imaginative details developed in previous eras which were now unified into serene ensembles of immense scale and grandeur. Isphahan was then much larger than it is today – its population was estimated at some 650,000 people – and with its new mosques, palaces, bridges, avenues and parks, it deeply impressed numerous European travellers, as it still does. The Pol-i Khwaju, the bridge linking the capital with Julfa across the river, is in the Sassanian tradition, being a weir as well as a bridge. The centrepiece of the city is the Maidan-i Shah, the Royal Square. This rectangular open space, a centre for manoeuvres, parades and games – especially polo – is flanked by two-storeyed arcades broken by the entrances, one on each side, to the royal caravanserai and bazaar, the mosque of Shaikh Lutfullah, the 'Ali Qapu (the main portal of the palace, serving as a grandstand for the Shah and his entourage), and the superb Masjid-i Shah, the focus of the whole complex.

Under Shah 'Abbas the roads between the various cities were improved, even in the wooded provinces of the Caspian Sea, which his famous causeway, known as Sang-Farsh or the 'Stone Carpet', traverses from end to end, a distance of 300 miles.

There is hardly a single difficult mountain pass in Iran which does not boast a caravanserai built in the reign of Shah 'Abbas, where the traveller can shelter from the snow and rain. E. G. Browne speaks of them as 'fine, spacious, solidly constructed buildings which can be referred, almost at a glance, to the time of the Safavid kings, and which the tradition of muleteers, recognising as a rule, only two great periods in history – that of Feridun, and that of Shah 'Abbas the Great – unhesitatingly attributes to the latter'.

The arts, notably ceramics, carpet-weaving, painting and metal-work, were also strongly encouraged. It has been said that the literature of the Safavid period did not reach the heights of that which preceded it, but this was probably due to the fact that the Persians' energy found a new outlet in practical and productive activities, which explains a lesser interest in mysticism and doctrines enjoining the renunciation of the world.

Shah 'Abbas was given to sudden fits of rage, which often horrified Europeans, his wrath being directed above all towards foreign enemies and the aristocracy. Consequently his people favoured this energetic sovereign, who had obtained peace for their country. It is not for nothing that he is associated in folk memory with the mythical Feridun, who is said to have slain the tyrant Zahhak and to have ruled Iran with justice and splendour for a period of five hundred years.

Although his successors failed to match his achievements, they continued Shah 'Abbas's traditions. A new treaty was signed with Turkey in 1639, which was until recently the basic document for fixing the boundaries between the two states: thus a kind of truce was secured on the main front. On the Central Asian frontier a new migration of Western Mongolian tribes (the Kalmucks), from near the Volga, came to threaten Iran's neighbours, thus easing their pressure on her. However, the movements of Afghan tribes constituted a new and serious threat.

Internally the process of splitting up the Turkmen tribes continued, while the unity of the state was gradually established. Religion was losing its ecstatic extremism, and Syrian and Mesopotamian scholars from Mount 'Amil were endeavouring to give it a moderated character of theological Shi'ism. The old supporters of the throne, the Turkmen dervishes with their red turbans and long moustaches, were relegated to their chapels (*tauhidkhaneh*) or to the decorative office of Royal Guards.

These gradual changes took place amid certain limitations, tempering the harsh

energy of the days of war. By his outrageous acts to the detriment of the provinces (*mamalik*) the Shah's personal treasury, by confiscating the wealth and resources of many great land-owning families, was weakening their loyalty. 'Abbas II (1642–67) was given to excesses which undoubtedly hastened his end. Yet he still retained some of the qualities of his ancestor and namesake. At the age of sixteen he led the army in person against the Moghuls, from whom he recovered Qandahar, and he was, like all the Safavids, a great patron of the arts. His reign was distinguished by the large number of diplomatic missions dispatched from Europe, including the first Russian embassy to Persia.

The symptoms of decadence already distinguishable in this prince showed themselves above all in Sultan Husain (1694–1722). The young Shah, who had been brought up in a harem, was in the hands of courtiers, theologians and astrologers, in whose company he spent his days. By that time the *mulla* had completely curbed the movement of the dervishes, the old supporters of the throne, against whom the omnipotent *mulla-bashi*, Muhammad Baqir Majlisi (d. 1699), had instigated a severe persecution. The knowledge of these court intrigues discouraged the generals and the more able administrators.

In 1706 and 1711 the Ghilzai Afghans of Qandahar assassinated the Georgian princes who were acting as Persian governors. Even the Abdali Afghans of Herat defeated several generals who had been sent against them by the Shah.

The Afghan domination lasted seven years. The cruel Mahmud massacred the Safavid princes, but finally went mad and was replaced by his cousin Ashraf (1725). The Ghilza'i seized the central plateau, but were not strong enough to cope with the situation precipitated by the Afghans' presence. The Ottomans at once hurled themselves into the north-western Persian territories. To ward off the threat to the Caspian Sea, Peter the Great quickly occupied Derbend (1722). The following year he concluded with Tahmasp II, the son of Sultan Husain, a treaty under which he was granted Gilan, Mazandaran and Astarabad in exchange for a promise of help against the Afghan rebels. With France acting as mediator, a treaty was signed between Turkey and Russia in 1724, and the Turks occupied Tabriz (1725) and other areas of western Persia. After a skirmish with the Ottomans, Ashraf surrendered all the territories that had been taken and in 1729 it was confirmed that Gilan would be granted to the Russians.

Tahmasp, who had proclaimed himself king after his flight from Isphahan, was

In Samarkand are the remains of three great mosques. *Above left:* a minaret and (*right*) the dome of Shir-Dar, *c.* 1648; (*above*) a lattice framed with decorative tiles, from Gur-Amir, the tomb of Tamerlaine (Timur), *c.* 1404; and (*left*) the shattered walls of Bibi Khanum.

gradually withdrawing before the Afghans. He was to find in Khorasan a powerful champion, the celebrated Nader Shah. At the age of fifteen Nader had left his parents' humble home to enter the service of the governor of Abivard. From this position he rose rapidly and in course of time achieved the post of Tahmasp's commander-in-chief. Later his relations with Tahmasp became strained, partly owing to the intrigues of the latter's ministers; but in 1729 Nader persuaded his master to accompany him on

an expedition against the Abdalis of Herat. The success of this campaign enabled Nader to turn his attention to the task of expelling the Ghilza'i from Persia and setting Tahmasp upon the throne. Victory over the invaders provided one of the first indications of Nader's military talents, and within a few weeks he made a triumphal entry into Isphahan, where shortly afterwards Tahmasp, summoned from Tehran, ascended the throne of his fathers. Pursuing the fleeing Ashraf, leader of the Ghilza'i and the last Afghan ruler of Persia, Nader inflicted a final defeat on him near Pasargadae, and at length, deserted by his followers, Ashraf met a violent death somewhere to the west of Qandahar.

The expulsion of the Ghilza'i having been accomplished, Nader applied himself to the more formidable problem of the Ottomans, who as a result of the Turco-Afghan war were in possession not only of the Caucasus, but also of Azerbaijan and much of central and western Persia. Setting out from Shiraz early in 1730, Nader freed the whole of Kurdistan and occupied Hamadan, and then embarked on a campaign to liberate Azerbaijan. After a series of spectacular victories, news of a revolt of the Abdalis forced Nader to quit Tabriz and go to eastern Iran, where in 1732, after a ten-months' siege of Herat, the Afghans surrendered.

Left: Helmet of Shah 'Abbas I, dated 1625–6, made of chased steel inlaid with gold.

Far left: Shield, of steel inlaid with gold.

Below: Pen box (early 19th century) of painted and lacquered papier-maché, depicting the Battle of Chaldiran (1514) between the Persians and the Turks. Beneath the box is a detail from the scene, showing Shah Isma'il about to kill the chief of the janissaries.

Right: Dagger with a carved jade hilt (17th century).

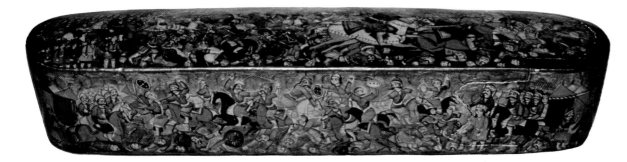

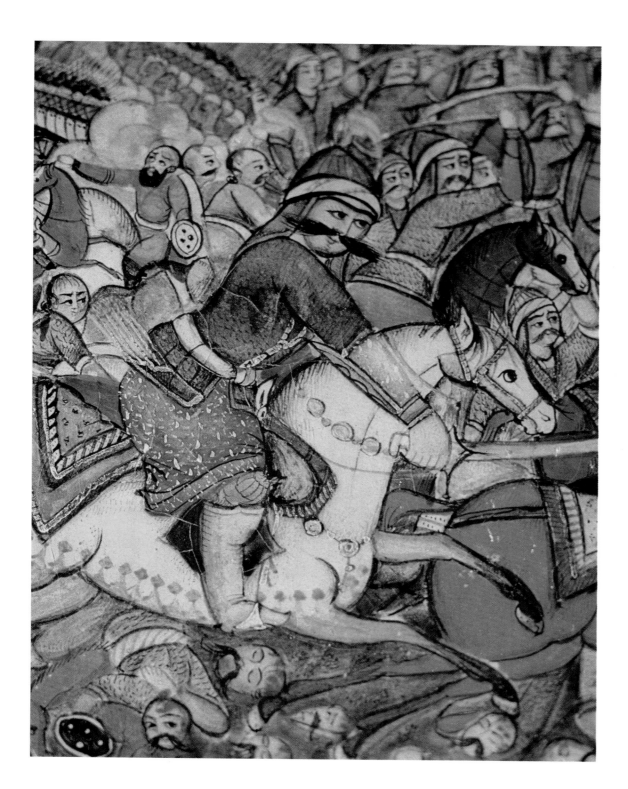

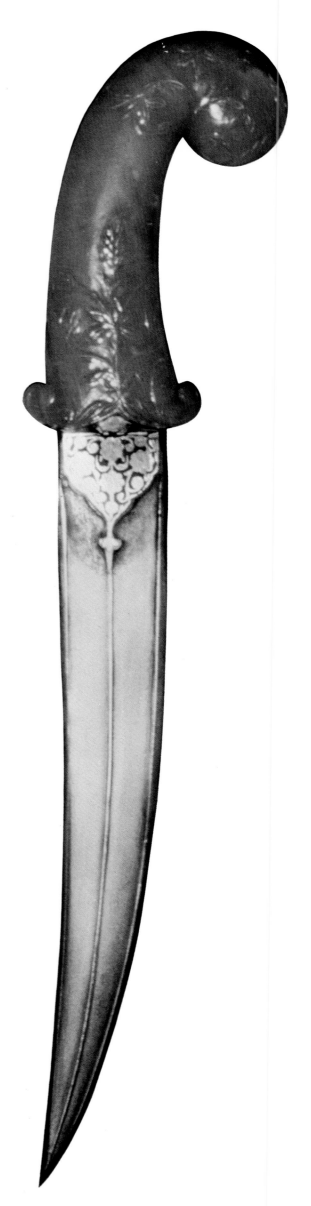

Below: The Khwaju Bridge at Isphahan, 429 feet long and 39 feet wide, was built during the reign of Shah 'Abbas II (1642–47). It served not only for irrigation, but also to create an artificial lake in front of the mansions which, in Safavid days, stood along the riverbank.

Below centre: Although dating from the 18th century, this ewer of inlaid silver with a body of blue and gold enamel retains almost unaltered the traditional shape common to such vessels for centuries.

Right: The main court of the Madrasseh Madar-i-Shah at Isphahan. This peaceful sanctuary in the centre of the city was built (1706–14) as a theological seminary by the mother of Shah Sultan Husain.

Meanwhile, in Nader's absence Tahmasp had re-opened hostilities with the Turks, a disastrous campaign which resulted in their re-occupying most of the territories which Nader had liberated. Returning to Isphahan, Nader seized and imprisoned Tahmasp and proclaimed his infant son, 'Abbas, as Shah. He now adopted the title of Vakil ad-Daula, or Regent, and resumed the war with Turkey. After freeing Kermanshah, he set out for the Turkish frontier. The Taq-i Girra pass being strongly guarded, he crossed the mountains by devious tracks and took the defenders by surprise. He then led his forces southwards against Baghdad, which by February 1733, was blockaded from every side; the siege continued till July, when the garrison was on the verge of surrender. However, a large army was approaching under the famous general and ex-Grand Vizier, Topal Osman Pasha. Nader, leaving only a token force behind, advanced at the head of his whole army to meet the attack and in the battle which followed the Persians were defeated and the Turks then raised the siege of Baghdad.

Nader's resilience after this battle is further proof of his military genius. Rallying the remnants of his forces, he re-organised his army, and two months later invaded Iraq for

the second time. Another battle was fought with Topal Osman Pasha at Leilan near Kirkuk in November, and this time the tables were turned: the Turks were defeated with great losses and Topal Osman himself was among the slain.

After negotiating peace terms with the Ottoman government of Baghdad, Nader made his way to Fars to quell a rising in that province. But the Sultan refused to ratify the treaty and hostilities broke out again in the Caucasus, where Nader laid siege to Tiflis, Ganja, and Erivan. In June 1735, a great victory was won over a Turkish army at Baghavand, news of which prompted the surrender of Tiflis and Ganja; Erivan capitulated soon afterwards. In the meantime Nader had reached an agreement with Russia regarding the evacuation of Baku and Darband, thus bringing to an end the Russian occupation of northern Persia which had begun under Peter the Great. At the beginning of 1736, Nader summoned all the notables of his kingdom to a special assembly on the Moghan Steppe to confer 'the crown of Persia upon the person whom they considered most worthy to receive it'. He declared that he himself was old and worn out and wished to retire. In his place he proposed that they should choose Tahmasp or another Safavid as their Shah. This

Sistan-Qandahar border in February 1737. By the beginning of 1738 the greater part of Mahmud's territory was subdued, and by March Qandahar itself was taken.

Having thus restored the boundaries of the Safavid Empire, Nader determined to extend them by foreign conquest. He crossed the frontier of the Moghul Empire and advanced on Ghazna and Kabul, the pretext for the invasion being the Moghuls' failure to close their borders to Afghan fugitives. Learning that an army had been gathered together to oppose him at the foot of the Khyber Pass, he adopted the same tactics that he had used at the beginning of his second Turkish campaign and turned the enemy's position by making a detour and attacking him from the rear. In a great battle at Karnal the Moghuls were defeated, and on March 20 Nader entered Delhi in triumph. The next day rioting led to the death of some 3,000 Persian soldiers, and Nader ordered reprisals. But when, on the Moghul Emperor's plea for mercy, Nader called a halt to the killing and looting, his command was instantly obeyed: his control over his troops in such conditions was described by a contemporary historian as 'one of the most wonderful things in the world'.

While at Delhi Nader asked for the hand of a Moghul princess for one of his sons. It was Moghul etiquette on such occasions to demand an account of the bridegroom's male ancestors for seven generations, and Nader is said to have exclaimed: 'Tell them he is the son of Nader Shah, the son of the sword, the grandson of the sword; and so on till they have a descent of seventy instead of seven generations.' On May 12 Nader held a durbar, at which he reinstated Muhammad Shah as Emperor, crowning him in person with the crown of Hindustan, and the Emperor in gratitude ceded to him all the territories of the Empire lying to the west of the Indus, 'from the frontier of Tibet and Kashmir to the place where that river flows into the ocean', in other words, the greater part of what is now West Pakistan. Four days later Nader left Delhi on the long trek northwards, accompanied by an immense baggage train of treasure, the spoils of his victory, including the famous Peacock Throne and the Koh-i-Noor diamond. At Kabul which he reached on December 2, Nader received news that the governor of the now Persian province of Sind had risen in revolt, thinking himself safe at so great a distance. Nader's march across the mountains and rivers of Afghanistan and through the deserts of the Indus Valley was one of his greatest military feats: at the end of February 1740, he accepted the rebels' surrender and

proposal was not meant to be taken seriously, and it was made plain by acclamation that Nader himself was the only possible candidate. He accepted the crown offered to him on condition that the Persians gave up the Shi'ite practices introduced by Shah Isma'il and formed a new 'column' of orthodoxy, that of the Imam Ja'far Sadiq. This condition being accepted, it serve as a basis for further proposals that the new Shah was to make to the Sultan, including the Ottomans' recognition of the Ja'farite creed as the fifth orthodox sect (*madhhab*) and the granting of a fifth column in the Ka'ba, like those assigned to the four existing

sects. Nader was crowned on March 8, and changed his name, Nadr, and assumed that of Nader ('Rare', 'Uncommon').

Shortly afterwards he received news of rebellion among the Bakhtiyaris, the suppression of which he directed in person. Impressed by the fighting qualities of the Bakhtiyaris, he enrolled a large number of these tribesmen in the army, which he was about to lead against the only territory lost to the Safavids which was still unrecovered: the town and province of Qandahar, held by Husain Sultan, brother of Mahmud. In November 1736, Nader left Isphahan at the head of an army of 80,000 men, reaching the

Right centre: Shah 'Abbas I, detail of a painting from the saloon at the Chihil Sutun in Isphahan.

Below: The ceiling of Hasht Behesht palace in Isphahan (17th century).

Right: Blue glass ewer decorated with a gilt pattern (17th century).

then returned to the Qandahar region.

Nader now gave his attention to the securing of Persia's north-eastern frontiers. Already in 1737 his son, Reza Quli, acting as viceroy during his father's absence, had recovered the amirate of Balkh and had crossed the Oxus to clash with the Uzbeks. In 1740 Nader, after constructing a flotilla of boats, moved large forces along the river, defeated the Uzbeks, and occupied their capital at Bokhara, whence he proceeded against Khiva, whose Khan was drawn out of his fortress to meet defeat in the open field. The Khan was executed for his treachery towards ambassadors and replaced by a rival. By these operations Nader re-established the Oxus as the Persian frontier and arrested Uzbek encroachments.

In 1741–42 he was involved in a protracted campaign against the mountain tribes of Daghestan, whom even the Mongols had been unable to subdue. During this campaign Reza Quli, who had incurred his father's displeasure by the murder of all the surviving members of the Safavid dynasty during Nader's absence in India, was accused of complicity in an attempt on his life. Wrongly believing his son to be guilty, Nader condemned him to be blinded and so debarred him from succeeding to the throne. This dreadful decision was to cast a shadow over the remaining years of his life.

Since 1736 there had been an uneasy truce with Turkey. Hostilities were resumed in 1743, when Nader invaded Iraq, captured Kirkuk, and laid siege to Mosul, while in the

extreme south another force invested Basra. However, news of risings in the Caucasus and elsewhere induced him to offer peace to the Ottomans, and in January 1744 he withdrew to Persia. But his offer proving fruitless, war broke out again in the southern Caucasus area. It lasted until September 1746 when, by the Treaty of Kurdan, the 1639 frontiers with the Ottoman Empire were restored. These frontiers were destined to remain unaltered until the nineteenth century. Nader had long been a sick man, and there can be little doubt that there were physical reasons for the melancholia and outbursts of rage to which he was subject in his last years. These frailties, combined with remorse for his treatment of his son, seem in the end to have unhinged his mind. His last stay in Isphahan in the winter of 1746–47 was characterised by terrible acts of cruelty. Proceeding eastwards to put down a revolt in Sistan and Baluchistan, he behaved with barbarity in the towns along the route. In the evening of June 19, 1747 he pitched his camp near Quchan, and here two conspirators from his own household, impelled by fears of their own imminent execution, broke into his tent and made an end of him. He was in his fifty-ninth year.

As a military genius Nader Shah was on a par with Timur, on whom he seems consciously to have modelled his career, and with Napoleon, with both of whom he has been aptly compared. He was the only Persian ruler since the Achaemenids to grasp the importance of naval power, and he endeavoured to build up a fleet both in the Persian Gulf and in the Caspian Sea. War has been said to have been Nader's hobby. A story is told of his conversing with a holy man about the pleasures of Paradise. Would there be such things, he asked, as war and the overcoming of one's enemies in the Hereafter? The holy man replied that there would not, to which Nader retorted 'How then can there be any delights there?' In fact, it was Nader's love of war that saved his country. His conquests restored Persia's prestige after the humiliation of the Safavid collapse and, by weakening her enemies, allowed her to survive the long years of internecine strife that preceded the establishment of the Qajars.

Nader's nephew, 'Ali, was proud to claim responsibility for having hatched the plot against his uncle. He restored to the Shi'ite clergy their confiscated property and thus won the title of 'Adil (the Just). Soon, however, he and his successor were murdered. The child of his son and of a Safavid princess, Shah-Rukh, was acknowledged prince of Khorasan and ruled for many years (1748–96). His reign was

twice interrupted and he himself was blinded by a pretender of the Safavid line on his mother's side; finally, he found a protector in the person of Ahmad Khan 'Abdali, who had been one of his grandfather's generals and who had founded the Durrani dynasty in Afghanistan.

With the exception of Khorasan, the rest of Persia now became a battleground for minor chieftains. Isphahan was occupied by 'Ali Mardan, the leader of the neighbouring Bakhtiyari tribes, who had allied himself with Karim Khan Zand. In the meantime, in the south-eastern Caspian area, the Qajars, an ancient Shahi-seven tribe, predominated, while Azerbaijan was in the hands of Azad Khan, a survivor of the Afghan invaders.

After 'Ali Mardan's assassination in 1751, the leadership passed into the hands of Karim Khan. This prince of a minor Kurdish tribe of Zand gave the country a long period of much-needed peace (1751–79). He was a courageous but modest man, and was content to hold the title of Vakil (delegate, lieutenant). By his clemency he subdued Azad Khan, the Afghan, who became one of his faithful supporters. In 1759 he ended the struggle with the Qajars. Only in 1776 did Karim Khan's troops pass to the offensive, when they attacked the Turks and gained possession of Basra. Karim Khan's government was paternalistic: he encouraged trade and contributed considerably to the beautifying of Shiraz, the capital.

His death was followed by family disputes. Five of his family occupied the throne one after another until the advent of the youthful and magnanimous Lutf 'Ali (1789), whose reign seemed to presage better times, but ended tragically in 1794. Betrayed by his vizier, the 'King-Maker' Hajji Ibrahim, he lost both his throne and his life in a struggle with Aga Muhammad, the founder of the Qajar dynasty, which ruled from the end of the eighteenth to the third decade of the twentieth century and witnessed the emergence of Persia as a modern state.

'...the recent dramatic changes in my country
testify that we welcome constructive change,
but at the same time we stand fast
in support of certain superior values
that I believe to be classically ours...
We acclaim this land of deserts and snow-capped mountains,
of cedars and plane trees, of rivers and fountains...
and we are proud of our political and social institutions.'

Ramesh Sanghvi

IRAN TODAY AND TOMORROW

Power and authority were centralised in the hands of the monarch, who encouraged not only agriculture, but also industry and trade, keeping these under strict imperial supervision.

Iran faced a severe internal crisis during most of the eighteenth century, once the centralised authority of the Safavi Shahs began to wither. It was a traditional test of the vitality of her civilisation not uncommon in her cyclical history. The monarch, his subordinate feudal underlings, including the tribal chiefs, and the peasantry, had formed the basic elements of the Iranian social fabric ever since the first state of the Persian nation was founded by the Achaemenians. The patrimonial role of the monarch was the key to the country's stability and prosperity. His special position kept under control the feudal elements who, as his agents, preserved administrative and political contacts with numerous village communities. However, it was to the monarch and not to their immediate feudal superiors that the peasants looked for protection, justice and guidance. Because of their paternal relationship with the king the feudal elements were the latter's *benefice* and not the *fief*, as in the European feudal pattern, and this was the reason that they were unable to constitute themselves as a class through the long centuries of Iranian civilisation. Power and authority were thus centralised in the hands of the monarch, who encouraged not only agriculture, but also industry and trade, keeping these under strict imperial supervision.

This inherent equilibrium between the three major divisions of Iranian society gave it the essential strength and momentum to survive and progress. This was witnessed during the two prosperous centuries of the Safavi dynasty and especially during the four decades between 1587 and 1629, when Shah Abbas the Great ruled Iran from his magnificent Court at Isphahan. Whenever the country was ruled by a weak king or during the periods between dynasties, Iranian society lost this basic equilibrium and administrative chaos, territorial disintegration, and oppression of the peasantry ensued. Normally, the emergence of the new monarch and the founding of a new dynasty ended this interregnum once the new monarch and the new dynasty had re-established the original equation between the three major constituents of society.

Though weaknesses had set in during the rule of Shah Sultan Hussain and Shah Tahmasp II and their immediate predecessor of the Safavi dynasty, the vitality of the social structure of this period had not been entirely exhausted. Within eight years of the Afghan onslaught, Nader Quli, a general of the regime, had risen like a meteor, consolidated the power of the monarchy, and expelled the Afghans. Later, after the death of Abbas, this legendary hero, as Nader Shah, reunited Iran, and carried the arms of the nation to Delhi in the east, Bokhara and Khiva in the north, Georgia in the north-west, and across the Persian Gulf in the south. He also began to convert Iran into a maritime power. Nader, however, ruled only for eleven years and his aim of establishing the traditional political and social equilibrium failed to materialise. After his assassination in 1747, Karim Khan Zand strove bravely between 1750 and 1779 to continue Nader's work. At the end of the Zand regime, which was based in Shiraz, Iran was plunged into a deeper crisis. It must be said to the credit of the new contender for power, Agha Mohammed Khan Qajar, that he was fully aware of the gravity of the situation and took upon himself the task of saving the country.

He was the leader of the Qajars, who fought for fifteen years to gain the upper hand. He captured Kerman and later Bam, and there Lutf Ali Khan, the young Zand chief was blinded and killed, leaving the Qajars in undisputed possession of the throne in 1794. In 1795 Agha Mohammed Khan marched to restore Persian power over Georgia, which after Nader Shah's death had renounced all connection with Persia and signed a treaty with Russia in 1783. Agha Mohammed Khan overpowered the Georgians and captured Tiflis and Erivan. He was proclaimed Shah in 1796 after this successful campaign. He established Tehran as the capital of the country (which it has since remained) because of its proximity to Mazandaran, his native province. He succeeded in bringing the period of internal confusion to an end, and finally reaffirmed the Shi'a faith as the State religion. On his assassination in the following year, his nephew, Fath Ali, inherited his tremendous responsibilities. But as this same moment Iran found herself drawn into the maelstrom of nineteenth-century European power-politics. The second Qajar monarch was unequal to this twin challenge of internal and external crisis.

Iran could not escape the profound changes brought about by these developments, even though the preoccupation of the Europeans with India and China brought her rather late within the ambit of the general European dominance over Asia. During the first phase of this epoch, that of European expansion in Asia between 1498 and 1750, Iran had had some experience of European designs. Within eight years of the arrival of Vasco da Gama at Calicut, the Portuguese Governor, Affonso de Albuquerque, and the Portuguese fleet under Tristan da Cunha, attacked and occupied the island of Hormuz, five miles off the Iranian coast in the Persian Gulf. The Portuguese occupation of Hormuz and other strategic ports and islands of the Persian Gulf continued for almost a century until Shah Abbas the Great decided to put an end to European intrusion. Between 1602 and 1619 he drove the Portuguese out of Persian waters: from Bahrein in 1602, Gombrun (Bandar Abbas) in 1615, and Ras al Khaimah in 1619.

The English East India Company, seeing that the Shah was bringing the era of Portuguese supremacy in the Gulf to an end, made an approach to the Court of Isphahan in 1615 and received a firman from the Shah to sell woollen textiles and to export Persian silks. The first English agency was opened at Shiraz in 1617. In the following year the Shah granted the Company a monopoly to export silks and also permitted it to open another trading station at Jask in 1619. This explains why English ships participated in the Persian expedition against the Portuguese to liberate Hormuz in 1621. At the end of the victorious expedition, the Shah granted the customs franchise of the port of Bandar Abbas to the Company. The period between the death of Shah Abbas in 1629 and the dethronement of Shah Tahmasp II in 1732 witnessed the establishment of English supremacy in the Persian Gulf, the Portuguese having been defeated in 1650.

After Nader Shah, Karim Khan Zand occupies an honoured place in the eighteenth-century annals of Iran. It fell to him to bring peace and stability to Persia following the turbulence created by the Afghan invasion. Karim Khan was not born to high estate, but having won supreme power he continued to maintain close links with the common people and won their hearts through his love for them. He was a just, courageous and constructive ruler, inspired by the finest ideals of Persian statesmanship. Being strong as well as good he was able to achieve stability for the country – something which even Nader Shah had not been able to accomplish, despite his stupendous military feats both inside and outside the country. After he had consolidated his position Karim Khan refused the title of Shah but modestly termed himself Vakil or representative of the people. He endowed his capital Shiraz, in whose vicinity he was born, with many fine monuments and buildings. The famous Vakil Mosque and Bazaar, schools and other monuments still to be seen in Shiraz are a living testimony to his constructive munificence and devotion to culture. Karim Khan was anxious to foster Persia's economic well-being and trade in the Persian Gulf. To this end, in answer to British requests he issued a firman in 1763 giving the East India Company rights to establish a factory at Bushire, which soon began to

Below: Lacquered papier-maché book cover (early 19th century), painted with a picture of the battle of Karnal (1739), in which the Great Moghul, Mohammed Shah, was defeated by the Persians under their leader, Nader Shah.

Far right: Portrait of a young Zand prince, painted in 1793. This style of painting, which is markedly different from that of the more familiar Persian miniature, began to emerge in the latter half of the 18th century and was continued during the period of the Qajar dynasty.

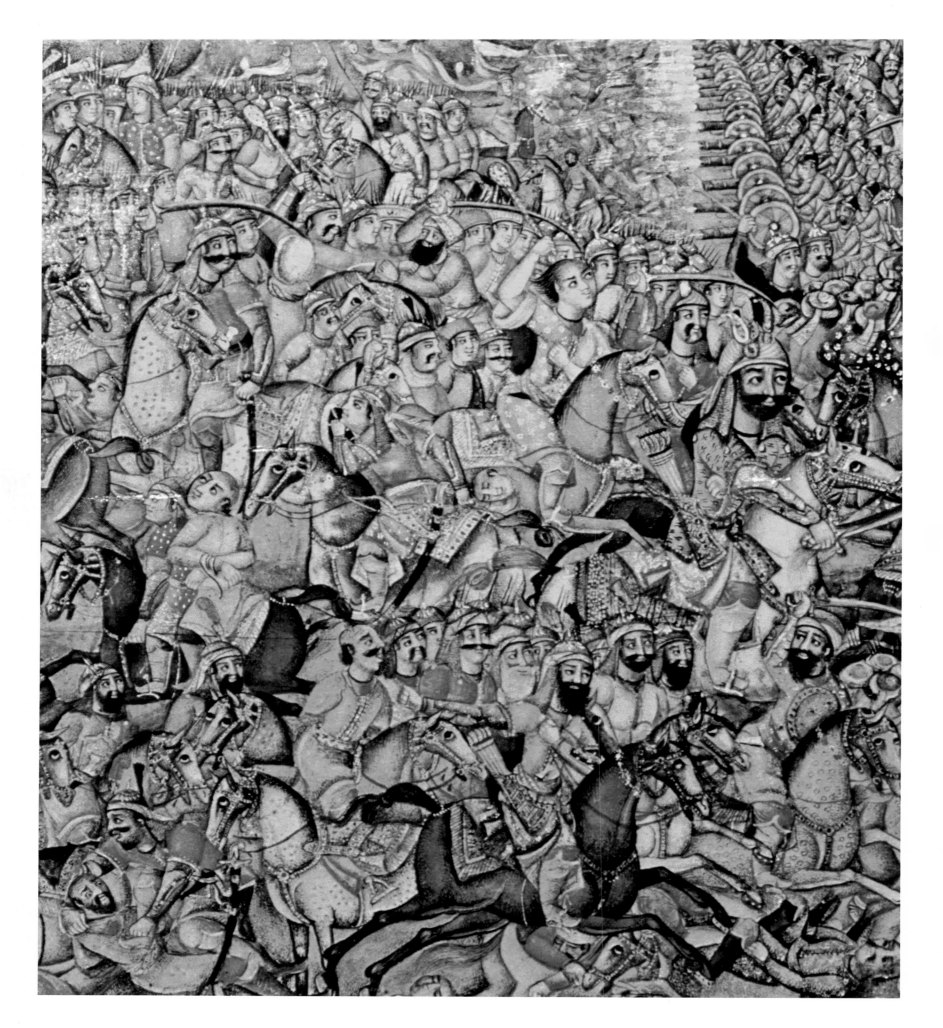

flourish as a centre of commercial activity. The Company also received a monopoly of woollen imports and freedom from all taxes, and received a promise that all other Europeans would be excluded from Bushire as long as the British remained. The Vakil may not have thought of these favours as unusual, but later events proved that this firm foothold was to lead to the eventual predominance of the British in southern Iran.

The granting of these favours occurred at a time when a complete change was about to come over the character of the Company. The Gulf and the land route to India passing through Iran had begun to receive major attention both in Calcutta and in London at this period. In 1784, the British government introduced legislation to bring the Company under its political control. Henceforth, it was to act as an undisguised instrument of British colonial policy.

While the British consolidated their position and power in the Gulf, another danger to Iran and her independence appeared in the north. The Empress Catherine of Russia was waking up to the realisation that if she did not move speedily she would be left behind in the race for the domination of Asia. The Russian shadow had already begun to lengthen over the Iranian provinces around the Caspian. The sword of Nader Shah had restored to Iran her lost provinces in the north-west, notably Georgia, but in the years of weakness following Nader's reign Georgia again moved away to enter into a defence agreement with Moscow. Agha Mohammed Khan Qajar, who had won power after defeating Lutf Ali Khan, the last of the Zand rulers, tested the strength of this alliance in 1795 by marching to Tiflis. Catherine, in annoyance and anger, ordered an invasion of Georgia, which failed to materialise only because of her death. When Fath Ali Shah ascended the throne in 1797, Iran knew that the Russian blow would come sooner rather than later.

The first attack came in 1800 when Russia annexed Georgia, which had long been a friendly tributary of Persia. This compelled Persia to go to war with Russia in 1804. The Persian armies won several successes, but later suffered severe reverses and in 1813 Persia ended the war and Fath Ali Shah was compelled to sign the treaty of Gulistan, which ironically was made possible through the influence of the British representative, Sir Gore Ouseley. She had to abandon all rights to Georgia, which included giving up the right to maintain a navy in Caspian waters, and to cede certain other districts to Russia in the trans-Caucasian region.

But the treaty of Gulistan was vaguely worded in respect of three districts lying between Erivan and the Gokcha Lake which remained in dispute, and in 1815 the Russians eventually seized the important Gokcha district, a move which led to the second Russo-Persian war. Russia's expansionist aims roused public resentment among the masses of the Persian people and volunteers from all over the country flocked to the standard of Prince Abbas Mirza, son and heir-apparent of Fath Ali Shah. The Crown Prince, who was Governor of Azerbaijan, was one of the most courageous military leaders of the Qajar period and a staunch patriot. He was also a zealous administrative and cultural reformer, and had considerably improved and modernised the Persian forces under his command, which he led with conspicuous ability in the first war which was forced upon the country by Russia's ambitions. At his side was his minister, Mirza Abu'l Qasim, Qa'im Maqam Farahani, one of the most notable administrators of his time. An outstanding politician with a keen knowledge of foreign affairs, he fully appreciated the new menaces from abroad with which Persia would have to contend to maintain her integrity and sovereignty. But beyond this, he realised the urgent need to carry out internal reforms in all fields of public life – spiritual, political, military, and literary.

In the second war with Russia, Abbas Mirza again led the Persian forces into battle and in the first phase the troops under his command gained a series of victories, retaking many of the places lost in the first war; but as before, the weight of Russian material and man-power proved too great. Abbas Mirza and the Qa'im Maqam were unfortunately unsuccessful against Russia's might, but the Crown Prince later performed great military services for his country on the eastern frontier of Khorassan against fresh Afghan and Turkoman encroachments. His premature death in 1833, a year before that of his father, was a grievous loss to the country. Not long afterwards the Qa'im Maqam also fell a victim to intrigues against him in the reign of Mohammed Shah, who in 1834 succeeded Fath Ali Shah.

Those of the Qajar rulers who followed Fath Ali Shah were mere shadows of the true kings of Iran. Fath Ali Shah himself had to wage five wars: two against Russia, two against Afghanistan, and one against Turkey. His court became a centre of treacherous European intrigue. The British East India Company sent several missions from Calcutta to Tehran, and the British government, not to be left behind, twice sent representatives. Napoleonic France sent two embassies and the Russians one. Fath Ali indirectly involved Iran in European wars and directly participated in alliances and counter-alliances with the European powers, which left his country betrayed and helpless on every occasion. She not only lost her northern territories to Russia, but gave in to other European demands which compromised her political sovereignty.

The rise of Napoleon and his alleged plan to invade India through Iranian territory was the formal starting point of European intrigue. The plan, conceived in 1801 in collaboration with the Czar Paul, was for Russian troops to descend upon Iran and join Napoleon's armies in a march against India. Russia's role remained unfulfilled because Paul was assassinated immediately afterwards. Whether the plan would have been feasible or not, nobody seems to have tried to find out. In any event, it gave considerable alarm to the British in India, and, in turn, provided the final impetus for their desire to bring Iran into their sphere of influence.

Besides Iran, Afghanistan lay on the road to India. Kabul was under the control of Zaman Shah, who had also been contacted by Napoleon's agents. The British decided to use the recent Herat question to their own advantage. The first mission from Bombay came to the Court of Fath Ali Shah in 1799 to convince him that his safety lay in alliance with the British. A second mission followed in 1800, under Captain Malcolm. This Malcolm mission ended in a treaty whereby Fath Ali Shah agreed not to make peace with the Afghan Amir till Kabul renounced its desire to attack British possessions in India. The Shah also accepted the British demand for the expulsion of the French from Iran. The East India Company gained more commercial privileges: British and Indian merchants were to be permitted to settle at Iranian ports, free of tax, and English broadcloth, iron, steel and lead were to be admitted to Iran, also free of tax. The

Left: Fath Ali Shah (1798–1834), the second of the Qajar monarchs; from a contemporary portrait. He was famous for the splendour of his appearance. His head-dress is decorated with egret plumes dyed to match his beard, and over the sleeves of his cloth-of-gold tunic he wears a pair of jewelled armlets in each of which is set a diamond of fabulous size.

Right: The minaret at Sepah-Salar, the largest mosque in Tehran, built in the latter half of the 19th century by Nassereddin Shah and named after his Minister for War.

British were to assist Iran militarily in case of an attack by the Afghans or the French, and also to assist generally in equipping Iranian troops.

Fath Ali Shah was more interested in getting equipment for his army, as he saw the real danger to Iran coming from Russia's aggressive designs. His faith in British promises was so strong that French approaches were temporarily rejected. But British assistance failed to materialise, despite the sending of reminders. In 1804 the French again offered Iran an alliance against Russia. Fath Ali Shah made one more attempt to make the British keep their word. The French, yet again through a special ambassador, sought to finalize an alliance with Iran in 1806, when the Franco-Russian war broke out; however, Fath Ali still pinned his hopes on the British. After waiting for four years and failing to obtain the promised assistance, he turned to the French. Their victories in Europe at this time seemed to provide the Shah and his advisers with some hope that if an alliance could be brought about between Iran and France, this would help to ward off the danger from Russia and also perhaps provide a counter-balance to British influence. In 1807, Iran and France signed the treaty of Finkenstein, which aimed to provide for mutual aid against Russia and Britain. While one salutary result of this Franco-Iranian understanding was the laying of an enduring cultural bond between the two countries, the political and military aspects of the treaty were negatived almost immediately by Napoleon's signing of the treaty of Tilsit with Russia, after which the latter seized Nakhchivan and Erivan, cities that Agha Mohammed Khan had reoccupied only twelve years before.

Once again, the British were on the scene, appearing both from India and London, in the person of Captain Malcolm and Sir Harford Jones, who signed a preliminary treaty with Iran in 1809 by which England promised military and financial aid. The treaty was ratified by London in 1811, but it proved no more than a scrap of paper when the Russians attacked again in 1813, since London meanwhile had come to terms with St Petersburg, and so Iran lost out to the Russians. As a result of this, Fath Ali ceded Derbent, Baku, Shirwan, Shaki, Karabagh, and part of Talish and gave up historic Iranian claims to Georgia, Daghestan, Mingrelia, Imertitia and Abkhasia. The Iranian navy was exiled from the Caspian. The Russians set up an embassy at Tehran and though Russia was to gain much more in yet another war, the treaty of 1813 was the beginning of Russian influence at the Qajar courts.

The defeat by Russia led Fath Ali to lean more heavily on the British and a definitive treaty with Britain was signed in 1814. But when hostilities with Russia broke out again in 1826 there were no signs of British aid. Iran, after some initial successes, lost the war, which ended with the Treaty of Turkomanchai in 1828. She not only surrendered all her territory north of the Aras river, but agreed to pay a heavy indemnity to Russia, and Russian citizens were granted extra-territorial privileges. Once again, the British Minister, Sir John Macdonald, used his influence to compel the aged Fath Ali to agree to the Russian demands. The means by which these terms were exacted from Iran came to be taken by other Europeans as a model for treatment of Iran in later years.

During the last three quarters of the nineteenth century Iran's ancient society became a defenceless victim of Western pressures. It was in the reign of Mohammed Shah, 1848–96, that the Western imperial system prospered on the Asian continent. By the time Mohammed Shah ascended the throne, British rule over the entire sub-continent of India was nearly established.

The new rulers of India contrived the theory from 1800 that the defence of the frontiers of their empire lay deep inside the territories of Iran. Firmly in the saddle in the Persian Gulf and enjoying unchallenged maritime supremacy, they were determined to bend the Qajar monarchs to their will. This danger to Iranian survival became all the greater with the spread of the Russian empire in the east. Russia, having annexed all the Iranian provinces north of the Aras river between 1800 and 1828, now moved its troops in a bid to include the whole of outer Iran, which lay in the north and north-east of the plateau, in her eastern empire. The Russian expansion began with the First Expedition to Khiva in 1838–40. After the Russian armies had advanced gradually to the Sea of Aral between 1849–64, the Czarist regime occupied the historic Valley of the Syr Darya, for centuries an advanced centre of Iranian civilisation. The Amir of Bokhara was defeated in 1868 and the Khanate of Khokand was annexed in 1876, Khiva having been conquered in 1873. The Czarist empire loomed heavy and large over Iran by 1881, when the Russian armies defeated the Turkomans. Iran now lay helpless between the cruel pincers of the British and Russian empires in the East.

The new realities of Western dominance became depressingly clear on Fath Ali Shah's death and during the short contest for the succession which followed. Mohammed Shah's accession to the throne was a direct consequence of his having won the favour of the two Western powers. Mohammed Shah marched from Tabriz to Tehran, but his uncle, Farman Farma, who had challenged the choice, was chased to Kuminshah and his forces routed.

During the reigns of Mohammed Shah and Nassereddin Shah, the Russian and British representatives alternately exercised their influence at Tehran Court. Russia no longer found resistance to her attempt to dominate the five northern provinces of Iran. The only military conflict with Iran after 1834 in which the British became involved was related to the fate of Afghanistan. Iran was preoccupied in the Herat area with an attempt to restore what she considered her historic rights, namely that it was Persian territory and had once been a centre of Persian culture. In this she at first received support and encouragement from the British in India, who were anxious about the security of the Indo-Afghan frontier following the consolidation of the forces of successive Afghan amirs, who sought to extend their power into northern India. Later, however, when Iran was about to succeed, the British position changed. Growing Anglo-Russian rivalry and British fears that if Herat were restored to Persia, Russia would have the right, under the terms of the Treaty of Turkomanchai, to appoint consular and commercial representatives there caused the British to alter their minds. Britain's efforts were now directed against Persia, with the result that even though Persian forces, in Nassereddin Shah's time, occupied Herat, they eventually had to agree to withdraw and some years later a series of boundary negotiations between Persia and Britain were concluded by an agreed demarcation of the frontier between Afghanistan and Persia in Sistan and along sectors of the Baluchistan borders further south with British India. Besides the need at times to defend Persia's historic rights in these regions by military means, the country's representatives had to use all their diplomatic skill to secure just settlements, insofar as these were possible, in tough negotiations with British representatives during the latter half of the nineteenth and the early years of the twentieth century.

And but for the determined stand of the Shah and his nominees many regions inhabited by Persian subjects might well have been lost. While the Herat region had to be abandoned because of a British military expedition to the Persian Gulf, which occupied the island of Kharg and strengthened the British hold on Bushire, other major territorial disasters of the kind imposed by the Russians in the Caucasus and Central Asia were happily avoided by active Persian resistance and vigilance on the eastern Frontier. By the Anglo-Persian Treaty of Paris (1857) Persia undertook to withdraw her troops from Herat and to give up her claim in that and other regions of Afghanistan, while the aims of the British expedition to the Persian Gulf were rendered useless, as General Outram, who commanded it, had to relinquish Kharg island, as well as the cities of Mohammerah and Ahwaz which he had occupied on the mainland.

There is a considerable amount of data to show the devastation which industrial dumping by the British wrought in the manufacturing centres of the country. This is broadly reflected in the change in the character of Iran's foreign trade during this period. The Treaty of Turkomanchai (1828) contained a most-favoured nation clause whereby a maximum of only 5 per cent customs duty on all imported goods from Russia was agreed to by Fath Ali Shah. As the government became more susceptible to foreign influence, the application of this clause was subsequently extended to all European countries and British India. Further, foreign merchants were granted immunity from road-tolls and internal transit taxes, which, however, remained mandatory for Iranian merchants. These exceptional facilities granted to foreigners made it possible for them to flood the markets of Iran with cheap machine-made goods and with this the bell began to toll for traditional Iranian manufactures.

Iranian manufactured goods, which had made a name for themselves during the centuries of Safavi power, received a tremendous setback. They were replaced by goods from Europe and instead of manufactured goods, Iran began to export raw materials. In 1849 Flandin reported that

the import of British materials had destroyed all the large silk factories of Kashan. Since foreign merchants paid only minimum taxes, they could easily afford the luxury of dumping their goods. Flandin also reported that Isphahan, which was famous for its textiles, had become a consumer of manufactured cotton goods, imported almost wholly from Manchester and Glasgow. The exports from Iran were mainly limited to opium, tobacco, cotton, almonds and rice. Lord Curzon was to report the same sad story with reference to Yazd. Yazd possessed 1,800 silk factories in the middle of the nineteenth century. By the time Curzon was in Iran, they were bankrupt, and the ground on which they stood was taken over for the cultivation of the poppy, from which 2,000 chests of opium extract were being exported annually! Curzon also lamented the fate of Kerman and Meshed, formerly centres famous for arms manufactures, whose metal industries suffered from the devastation caused by imports of British steel. In the fifteen years from 1873 to 1888 the value of imports and exports through Bushire increased by about five million rupees. During the decade between 1878 and 1888, the trade of Bandar Abbas increased to a similar extent. The value of the customs franchise at the southern ports went up proportionately: at Bushire from 40,000 *tomans* in 1874 to 99,000 in 1889; at Bandar Abbas from 30,000 to 53,000; and at Lingah from 6,500 to 12,000.

The miseries of famous manufacturing towns, some of which were turned into ruined villages within a decade, led to the flight of traders, craftsmen and artisans, either to overcrowded villages or to new commercial cities, such as Tehran, whose population doubled itself in the second half of the nineteenth century.

Like other ancient societies of Asia, Iran was in need of re-adjustment to the realities of the new industrial world which had risen in Europe and was now sitting on her doorstep. The leadership for such a movement of revival, in the context of the historic traditions of Iranian civilisation, could come only from the monarchs, who in the past had led the nation to greatness.

Nassereddin Shah was ready to compromise. He granted comprehensive national monopolies to foreigners. The case of Baron Julius de Reuter, a naturalised British subject, set an example which was to be followed by others. In 1872 the Shah granted Reuter rights to build railways, work mines, and set up a state bank. The Shah even agreed to place the total customs rights of the country in the Baron's hands and pledged almost the whole of Iran's resources to him in return for completely hypothetical benefits. In fact, these extensive rights had to be cancelled the next year because neither the Russians nor the British approved of this virtual sale of the resources of Iran to a private individual. But the Baron did not give up easily. He claimed compensation, and was satisfied only when he received £40,000. Later, he was given the privilege of founding a national bank, and was granted the right to exploit all the country's mineral resources (other than gold, silver and precious stones) outside the five northern provinces dominated by Russia. Reuter's bank, the Imperial Bank of Persia, which was allowed to issue currency notes, exercised enormous influence over the economy of Iran. In 1888, a contract was granted to Messrs Lynch Bros., of England, by which the lower reaches of the Karun River were opened to commerce. This venture became very profitable once oil was discovered nearby in the Bakhtiari mountains. After Reuter's acquisition of banking rights, the Russians received a similar right to set up Iran's sole discount bank. In 1890, a British citizen was the recipient of an extraordinary right which gave him control over the production, sale and export of all tobacco in Iran, which affected large sections of the population, including the numerous tobacco growers. The popular agitation against this move became a landmark in the movement to aid Iran's renaissance. Nassereddin Shah was compelled to cancel the tobacco right, but Iran had to pay compensation to the extent of half a million pounds sterling! The money, borrowed from Reuter's Imperial Bank, was the genesis of the Persian national debt.

During this period, however, some superficial features of a modern state were introduced. The first telegraph line of the country was laid in 1864. Six years after this, a complex of Indo-European telegraph lines was built. By 1898 several lines crossed the country, linking India, Europe, Russia and Great Britain. The lines were laid by English and German firms. Technically, the Iranian government, through its Minister of Telegraphs, managed the whole complex. The real power, however, lay with the English advisers, whose appointment was mandatory and whose choice lay with the British government. Several foreign powers sought to build up a modern army for Iran. At the beginning of the century, this task was attempted by military missions from Britain and France. In 1804, when Mohammed Shah dispensed with the English military mission, the French returned. Then came the Italians, who were followed by the French once again. But all these attempts failed. In 1878, Britain refused a request from Nassereddin Shah for assistance and this resulted in the employment of Austrians to do the job. The Russians also took a hand and organised a regiment on the Cossack model. The Czar presented one thousand rifles and some guns and lent Russian officers and material support. This regiment was to expand into a brigade, armed with its complement of guns, and to become the most efficient part of the Iranian army.

The alternate supremacy of Britain and Russia was recognised by the ruling minority of tribal khans and feudal land-lords and a small group of the merchant class, who were only too pleased to work in collaboration with foreigners. Some became willing tools in the hands of foreign powers which were seeking to execute their aims.

British policy during this period was guided by a dual objective: to establish and expand British trade; and to defend the British Empire in India. Russia, on the other hand, ever since the time of Peter the Great, had been seeking warm-water ports and this led her in the direction of the Black Sea and the Caspian Sea, bringing her into conflict with Turkey and Iran, and finally with Britain, over the issue of their commercial and political imperialist rivalry. These selfish objectives of the two great powers required that neither of them should be in a position to control the whole of Iran. This Anglo-Russian rivalry was one of the factors that prevented Iran from being dominated exclusively by either during the nineteenth century. Both powers fostered the weakness of the country's political structure and of the Qajar monarchy. When this rivalry temporarily abated, they agreed to divide Iran into spheres of influence, as in 1907. In 1917, when the Czarist regime collapsed, Britain made the first – and indeed

last – effort to dominate Iran. The *coup d'état* led by Reza Shah frustrated the attempt and opened a new era of national renaissance.

The national setback at Turkomanchai set in motion developments which ultimately gave rise to a movement of national revival. The build-up of this movement was gradual and spread over a period of some eighty years. It was complex in its formation and its immediate motivation varied at each phase. From the beginning, however, there was a general realisation that Iran's ancient society must accept adjustments in order to achieve the growing national desire to resist foreigners and assert the country's natural and historic position in the world. That this became a reality was due to the national character of the Iranian people. They had met with catastrophic situations in the past

when their society had been challenged by others – the Greeks, the Romans and, above all, the Arabs. Their civilisation had suffered temporary and terrible declines in the course of some of these encounters. However, they had risen again on each occasion because of their pragmatic and resilient character. This capacity of the people came into play again immediately after the Treaty of Turkomanchai and, after a struggle of eight decades, carried them forward to national liberation and the revolution of 1921.

The first glimmer of realisation that Iran's ancient society must discard some of its obsolete features came to a few enlightened representatives of the upper classes and the Court. They were not inspired by any kind of idealism, and were even loathe to make any alteration in the oppressive economic

structure of society. They were guided rather by their knowledge that the only way Iran could stand up to Russian and British dominance was by gaining national strength.

Prince Abbas Mirza, the distinguished military leader, began the introduction of European methods of training for the Persian armed forces. His able minister Mirza Abu'l Qasim, Qa'im Maqam Farahani, began the movement for administrative, literary, and educational reform. (The first lithographic press was established in Persia in Tabriz in 1812.) One of Qasim's literary works, *Munshiat-e Qa'im Maqam*, is characterised by the use for the first time of simple Farsi.

Another great reformer and progressive figure of Qajar times was Mirza Taqi Khan, who began life as a protégé of Mirza Abu'l Qasim and later rose to be Nassereddin Shah's

chief minister. Mirza Taqi Khan founded in Tehran the Dar ul-Funoon, a college run on modern lines. This helped to raise the level of education in Persia. He kept a watchful eye on the growth of foreign influences in Persian affairs and sought to keep them in check. He also made efforts to improve the country's finances and he took steps to end the rebellion that had broken out in Khorassan and to curb the power of the most conservative elements of the clergy in public affairs. Like Prince Abbas Mirza and the Qa'im Maqam, Taqi Khan, who earned the title of Amir Kabir, was the victim of intrigues and plots among those forces who opposed his reforms and in 1851 he was dismissed. He died in the following year. His death came as a bitter blow to all those who favoured the newly-emerging healthy trends of the time and the following years of Nassereddin Shah's reign were the poorer for his loss.

The noble efforts of these outstanding figures of the Qajar period during the reigns of both Fath Ali Shah and Nassereddin Shah, pointed the way to, if they did not actually establish the basis for, the rise and later fulfilment of modern Persian nationalism.

Besides these notable leaders there was a growing number of patriotic Iranians who felt that since Iran did not possess adequate military strength to throw back the Europeans, her salvation lay in a genuine spiritual revival. Some advocated the purification of religious practices and a return to the strict adherence to the religion of the Prophet, a type of thinking engendered by adherence to the concept of pan-Islamism and the unity of all Moslem nations. This trend was not limited to Iran, but spread to various Moslem countries, including Moslem India. The reformist clergy gained support from the new mercantile class which had grown up, initially in the southern ports and in the course of trade with India. Iranian merchants in the latter half of the nineteenth century traded largely with Bombay and Calcutta. They visited not only India, but went also to Egypt and Turkey; some even travelled to Europe. These merchants, in the course of their dealings with foreigners, came to believe strongly that the solution of Iran's problems lay in religious reformation. They were to remain a powerful force in the movement of revival till the revolution of Reza Shah.

Another trend was a desire to assimilate the learning of the West. This trend grew up in the new urban areas. A Western type of

college was set up in Tehran in 1851; the Masonic cult was introduced in 1860; and in 1865 a girls' school was founded. Thus by the 1890s a more widely educated class had come into existence to influence fresh thinking among the people.

All these developments led to a new spirit of nationalism. It is important to note that the common aspiration among the merchants, the progressive clergy, and the new educated class was to readjust the structure of Iranian society, so as to build up a strong and powerful nation. Though there were differences among them, there was this area of common agreement.

It is often said that this was a movement for the 'Westernisation' of Iran, which was true. But it was also much more. It was a matter of the Persians' pride in their history and in their ancient heritage as a people. A nation with a continuous history of 2,500 years, one which had initiated civilisations in other countries that came under its influence, could hardly be content to accept only the customs and traditions of the West. But the people were not slow to appreciate that unless the new forces arising in the modern world were identified with and adjusted to the conditions of Iran, the nation would not be able to re-establish its traditional stature in the new world conditions.

This growing movement, which was many-sided, made its first political impact in the reaction to Nassereddin Shah's tobacco rights, given to a British company in 1890. By itself, this episode might not have provoked so strong a national resistance. But it was seen in a sense as the culmination of the 'concession' policy put forward by some of the misguided advisers close to the Shah. Other such privileges did not affect the day-to-day life of the people, though they contained disadvantages from the national point of view. The grant of the tobacco monopoly to a foreign company touched everyone, since the tobacco habit was national. The call for resistance came from the clergy and Sayyid Jamalu'd-Din Assa'd Abadi played an important part in stimulating popular indignation over the action of the Shah. The merchants supported the clergy and the educated class became the moving spirit of the movement. The people responded by boycotting tobacco on a nation-wide basis. All pipe and cigarette smoking ceased. Even the courtiers stopped smoking. The Shah, amazed at first, realised that the people had become united in an impregnable front. Early in 1892 he was compelled to cancel the British

company's tobacco rights. This, however, did little to subdue the antagonism which his policy had provoked. His assassination in 1896, however, cannot be put down to any single factor. Extremist clerics, political malcontents among certain economically dissatisfied sections of the population, and foreign intrigues were among the causes of this event.

The new monarch, Mozaffareddin Shah, had learnt little from the experiences of his predecessor. Unmindful of the national resentment against the granting of exceptional economic privileges to foreigners, he continued to follow this harmful practice, and in 1901, agreed to a tariff preference being given to Russia and rights in oil to Britain.

It is significant that Iranian resistance should have crystallised into a movement in the very year when these rights were given to foreigners. For this was the year in which there arose a popular demand for a constitution. The leaders of this movement came to be known as Constitutionalists. The British representative in Tehran, who saw the potential strength of the movement, was already familiar with the mortal disease, which by now had begun to sap the strength of the Qajar dynasty itself. It was therefore not surprising to find Britain coming out in support of the Constitutionalists. Once they began to agitate vociferously against the pro-Russian policy of the court, the British authorities in Tehran began to give moral and material sustenance to their movement.

The influence of the Constitutionalists was at first limited to the urban population. The victory of Japan in the Russo-Japanese war and the Russian revolution of 1905 made a deep impact on the minds of educated Iranians. From 1906, the constitutional movement spread throughout the country and demonstrations in support of the Constitutionalists continued in major urban and rural centres during the first five months of that year. Emboldened by this popular support, the leaders of the Constitutional movement served an ultimatum on the Shah that he must grant a constitution without delay. Mozaffareddin Shah retaliated by imprisoning a large number of the popular leaders. The British legation in Tehran became a sanctuary for those who escaped or were afraid of being arrested. This was a peculiar situation for the Qajar king. One of his patrons, the Czar, who had his own troubles, failed to assist him, while the other was openly giving support to his enemies,

Right: Nassereddin Shah (*reg.* 1848–1896) with his entourage.

Below: Chained to his guard, Mirza Reza Kermani, the assassin of Nassereddin Shah, awaits his execution.

Right: Supporters of the Constitutional movement captured during the revolts that broke out in various parts of Persia at the beginning of the 20th century.

Lower right: Mozaffareddin Shah (*reg.* 1896–1907) with his Prime Minister, Mirza Ali Asghar Khan.

the Constitutionalists. He himself had little power to sweep back the rising tide of popular anger. Under these circumstances he was compelled to accept some of the demands, including that of the formation of a national assembly – the majlis. In October of the same year, members of the National Assembly were elected for the first time and drew up a constitution, which the Shah had no alternative but to ratify.

Mohammed Ali, Mozaffareddin's son, who came to the throne in 1907, attempted a *coup* against the Constitutionalists and provoked nationalist reaction. The Qajar monarchy could have been ended at this moment; however, greater forces were at work in Iran at the time. The traditional rivals for domination of the country, Britain and Russia, were now faced with a new challenge from a unified Germany. In face of this increasing threat, they arrived at an agreement in which Iran had a major role to play. The *détente* between London and St Petersburg, the terms of which were embodied in the Anglo-Russian Convention of August 31, 1907, enabled Mohammed Ali Shah to retain his throne, and postponed the imminent demise of the Qajar monarchy.

Under the 1907 Convention, Iran was divided into rival spheres of influence. Britain secured for herself the south, including all territory south of a line drawn from the Afghan frontier, via Gazik, Birjand and Kerman to the sea at Bandar Abbas. Thus Seistan and most of the provinces of Kerman and of Makran fell within her sphere of influence. Russia controlled the whole of northern Iran above a line drawn from Kasr-i-Shirin on the Turkish frontier, through Isphahan, Yazd and Kahk to the point on the Iranian frontier where the Russian and Afghan borders intersected. This arrangement meant that almost all the major towns of Iran – Tabriz, Rasht, Tehran, Mashad and Isphahan – fell within the Russian sphere of influence. The government of Mohammed Ali Shah was left with an area between the two zones, a buffer strip which comprised the greater part of southern Iran and the whole of the Persian Gulf coast on the Iranian side. The Convention did not specify this as a third zone and the Shah's sovereignty over it was at best dubious. The reasons for this became clear in 1911. By an informal and unwritten understanding, the two powers agreed to the complete domination of the northern areas by Russia, and the inclusion of this third zone in the British sphere of influence.

The Anglo-Russian Convention created a new political situation in Iran. Mohammed Ali Shah realised that Britain would now withdraw the support previously granted to the Constitutionalists, since her interests in Iran were guaranteed, at least for the time being. On the other hand, Russia was extremely concerned with the revolutionary element in the constitutional movement, with which she was becoming increasingly familiar at home. The movement itself was primarily based in the cities which fell within the Russian sphere of influence. The Czarist government encouraged Mohammed Ali Shah to suppress the Constitutionalists. Mohammed Ali Shah, for his part needed only the promise of Russian support should matters get out of hand. He therefore lost no time in staging a second *coup* against the Constitutionalists with the assistance of the Cossack Brigade. In June 1908, he ordered Colonel Liakhoff, the Russian commander of the Brigade, to mount an artillery attack on the parliament building in Tehran. On June 23, Liakhoff bombarded parliament whilst the majlis was in session, and six regiments

of the Brigade occupied Tehran. On the same day, a state of siege was proclaimed in Tehran, and Liakhoff was named the Governor of the capital.

The Constitutionalists retaliated swiftly and effectively. Revolt was proclaimed by the clergy at Nadjaf, Khorassan, Mazandaran and other places. Tabriz became the headquarters of the Constitutionalists, who had now taken up arms. At this stage the Czar intervened with his promised support. Russian troops entered Tabriz and a period of violence and cruelty began. The revolt spread to Rasht and Isphahan. The re-grouped revolutionary forces marched towards Tehran, where they defeated the half-hearted soldiers of the Cossack Brigade. The Constitutionalists' entry into the capital compelled Mohammed Ali Shah to flee, first as a refugee to the Russian Legation and then to Russia. His eleven-year-old son, Crown Prince Ahmad, was placed on the throne by the Constitutionalists.

The defeat of Mohammed Ali Shah was a distinct setback to Russian ambitions, for which the Czarist regime took its revenge in 1911. The Czar ordered the Constitutionalists to terminate the services of an American financial expert, Morgan Shuster. This order was followed by an ultimatum, which in turn was followed by an invasion, another massacre of liberals and revolutionaries at Tabriz, and the bombardment of the Holy Shrine of Imam Reza at Meshed. The government, fearing the occupation of the capital by Russian troops, accepted Russian demands and dismissed Shuster. Before doing so it had turned to the British for support, but true to the spirit of the Convention of 1907, Britain abandoned the Constitutionalists, whom she had encouraged earlier. Russian troops were still in occupation of northern Iran when the First World War broke out in 1914. The war years were a time of alien and military occupation, of untold misery and vast desolation for Iran. Her neutrality was violated first by the Russians and Turks, in the north-west, and then by the Turks and the British in the south-west. After the revolution in Russia, in February, 1917, northern Iran became a battlefield, while the Turkish, British, White Russian and Bolshevik forces sought to settle their scores against each other, primarily at the cost of Iranian peasants. By the time the War ended, White Russian troops were in occupation of the Caspian seaboard, and the rest of the country was virtually under British military occupation.

At the end of the war, Iran made one last attempt to seek justice from the victorious powers, who had formally sanctified the principle of national self-determination. The government prepared a document in which

Right: One of the Tabriz revolutionaries who died for his cause.

Lower right: A group of revolutionary volunteers inside the citadel at Tabriz.

her case for political, judicial and economic independence and her right to territorial restorations and reparation was pleaded. It requested the abrogation of the Anglo-Russian Convention of 1907, and demanded the withdrawal of Consular guards and the abolition of Consular courts. Iran never reached the stage of pleading her case, and was dismissed in a summary fashion. Lloyd George, prompted by Lord Curzon, was primarily responsible for this iniquity, the reasons for which became clear on August 9, 1919, when the British decision to convert Iran into a protectorate was gently announced in the form of a new Anglo-Persian treaty.

The new treaty consisted of a short document containing a preamble and six articles. By the first article the British government reiterated its past undertakings to respect the independence and integrity of Iran. Having stated this, Britain, in the remaining articles, acquired for herself

complete control over the Iranian army and finances: British military experts were to reorganise and equip Iranian armed forces at Iran's expense; British technical experts were to construct railways and other forms of transport, for which Iran was to pay. In return for all this, Britain was to advance a loan, the terms of which were defined by a second agreement. The loan of £2 million at 7 per cent, redeemable in twenty years, was to remain under British control. Even before the treaty was submitted to the Majlis for ratification, several of its provisions had been put into operation. A British financial commission arrived at Tehran and General Dickson, whose troops had occupied eastern Iran during the War, headed a military commission. The terms of the treaty angered other Western governments. The United States registered a public protest, while the French Government let their displeasure be known diplomatically.

The treaty of 1919 was the culmination of a policy which Britain had pursued from the beginning of the nineteenth century in the Persian Gulf and India. Its author, Lord Curzon, never concealed his belief that British supremacy in Iran and the Persian Gulf was unquestionably bound up with supremacy in India. His conviction that if Britain lost the Gulf, she would lose India, was well publicised. Even the consideration of this treaty by the central government inflamed national feelings. The movement for resistance, which had suffered setbacks, and was, ironically, leaderless, found the solution to its problems in a strong new leadership. Once again an old tradition was revived. In the long history of Iran, whenever the country reached its nadir, a leader had emerged to take control of the situation and lead the nation into a new era of unity and progress. In 1919–20, such a leader was found in the person of Reza Khan, who was

179

Below: In 1933, Reza Shah accepted an
invitation from Kemal Ataturk to visit Turkey.
Here Reza Shah (far right) is greeted by his host
(centre). On the Shah's right is Rashidi Aras,
Turkey's foreign minister, and on the extreme
left is Ismet Inonou, then Prime Minister, and
later President of Turkey.

Far right: Reza Shah, accompanied by the Crown
Prince, visits a girls' school and listens to the
choir. (*Below*) A visit to a girls' college in
Tehran.

Following pages: Fishing for sturgeon in the
Caspian Sea, the last catch of the 1971 season.
The caviar extracted from the fish is processed in
northern Iran.

signed on the very day on which Reza Shah
put a match to the Anglo-Persian treaty of
1919. Lenin agreed to the renunciation of the
Czarist interests in Iran, though later
Kuchlik Khan's revolt in Gilan received
support from the Bolsheviks. Its defeat by
Reza Shah ended the era of Russian inter-
vention, which was not to re-occur till the
Second World War. In the process of ending
the Balkanisation of the country, and
liquidating the rebellious tribal and provincial
chiefs, he succeeded also in weakening the
influence of foreign powers with whom
these chiefs were in league.

Yet Reza Shah knew that the primary

guarantee of national unity and defence lay
in the existence of a strong modern army. No
sooner had he become Minister of Defence
than he merged the various units of the
armed forces into a regular army and
introduced conscription, which in turn
changed the character of the officer class. In
1936 he reorganised the army, introducing
Persian names for its ranks, revising battle
orders, and instituting new bases for
promotion, retirement age, and pensions.
Four years earlier he had organised, for the
first time since the days of Nader Shah, an
Iranian navy, based on the Persian Gulf. He
had also laid the foundation of an Iranian air

force. In order to train personnel for the
three armed services he had chosen Swedish
officers for the army, sent the pilots to
Russia, and later to France, and arranged
for the training of his naval officers at
Iranian academies.

Reza Shah assiduously applied himself to
the difficult task of modernisation within
the framework of the society to be built on
the foundation of a patrimonial monarchy.
The state which he inherited as the first
Pahlavi Shahanshah was bankrupt. Its
economy was still overwhelmingly dominated
by foreigners. Its only bank was outside the
control of the government; even the currency

notes which it circulated had been issued by this foreign-owned bank. Its natural wealth, that is, its oil, was being exploited by others, and it received negligible returns in the form of royalties. No budget or any financial administrative system existed. Iran in the twenties had neither a secular judicial court nor a public health system. She lacked means of communication and the people in the different areas lived in a constant and dangerous state of separation. It would have been a difficult task to remedy such a situation and create the infra-structure of a modern state even if the resources had been available. Yet Reza Shah was determined to accomplish all this and much more, for he had faith in the capacity of his people to convert their ancient society into a modern state.

He introduced a budgetary system and nationalised the issue of bank notes. He established the first large and efficient national bank. He was willing to accept foreign technical advisors on condition that they worked under his own directors. He set in motion a small industrial revolution and established light industries under the control of the state. The inspiration for state ownership did not flow from any socialistic leanings: it was part of the revival of the Iranian tradition of the Safavid period, when manufactures were totally controlled and largely owned by the state. The new factories, the first of their kind in Iran, produced among other things, cotton, woollen and silk materials, cement, sugar, glass, chemicals and munitions. In order to counteract the Western practice of dumping foods on the Iranian market, a system of government monopolies was created to handle the nation's foreign trade. Units of money and weights and measures were rationalised and standardised, so as to make the flow of commerce easy and rapid. All these steps were taken by Reza Shah with the aim of assuring the financial and monetary independence of Iran.

Once he had accepted secularism as a cardinal principle of his policy, Reza Shah was bound to introduce secular judicial courts. All the Iranian courts before this time were clerical tribunals which administered justice by rule of thumb and on the basis of the religious injunctions of Islam. Besides these clerical courts, the country was infested with what were called the consular courts. Each Western power had set up its own court and Western citizens could be tried by no others. This was a part of the monstrous system of capitulations which the Qajar monarchs had accepted. Reza Shah abolished all the consular courts. In framing the new judicial code which, with some alteration,

exists today in Iran, he drew largely on the French legal system. Next, he introduced social and educational reforms. An educational system and service, once again based on the French pattern, were introduced into the country for the first time. A public health system was also set up. In 1934, Iran's first university was founded in Tehran. A little earlier, Reza Shah had abolished the rule which made it obligatory for women to wear veils, and at the opening of the university the ladies of the royal family appeared in public without them. However, his greatest achievement – a monument to his foresight, courage and determination – was the construction of the trans-Iranian railway. Work on this project began in 1927 and ended in 1939. It was a difficult engineering task since the railway had to cross more than 4,100 bridges and pass through 224 bored tunnels, the total length of which was 54 miles. It was also a tremendous financial enterprise, the money for which came exclusively from revenues raised internally by taxes on sugar and tea. Ironically, the use of this magnificent railway, which originally ran over a distance of 900 miles, was to become one of the reasons for the Anglo-Russian invasion during the Second World War; the only land route by which the Allies could send war material to Russia ran through Iran.

Of all the changes which characterised the rebirth of Iran under Reza Shah the most significant was the one which concerned Iran's relations with the Anglo-Persian Oil Company. Ever since 1926 Reza Shah had conducted, through the government, negotiations with the Company to improve the terms of the original concession granted in 1901. The Company had failed to respond favourably and the crisis in its relations with Iran came to a head in 1931. For various reasons, the Company decided to offer the government an insignificant sum as royalty. Reza Shah retaliated sharply and in November 1932 cancelled the concession, while still showing Iran's willingness to negotiate a new one. After the dispute had been brought before the Council of the League of Nations in January 1933, it was resolved through direct negotiations between the parties concerned, the Company undertaking to increase the size of the royalty. The Company's area of concession was reduced in size and its name was changed to the Anglo-Iranian Oil Company, since Reza Shah wanted his country to be known by its ancient name.

Reza Shah, like Nader Shah, had little time in which to accomplish all that he had dreamt of for his country. Unlike Nader Shah, he had made the beginnings of the readjustment

so acutely required for the regeneration of Iran. In all, he really ruled Iran for less than two decades. His reign as the Shahanshah was limited to sixteen years. During this period he worked ceaselessly and with enormous energy to accomplish the task which he had set himself. Within a short space of time he had achieved a modern miracle. He had dragged his country from the quagmire of stagnation and decay into which it had fallen before he came to power and had set it firmly on the path of progress. After a life-time of tireless activity, political realist that he had always tried to be, he knew that what he had started was but the beginning of a long process and that fresh thought and fresh energies would be needed to perform the herculean tasks that lay ahead. He had spared no energies to train the Crown Prince Mohammed Reza Pahlavi for the responsibilities of his succession as Shahanshah. He had even set a date, reportedly 1945, for his retirement and his assumption of the role of elder statesman, when it would have been his intention to hand over the powers of the throne to his heir. Unfortunately, the Second World War intervened and drew Iran into the vortex of that titanic struggle on whose outcome the destinies of mankind depended. So instead of being able to hand over power at a time of his own choice, his abdication came as a forced measure arising from a totally different and world-shaking set of circumstances. It was dictated by the sudden and harsh realities of the Allied invasion and occupation of Iran.

Reza Shah had proclaimed Iran's neutrality in the first phase of the War, when Britain and Germany were the two principal belligerents. There was hardly anything strange about this. The United States had not yet entered the war and Sweden and Switzerland were also neutral. Further, the overwhelming majority of Asian nationalist leaders had stood aside from the Anglo-German conflict. They, like Reza Shah, had no sympathy for either of the Axis powers. Yet they were not willing to accept that Britain, while refusing to give up its imperial position, was in the war for democratic aims. Broadly speaking, Reza Shah shared this outlook. He was, on the other hand, no admirer of the Nazis. As an intense nationalist he had sought economic assistance from all sources, including Germany, to advance his task of modernising Iran. Germany had given considerable help and shown sympathy with Reza Shah's aims even before the advent of the Nazis to power. Since there was no question of an ideological alliance with them, Reza Shah had allowed German-Iranian commercial and cultural relations to grow.

The *raison d'être* of this policy of neutralism during the first phase of the War was later summarised by the present Shah thus: 'My father wanted no entanglement of any kind in the war. Iran, he announced, was both ready and able to retain her neutrality in the face of provocation from either the Axis or the Allies. His declared policy, in a word, was one of neutrality backed by strength.'

The British were satisfied with this policy and hence Reza Shah was annoyed when on June 26, 1941, four days after Hitler's invasion of Russia, first the Soviet Union and then the British began to exercise pressure on Iran to abjure its neutrality. Several protests were delivered to the government of Iran by the British and Soviet governments. All were concerned with the presence of Germans in Iran and demanded that those who were residents should be immediately expelled. Reza Shah was annoyed by this demand because in all there were hardly a thousand Germans in Iran at that time, and this number could not prove dangerous either to Iran or the Allies. While Reza Shah sought clarification of these notes and notified the German Minister in Tehran of his plan to expel the Germans, the invasion of Iran took place on August 25, 1941.

In fact, in view of what the Allies required to help them win the war it is doubtful whether the invasion could have been avoided even if Reza Shah had complied with the demand for the expulsion of the Germans. The Allied powers required untrammelled control over Iran for building a supply line to the Soviet Union via the trans-Iranian railway from the Persian Gulf. Strangely enough, none of the Allied notes ever referred to the need for Iranian co-operation for such a supply line. As early as July 11, 1941, the British Cabinet had asked the

chiefs of staff 'to consider the desirability of joint military action in conjunction with the Russians' in Iran. Lord Wavell, who was Winston Churchill's main adviser about this invasion, proposed a classical colonial solution for the problem of the supply line. 'It is essential', he had written from Delhi to the Prime Minister, 'that we should join hands with Russia through Iran and if the present government [of Iran] is not willing to facilitate this, it must be made to give way to one which will.'

How the Russians prepared for the invasion still remains to be told. It is known that Stalin's government was equally keen to occupy Iran; only Stalin was unwilling to go it alone. On August 13, the Soviet Ambassador in London, M. Maisky, had informed the British Foreign Secretary, Anthony Eden (later Lord Avon), that the Soviet government were prepared to use troops for the invasion of Iran, but were unwilling to do so except in conjunction with Britain. Thus, the Anglo-Soviet notes were a mere façade behind which the plan for the joint invasion of Iran was perfected in London and Moscow.

The invasion led to the abdication of Reza Shah. On the morning of September 16, 1941, he called the Crown Prince to convey to him the news of his decision. He explained the reasons for it in some detail. 'In vivid language he told me,' the Shah has recorded, 'that the people had always known him as an independent monarch, respected and strong, representing the interests of his country as a sovereign. He said it was humanly impossible that he, who had such prestige and such a hold over his people, should act as the nominal ruler of an occupied country.' This grim situation provided the setting for the accession of Mohammed Reza Pahlavi as the Shahanshah of Iran. The

ceremony on the occasion of the new Shah's accession was limited to the absolute minimum: There was no question of the Shah being formally crowned on that fateful day of September 16, 1941, but the new Shahanshah's accession was applauded by the whole population of Iran.

The invasion and occupation of Iran in the autumn of 1941 pushed her into the mid-stream of international power politics. Reza Shah had intentionally kept the country relatively isolated from the main currents of European politics. While willing to benefit from the technological progress of the West, he was rightly suspicious of Western motives and averse to any form of military or political involvement with the major Western powers. His intense nationalism, partially a consequence of the long Anglo-Russian dominance of Iran, and his firm belief that there was no civilisation superior to that of Iran, led him inevitably to the formation of a cautious and limited foreign policy. Iran, as a consequence, was kept aloof from the main currents of inter-national, political and ideological life. Once the war came to Iran, the country moved in its wake into the complex of ideological and military motivations behind the great anti-fascist struggle.

The progressive and prosperous patrimonial society which Reza Shah had so bravely sought to build could not withstand the shock of his removal. After his abdication Iran desperately needed a new, dynamic leadership. Who was to provide it? A generation of able and idealistic statesmen had worked since the nationalist revolution for the betterment of the country. Now, even they felt shaken and insecure, since the leader from whom they drew their inspiration and strength had withdrawn.

The occupation was therefore a mortal blow to the patrimonial society. The arrival of foreign troops in large numbers after the short and disastrous military encounter led to the temporary collapse of central authority in Tehran. This could have been avoided. Reza Shah, and failing him, certainly his son, Mohammed Reza Shah, might well have reduced the impact of this national catastrophe, which inevitably followed the invasion, if only the Allies had had some sense of balance between their war-time needs and Iran's requirements.

The Allies, however, arrogant in their one-sided victory, extended to the new Shah the same animosity which they had felt against his father. They took several days to recognize his succession. Ultimately, when they had to accept the legitimacy of the reign of the new sovereign, Mohammed Reza Shah, they did so with bad grace.

Mohammad Reza Shah was now determined to complete the unfinished revolution of his father, but in his own way

The Allies expected to secure a pliant, if not subservient, regime in Tehran, but knew that the young Shah was far from likely to accept any form of subordination to their agents. He had never disguised his anger at the violation of Iran's national sovereignty. He would have adopted a policy of scorched earth if he had been in a position to do so. He was to make all this candidly clear in later years. 'We could have mined all the bridges, railroads and major highways', he said to his people while referring to the unhappy days of 1941, 'so that Iran could not be considered a communication link for the invading armies. We should have taken measures aimed at denying our vital oil resources to the invader.' His firm and determined sense of national resistance and pride were part of his upbringing. He had been trained by Reza Shah to rule over Iran as a sovereign whose devotion to the interest of his country would not be second to any other consideration. Even though the young Shah was in many ways a different person from his father, the founder of the Pahlavi dynasty, he shared with him the concept of absolute devotion to Iran. Thus the new Shah appeared to the people to be the only hope for them in those days of despondency.

Mohammed Reza Shah was still very young. Born on October 26, 1919, his character had been moulded by the intense nationalism of his father's period and by the rationalistic rebellion of intellectual Europe of the thirties. He had been under the personal tutelage of his father up to 1932 and had spent the following four years at the Le Rosey school in Switzerland. While he had been steeped in ancient Iranian cultural and historical traditions and the tenets of the religion of Islam since his boyhood, he had grown to manhood in a climate of intellectual quest and ideological conflicts. He returned from Europe to Iran in 1936 with an outlook which in many ways was revolutionary and different from that of his father. He then underwent intensive training in statecraft as an understudy to Reza Shah right up to the time of the wartime invasion of Iran.

The new Shah thus had had the opportunity to appreciate the enormity of all the tasks which his father had shouldered. He was now determined to complete the unfinished revolution of his father, but in his own way. While he recognised that his father had set Iran on a new course of economic development, he had no illusions about the revival which had taken place of some of the traditional forms of patrimonial society of the pre-Qajar period. He realised that the earlier success of such social forms was largely a consequence of Iran's isolated,

self-sufficient and primarily non-commercial economy. But this isolation had now ended. Iran had become linked with the international economy during a century of western dominance. In these circumstances, it was clear to Mohammed Reza Pahlavi that any further revival of the classical patrimonial society would be neither helpful nor feasible. What was required was a reorganisation of social-economic relations within society on a totally new, more democratic and equitable basis.

The toiling peasants of his country were close to the heart of the young Shah. Even as a boy he had been appalled by their poverty and misery. At an early age he had made up his mind to give away the Crown lands to the peasants who tilled them, once he became the king. It was at Le Rosey that his new outlook had gradually begun to take shape, influenced to some extent by the contemporary radical ideas of Europe. He had even found several similarities between the modern concept of a society based upon social justice, on the one hand, and the inherited social philosophy of Iranian civilisation on the other. Many plans for a more humane system formed in his mind, and he began to nurse his dream of setting up a new society in Iran. And yet all this appeared to be outside the bounds of possibility in the autumn of 1941, when he was compelled by a combination of

circumstances to step into the breach caused by Reza Shah's abrupt departure.

The diminished power of the central administration and the disorganisation of the armed forces were not the only catastrophies caused by the invasion. As has happened in many countries of Asia and Africa, military defeat and invasion by foreign troops brought to the surface all the main evils of foreign occupation. These evils were the end products of the social and economic rules which governed the life of the Iranian people. The nation was to be plagued by these evils not only during the occupation, but also for a decade and a half afterwards.

The dominant feature of old Iranian society was the existence of an influential and oppressive class of landlords and tribal khans. Since the Mongol invasion in the thirteenth century, the ownership and incontestable control of large tracts of cultivable land, grazing pastures, forests, and the limited supply of precious water in the arid plateau by a few landlords and tribal chiefs had become the central feature of the national socio-economic structure. The strength of such a powerful class was *ipso facto* a danger to the central authority. Time and again, these tribal leaders and landlords behaved like autonomous chieftans. But their defiance never lasted long. Great as was their strength, it was never equal to that of the Shahs. So the only manner in which they could hope to continue their defiance was by relying upon outside assistance, and this was hardly available in the pre-Qajar period. The strong Shahs always brought them to heel and curbed their rapacity towards the peasants and other sections of the rural population.

But a qualitative change in the equation of power between the Shah, on the one hand, and this feudal class on the other had come into operation since the reign of the third Qajar monarch. The Qajar Shahs, beginning with Mohammed Shah (1834–47), had weakened the traditional authority of the kings by their acceptance of the blandish-ments of the domineering Russian and British powers. The gradual collapse of the patrimonial society and the corresponding increase in the dominance of the Anglo-Russian governments had convinced the feudal class that its future lay in switching its loyalty from the Shahs to the alien powers. This belief had been proved valid, for both the Russians and the British frequently supported the landlords and tribal chiefs against the Shah. For a period, as we have seen, the defiance of this class had been brought under control by Reza Shah. However, unfortunately for Iran, Reza Shah through lack of time had been

concrete shape to the measures he intended to take. He began to spread the message of his understanding of the new society among the people. With missionary zeal he worked round the clock to fortify the bond of spirit and heart between himself and his people. By May, 1962, he was ready to act.

The twentieth Majlis, elected in 1960, was in being at this time, but like its predecessors, it was dominated by the big land-owners and their social allies, representing vested interests who were determined to block the land reforms proposed by the Shah and the government. But by now the issue had aroused nation-wide interest and support and neither the Shah nor the people were prepared to put up with the frequent misuse of parliament to hinder social reforms upon which the progress of the country depended. The Majlis was therefore dissolved by the Shah, exercising his constitutional rights, on 9 May 1961. Between the dissolution of this twentieth Majlis and the convening of the twenty-first in the latter part of 1963, Iran went through a peaceful revolutionary change which has become famous as the White (peaceful) Revolution of the Shah and the People.

In this period the Shah drew up a six-point plan of basic reforms which he placed before the people's representatives at a conference in Tehran on January 9, 1963. This conference, known as the National Congress of Rural Co-operatives, was a gathering of farmers' and peasants'

representatives from all over the country. The rural co-operatives were organisations which had grown out of the preliminary initiation of land reform measures begun by the Shah in the early fifties, starting with the distribution of Crown lands soon after he ascended the throne. At this historic Congress the Shah told the farmers' and peasants' representatives what he was going to do:

'By the nature of my responsibilities as Shah and the oath I took to protect the rights and honour of the Iranian nation, I cannot remain a neutral onlooker in the struggle against the forces of evil. I have taken up the banner myself. So that no power can reinstate the regime of slavery among the villagers, and plunder the nation's wealth for the benefit of a minority, I have decided as executive, legislative and judicial head of the state, to refer these reforms to a referendum. Henceforth, no individual or group will be able to cancel, for their private interests, the results of this reform, which will free the farmer from the yoke of feudalism, ensure a brighter future, based on justice and progress for the noble working class and a higher standard of living for honest and hard-working civil servants, members of the guilds, and craftsmen.'

Following this Congress, which unreservedly supported the Shah's action, he announced his revolutionary Six-Point Charter to the nation and named January 26, 1963 as the date on which the referendum would be held. The points of the Charter

may be briefly summarised thus:
1 The traditional landlord-and-peasant system will be brought to an end and farmers will henceforth operate independently or work on co-operative farms, according to what the farmers themselves may decide.
2 The forests and pastures of the country will be taken out of private ownership and declared national property.
3 All former landlords will be given shares in government-owned factories by way of compensation for their old rights and to enable them to invest their resources in new forms of economic development.
4 All factory workers will be given a part-share in the profits of the enterprise concerned.
5 The electoral system will be so reformed that all corrupt practices such as the registering of bogus votes or buying of votes will be eliminated and women (that is, half the population of the country) hitherto disenfranchised, will be given the vote and the right to stand for election to the Majlis.
6 The organisation of a Literacy Corps from the conscript recruits to the army, who will be encouraged to volunteer to join the Corps instead of performing military duties and will go out into the rural areas to help rid the country of the scourge of illiteracy.

These revolutionary proposals were truly epoch-making in their import and caught the imagination of the whole nation. The vote in the referendum was overwhelmingly in favour of the Shah's Charter.

'When there is a revolution in Iran, I shall be the one to lead it.' His Imperial Majesty Mohammed Reza Shah Pahlavi

At the same time, in his historic address to his people on January 9, the Shah had warned them that the battle for success in the Revolution he was starting would not be over quickly, that the forces of reaction and destruction would attempt to sabotage the programme he envisaged. And his forecast proved right. Within a few weeks, the reactionaries realised that they were about to lose the final battle and made a desperate bid to assassinate the Shah. On the morning of April 10, 1965, as he was going to his office in the Marble Palace, a left-wing extremist fired a machine gun at him. Miraculously, the Shah was unhurt, saved, as indeed he had been before, from what appeared to be certain death.

In June 1965, the reactionaries again organised a rebellion in the south of Iran, as well as riots in Tehran. The rebellion was led by the tribal Khans and feudal landlords. The urban riots were inspired by reactionary groups that falsely used religion to inflame feelings against the granting of equal rights to women. The attempt on the Shah's life in April 1965, the southern rebellion, and these urban riots were all connected with the activities of certain foreign powers. The Shah, with the zealous support of his people, defeated these final attempts by reactionary forces to gain their ends. The twenty-first Majlis, for which the elections were held on the basis of the Shah's electoral reforms, put its constitutional seal also on the revolutionary charter. The Revolution of the Shah and the People was now in full swing.

The revolution, heralded by the referendum held on January 26, 1963, has dominated all aspects of life in Iran for the past eight years. This great enterprise is called *Inquilab Safid* or the White Revolution, to signify its bloodless and non-violent character. It has often been called a legislative revolution from the top. To a limited extent this is true: its legality is dependent upon its legislative sanction. Its strength depends upon the support it receives from the mass of the people, who alone can guarantee its success. Its inspirer, architect and leader is the Shah. He alone worked on its blueprints in the days when its feasibility appeared negligible; he fought for nearly three decades to create social and political conditions within which it would be launched; and, he is now in command of the forces which are working towards the realisation of its aims. He repeatedly risked his own life to carry out this mission for his nation and even wagered his throne for the sake of its ultimate victory.

Herein lies the special character of the White Revolution. It is the revolution of the Shah and his people. The Shah had once said: 'When there is a revolution in Iran, I shall be the one to lead it.' This bold pledge, then dismissed as bold rhetoric, has been redeemed by him. All this sounds strange in the context of the accepted philosophy of political science. Monarchy, by tradition and self-interest, is generally wedded to the continuance of the *status quo* and conservatism. A revolution led by a monarch is by normal standards thought to be a political anachronism. It appears strange in terms of the ordinary pattern of political behaviour. And yet this is precisely what has happened in Iran. Even the bitter critics of the Shah and his policies have been compelled to recognise this reality. How, then, has such a development been made possible in Iran? To appreciate the Shah's crucial contribution one has to appreciate the Iranian mystique of the 'Shahanshah'.

The birth of the institution of monarchy in Iran is coeval with the rise of her first national state, set up by the leaders of the Aryan-Persian tribe, and the imperial state established by Cyrus the Great in 550 BC. Ever since, monarchy has continued to be the only and exclusive form of state in Iran. Even the seventh-century Arab invasion and the control of the country by the Turkish tribes and the Mongols made no difference to this broad form of the state. It is always to the monarch that the Persian people have looked for the maintenance of peace, stability, unity, and solidarity. The exceptional role of the king throughout the twenty-five centuries of Iran's history has led to the growth of a national concept of the King of Kings. In course of time, this mystique became part of the national character and a basic tradition of Iranian civilisation.

Within the Iranian tradition of the King of Kings, the monarch's role is not limited to political leadership. He must be possessed of 'kingly glory', described as *khvarnah* in the classical age, and later as *farn*. Iran's great kings, like the Achaemenians Cyrus, Darius and Xerxes; the Sassanians Ardeshir and Khrosrow Anushirvan; and the Safavi Abbas I, to mention only a few, gave substance to this national concept by their total leadership of society. They gave a specific meaning to the concept of 'kingly glory' and the role of King of Kings. This, in turn, was immensely enriched by historical experience and vivified in popular imagination. Thus was evolved the tradition of the King of Kings.

The king, according to this concept, has to have strong and intimate links with his people. He is one who has suffered privations and thus is capable of appreciating and identifying himself with the sufferings of the people. His political duties are only a subsidiary consequence of his basic role, which is to win popular esteem so as to be able to become a friend, leader, and ultimately, the father of the nation. His image as a saviour must conform to heroic and even superhuman standards.

Reza Shah the Great gave new impetus to this tradition when he became Iran's saviour in the first half of the twentieth century. Mohammed Reza Shah has enriched it in the second half, a more difficult period. It became his destiny to shake his people out of the temporary stupor which had overtaken them, to re-activate their lives, to dissipate the inertia and pessimism by which they had been overcome, and to bring out that inner strength and resilience that typifies their national character. His was the more difficult task since it had to be performed in a world torn asunder by ideological conflicts and a ruthless struggle for power. His success forged a close union between himself and his awakened nation and it laid the basis on which was remodelled an ancient society through the dynamics of the White Revolution.

The White Revolution is based upon the premise that unless Iran completely alters the archaic order of her ancient society, she will always remain outside the circle of progressive and dynamic nations. She must, therefore, end all social and economic inequalities and shed those features of her ancient society which in the past led to injustice, tyranny and the exploitation of her common people. The new society which is to replace the old, apart from being just and equitable, must be in harmony with the Persian spirit and character as well as with the needs of the Asian continent and Iran's geographical and historical requirements. It cannot be created if the ethical side of her civilisation is compromised. Neither the spiritual principles and religious beliefs of the nation nor individual and social freedoms can be sacrificed at the altar of material advancement. Thus, the new society must express the totality of human progress resting upon a true balance between the material and spiritual requirements. To say that it should be democratic is not enough. An effective democracy which prohibits the exploitation of the people by any private, governmental or class interests is the prerequisite of any system of political democracy. Only such a democratic society can render social justice and resolve the problems of production and distribution of wealth and the collection of revenues and their just disbursement.

The general aims of the White Revolution have themselves inspired a complete programme for their realisation. The Twelve-Point Programme of the revolution,

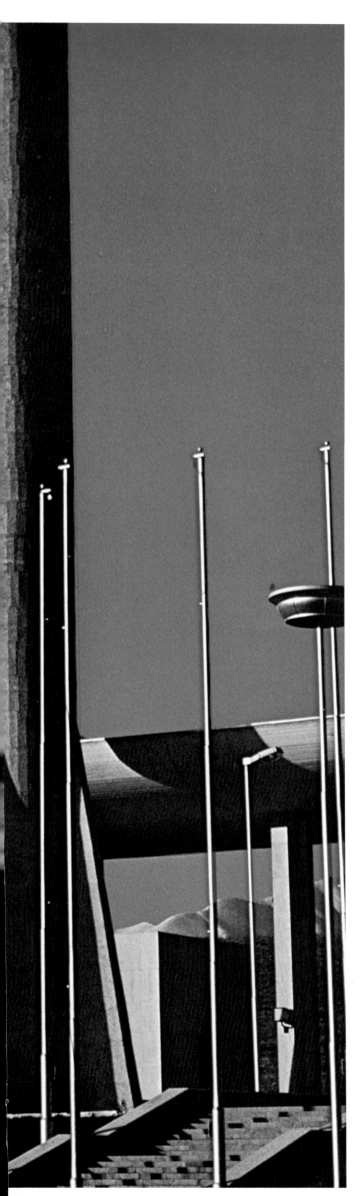

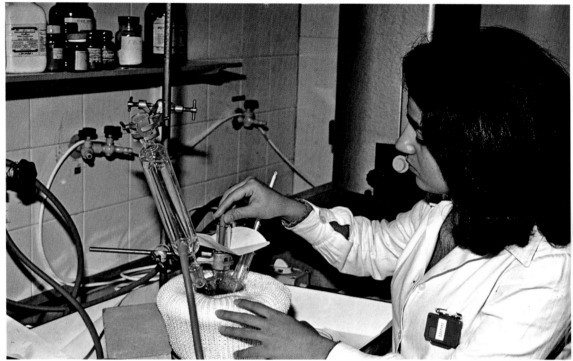

Left and below: The Atomic Research Centre at Tehran. Here young scientists are able to keep abreast of technical progress in the nuclear age.

which emerged by stages, includes land reform, aimed at abolition of the harsh landlord-and-peasant system inherited from the feudal age; reorganisation of the employer-employee relationship, to prevent the exploitation of labour and to allow workers a share of profits; eradication of illiteracy through formation of a Literacy Corps, so as to enable the common people to understand and defend their gains and exercise their rights in freedom; universal medical care by a specially organised Health Corps; the settlement of rural disputes by the setting up of arbitration courts, called Houses of Equity, and the establishment of an equilibrium between rural and urban centres with the aid of a Development and Extension Corps; and finally, the recognition of women's rights.

The main natural resources, and the basic and heavy industries are nationalised in order to destroy future possibility of the rise of trusts and cartels. The nationalisation concept flows from two beliefs: first, that the natural resources of the country, such as its oil and mineral deposits, fisheries, forests and pastures which no individual citizen had created himself, should not be in the hands of individuals or corporations for their private gain; and, secondly, that no new successors to the feudal minorities and the ruling class of the ancient society should be permitted to hold the new society to ransom by their control over major industries vital to the nation's economy.

The nationalisation of water resources; a plan for a massive reconstruction of town and country; and basic reforms in the educational and administrative systems complete the present programmes of the revolution. The participation of the people at all levels in the fulfilment of its objectives is accepted as imperative for its success. The peasants, on their own initiative, must form co-operatives and these co-operatives must in course of time convert themselves into the basic units of economic democracy.

The principles of the White Revolution govern Iran's political, social and economic policies. Her present and future course of action is based on them and the entire nation is engaged in bringing them to fruition. All the resources of the state and the energies of the people are devoted to one single aim: to translate into practice the twelve points of the White Revolution. It is now universally accepted that in the brief period since the revolution began Iran has changed. The best indication of this transformation is the fact that she is no longer classified as a developing nation. By the norms adopted by the United Nations, she is now a developed nation. She has passed the so-called take-off stage in her economy, which now generates its own self-propelled dynamism. Its average growth-rate during this period has remained at a steady 10 per cent and this places Iran among the front ranks of the fastest developing nations.

What has the revolution achieved during these past eight years? It is difficult to analyse all that a revolution of these dimensions introduces in an ancient society. Perhaps we may best begin to sketch the portrait of this new Iran with an examination of the effects of the land reform. In 1962 Iran was essentially an agricultural country. Her area, as large as that of the whole of Western Europe, does not lend itself easily to agriculture. Only 12 per cent of her land is arable. Her climate is so varied that there are seven distinct climatic zones. Besides, the land is water-hungry. There are 60,000 widely scattered villages, in which the majority of her population of nearly 29 million people live. Of these villages nearly 10,000, surrounded by the most fertile land, were completely owned by landlords in 1962. These were no ordinary landlords; their estates were in several cases as large as some of the smaller central European states. They not only owned the land, but also the water. The peasants received from them a mere one-fifth of the crops as payment, mostly in kind. If the peasant used his own oxen to pull the plough and helped to thresh grain, he received another one-fifth, also in kind. Thus, the landlord's control of the peasant's life in these estates was as complete as in serf-ridden medieval Europe.

Most of the land in the other 50,000 villages formed, with their mosques, part of various religious endowments to which they belonged, or was the property of landlords. Here, too, the peasants existed in the same wretched conditions. Only one hectare out of fifteen of arable land was owned by independent farmers, mainly in areas where surface irrigation water was available.

The land reform has now radically altered this situation. The big estates, including those owned by religious endowments, have been broken up. During the first phase of the reform 3,198,000 farmers received the title deeds to the land on which they and their forefathers had toiled for centuries. During the second phase, the scope of the reform was expanded and affected the lives of 12,058,000 rural inhabitants. The third phase, now approaching its end, is mainly concerned with mechanising agriculture, forming farmers' co-operatives, developing irrigation systems, and applying of modern scientific methods in farming.

The introduction of land reform by itself is not something exclusive to Iran. It has been the practice of all developing nations to make efforts for a change in the feudal basis of agriculture. However, there are some special distinguishing features of the reforms introduced in Iran. It was obvious to the Shah that the mere handing over of the land to the peasants would solve neither their difficulties nor the national problem. The land reform, important as it is, needed

to be a part of a wider agrarian revolution. Agriculture under the new conditions required a completely new system: an agricultural bank was needed to finance the operations of the new peasant proprietors, a body of expert helpers and advisers – an Expansion and Development Corps – was also required to assist him in the mechanisation of his methods and equipment; the introduction and extensive use of chemical fertilisers and new seeds was necessary; and finally, irrigation on an ever-expanding scale – all these became the means of putting into practice the comprehensive plans of the agrarian revolution.

One of the principal tests of the success of land reform in any country is the state of agricultural production in the post-reform period. According to the experts of the United Nations Food and Agriculture Organisation, Iran has passed the test. During the years of the revolution, the land under cultivation has increased by 16 per cent. The production of crops has shown a uniform growth: wheat has increased by 32 per cent, rice by 65 per cent, pulses by 38 per cent, vegetables and summer fruits by 23 per cent, fodder by 184 per cent, cotton by 66 per cent, and sugar by 38 per cent.

This rural prosperity has created an expanding domestic market for consumer goods which has helped Iran to become a major industrial power in western Asia. Between 1962–69 industrial production increased by 250 per cent. The mean annual rate of industrial growth has remained at approximately 14 per cent. The initial industrial expansion was centred on consumer goods. This phase is now over and the characteristics of industrial development today are a tendency towards major industries which require advanced technology, such as steel, engineering and chemicals. The growth of a machine-tool industry and the development of export-orientated industries constitute the most outstanding development. From being an importer Iran has converted herself into an exporter. She exported in 1970 about $7 million worth of textiles and knitwear, $5 million worth of soap and detergents, $4 million worth of shoes, about $4 million worth of vegetable oils, as well as automobiles, cement, refrigerators and tobacco in considerable quantities.

This high rate of industrial growth follows heavy investment, which is now one of the main characteristics of Iran's national economy. Whereas in 1962 total annual investment in industry was only 4,600,000 rials (75 rials = $1), in 1969 it rose to 21,400,000 rials. Foreign investment in this period has risen by 25 per cent.

The infra-structure required for such agro-industrial growth has been built rapidly. The length of asphalted roads has increased three times; new railway lines are being laid and shipping and air transport have witnessed an amazing growth. The energy sector has also witnessed a revolution. In 1962, the vast gas resources of the nation were totally wasted. In 1970 they supplied 14 per cent of the energy consumed and within the next five years, the share of natural gas in the consumption of total energy will rise to 34 per cent.

However, this economic 'miracle' is only a part of the goal of the revolution. It is by the investment made in the future generation that the revolution has scored its main success. Before the revolution only 15 per cent of the population above the age of seven was literate; now, the percentage stands at nearly 40 per cent. These figures refer to the work of the Literacy Corps. The Literacy Corps, like the Health Corps and the Development and Extension Corps, is composed of young men who spend a year of their eighteen-month period of national service in the villages to serve the nation in the areas assigned to them. Simultaneously, the ambit of primary, secondary and higher education has expanded. In 1962 1·5 million children attended primary schools; in 1970 the number was double that figure, and the number of pupils at secondary schools has increased three times. More than 85,000 post-graduate students are now studying in institutes of higher education.

Iran has succeeded in eradicating smallpox and malaria. The rate of infant mortality has dropped and life-expectancy has risen by a decade. The number of doctors has increased more than two-fold and it is planned to increase the number of beds in hospitals from 24,126 to 45,000.

The 1960s were to be a decade of development. This was the decision of the United Nations. Irrespective of what may have happened in other developing countries, Iran has indeed made the sixties her own decade of development. And this growth has been achieved against an adverse background. Iran lacks an adequate number of skilled workers, especially in agriculture, and has the grave disadvantage of a low rainfall. She has also suffered severe droughts and at the opposite extreme was inundated in 1968 with rain which caused floods and heavy losses. She has also been the victim recently of terrible earthquakes. But the momentum of the revolution has swept her on despite such adversities and is successfully taking the country forward along the path of the new society towards the era of a great civilisation.

Iran's renaissance will bring about a materially prosperous, spiritually rich, and culturally brilliant life for her people

Below: The Youth Palace in Tehran, where for a modest fee, young people may become members of a community that provides facilities for study and recreation.

The Iran of the White Revolution has moved far away from the Iran of the Qajar period. The country has put well behind it the dismal memories of those yesteryears. Her people, sensitive to the demands of a profound national rebirth, are concentrating on the tasks of today and tomorrow, though they never lose sight of the rich heritage of their ancient and classical past as a source of inspiration.

Any nation which increases its *per capita* income five-fold in almost as many years, as the Iranians have done recently, surely has reason to be proud of itself. Iranians, on the other hand, will be found insisting that this economic 'miracle' of theirs is less important for them than the underlying causes which produced their revolution. It is their earnest belief that this revolution has altered radically the equation of strength between the various social groups within their society. The stranglehold of the feudal landlords and tribal chiefs over the rural masses has been broken. The break-up of the larger estates by measures of land reform has transformed the pattern of the old society which took shape as far back as the time of the Mongols in the thirteenth century. To avoid neglect of the land, to sow it with seed, to irrigate it, plant it with trees and raise flocks on it – from these arts and practices of agriculture was woven, from ancient Achaemenian times, the very fabric of Iranian society. They were proof of Iranian man's love for Ahuramazda, his great God of light and truth. Agriculture was hallowed by the religious precepts of ancient Iran and its importance stressed by her very first imperial kings of the Achaemenian dynasty.

While oppressive groups such as the exploiting landlord class existed in similar societies in other countries, the feudal lords in Iran had been kept in check by the patrimonial form of her society and the moral code which that society engendered. The religion of Islam, when it came, was based upon the idea of the brotherhood of man and of equality. Both the Prophet Mohammed and Imam Ali inculcated this understanding among the Moslems. The Mongols after their conquest, had distributed large tracts of land among themselves. This Mongol policy of the deliberate creation of fiefs, combined with the practice of donating lands so as to provide for religious endowments, created the conditions for an oppressive feudal system. The transfer of water resources and pastures into private ownership gave the feudal lords power on a scale unparalleled in any oriental society.

The White Revolution has deprived this class of the power it had possessed for so long. The bourgeoisie, as a definite class, did not exist in the old Iranian society. However, the spread of industrialisation in the country would certainly have led to the rise of such a class, but for the way in which it has been controlled. The rise of such a class is no longer possible. As the Shah has said: 'The nationalised forests will never be returned to private owners. Land that has been distributed among the peasants will not be taken back from them. Such land may come to belong to the co-operatives of farmers or farm corporations, but there will never be large landowners. The nationalised water resources will never be distributed among individuals.

'The same is true of the pastures and of heavy industry, both of which should be owned and run by the government in the interest of the nation as a whole. Iran's oil, for example, will never be handed over to individual shareholders. The iron and steel industry will not be handed over to private enterprise.'

The revolution has thus given Iranian society a new foundation of public strength which cannot be undermined. No domination by an exploiting class will be tolerated by the productive and creative forces which the revolution has released.

An important aspect of the social reorganisation which has been in progress is the profound change which it has brought about in the status of women. For the first time in Iranian annals, the revolution has given to women the rights of equality with men in all respects, including the right of franchise. It is true that recognition of women's rights forms part of Iran's heritage. The concept of her equal status was repeatedly affirmed by the founders of Zoroastrianism, Iran's first religion. The Zoroastrians divided their principal angels into three male and three female, so as to inculcate the idea of equality between man and woman. They gave women the right to manage property, represent their husbands at law, and act as guardians of sons disinherited by their fathers; women had the right to be judges and in certain circumstances even to act as priests. Sassanian records show that women who became Queens, for example – Queen Pourandokht and Queen Azarmidokht, were sovereigns in their own right. In more recent times, the emergence of women from the veil was accomplished under Reza Shah. However, the current revolution has brought them an entirely new sense of dignity and involved them in all the creative endeavours of the nation. While old prejudices may still linger in the minds of some of the older generation, the future of Iranian women is assured. There can now be no going back from the position and status they have acquired.

The disenchantment of youth with many aspects of the existing order of things is a problem which plagues many countries today. This problem is being successfully tackled in Iran by the growth of the three corps – the Literacy Corps, the Health Corps, and the Development and Extension Corps. This is an unorthodox and original way of solving a complex problem by which the youth are identified with the revolution of the nation. In fact, it represents an Iranian innovation. Other countries besides Iran have national conscription, but in Iran it is put to a different use. Normally, a young man who becomes a conscript will spend eighteen months undergoing military training, but in Iran the period has been cut down and after it, the young recruits undergo an intensive course of tuition by qualified instructors.

They then go to the villages to work as members of one or other of the three Corps. Thousands of young men go to live among the villagers, whom they help to learn to read and write and to whom they teach the elements of sanitation and modern farming methods. The social impact of this movement has been tremendous, both on the rural population and on the young people, the future leaders of the country. They have broken down the wall which separated town from country. They have made such a rediscovery of their native land that large numbers of them have chosen to stay in the villages after the period of service with their Corps has ended. At first, it was only boys and young men who went out into the villages, but now girls, too, who want to take part in this adventure are being encouraged to do so.

These are some of the deep and fundamental social changes taking place in a society which remained moribund for several centuries. They are imparting to the new society an inner strength. On the basis of results that have been already achieved, plans are now being made for developments during the next quarter of a century and the future thus envisaged appears unquestionably bright. History in one sense will be repeating itself in Iran – it will enable the country to ride once more on the crest of its successes again to a greatness such as that for which it was famous in the ancient and medieval periods.

Iran's renaissance will bring about a materially prosperous, spiritually rich, and culturally brilliant life for her people. The Shah underlined the creed of this future some years ago thus: 'So precipitate is the world's metamorphosis that it has become easy for any society to lose its moorings. I think the recent dramatic changes in my country testify that we welcome constructive change, but at the same time we stand fast in support of certain superior values that I believe to be classically ours. We cherish the gardens and the poetry and the family life and the hospitality of Persia. We acclaim this land of deserts and snow-capped mountains, of cedars and plane trees, of rivers and fountains and tiled water courses, of roses and orange-blossom and nightingales and we are proud of our political and social institutions.'

The revolution has made a break with the past and yet kept the continuity alive. Iran today and tomorrow represents a new society, the edifice of which is raised upon the inspired heritage of the immortal kingdom.

ILLUSTRATIONS

The equipment used by Mr. MacQuitty was as follows: cameras: two Nikon F Photomic Tn; one Nikkormat FT; lenses: Nikkor Auto 20 mm F 3·5, 28 mm F 3·5, 35 mm F 2·8, Micro Auto 35 mm F 3·5, 105 mm F 2·5, 200 mm F 4. All lenses were fitted with lens hoods and protected with UV or skylight filters. Colour and neutral density filters were also used. The film stock was Kodachrome II and Kodak Tri-X; they were given normal exposure at meter readings with shutter speeds of usually 125th of a second or faster. Flash was supplied by three Megablitz with main charging units.

INDEX

222